DATE DUE

JY 27 '95	DE 19 '03		
FE 23 '96			
[illegible]			
DE 20 '96			
AP 7 '97			
[illegible]			
[illegible]			
[illegible]			
MY 13 '98			
JY 23 '98			
[illegible]			
MR 17 '01			
MY 30 '02			
[illegible]			

DEMCO 38-296

The NAFTA Debate

The NAFTA Debate

Grappling with Unconventional Trade Issues

edited by

M. Delal Baer

Sidney Weintraub

BOULDER
LONDON

Riverside Community College
Library

4800 Magnolia Avenue
Riverside, California 92506

HF1746 .N35 1994
The NAFTA debate : grappling with unconventional trade issues

Published in the United States of America in 1994 by
Lynne Rienner Publishers, Inc.
1800 30th Street, Boulder, Colorado 80301

and in the United Kingdom by
Lynne Rienner Publishers, Inc.
3 Henrietta Street, Covent Garden, London WC2E 8LU

© 1994 by Center for Strategic and International Studies. All rights reserved

Library of Congress Cataloging-in-Publication Data
The NAFTA debate : grappling with unconventional trade issues / edited by M. Delal Baer and Sidney Weintraub.
Includes bibliographical references and index.
ISBN 1-55587-464-9
1. Free trade—North America. 2. North America—Economic integration. 3. Free trade—Political aspects—North America.
I. Baer, M. Delal, 1953– . II. Weintraub, Sidney, 1922– .
HF1746.N333 1994
382'.917—dc20 93-38663
CIP

British Cataloguing in Publication Data
A Cataloguing in Publication record for this book is available from the British Library.

Printed and bound in the United States of America

The paper used in this publication meets the requirements of the American National Standard for Permanence of Paper for Printed Library Materials Z39.48-1984.

5 4 3 2

Contents

List of Tables and Figures vii
Preface ix

Part 1
The Economic and Social Dimensions of NAFTA

1 Assessing the Economic Impact of North American Free Trade, *Timothy J. Kehoe* 3

2 Adjustment and Transition Mechanisms for a U.S.-Mexico Free Trade Agreement, *Howard Rosen* 35

3 The Environment: Unwelcome Guest at the Free Trade Party, *Jan Gilbreath and John Benjamin Tonra* 53

Part 2
The Politics of NAFTA

4 North American Economic Integration and Canadian Sovereignty, *Alan M. Rugman* 97

5 The U.S. Domestic Politics of the U.S.-Mexico Free Trade Agreement, *Howard J. Wiarda* 117

6 The Changing Face of Mexican Nationalism, *Soledad Loaeza* 145

7 The Pressures for Political Reform in Mexico, *M. Delal Baer and Sidney Weintraub* 159

Part 3
Conclusion

8 New Patterns of Conflict and Cooperation, *M. Delal Baer* 183

List of Acronyms 193
The Contributors 195
Index 199
About the Book 211

Tables and Figures

Tables

1.1 U.S. Merchandise Trade by Commodity, 1989 8

1.2 Changes in Economic Welfare in Different Applied General Equilibrium Simulations of NAFTA 11

1.3 Comparison of Spanish Model's Prediction with the Data by Sector 14

1.4 Real Exchange Rate Indices: 1980–1991 15

1.5 Foreign Investment in Mexico and Spain, 1980–1991 17

1.6 Growth Rates of GDP and Various Components in Mexico and Spain, 1980–1991 17

1.7 Net Workers' Remittances, 1990, from Various Immigrant-Sending Countries 18

1.8 Total Population of Mexico, Spain, and the United States, 1930–1990 20

1.9 Population of Mexico, Spain, and the United States by Age Groups, 1990 23

2.1 U.S. Labor Market Adjustment Programs 38

2.2 International Comparison of Unemployment Insurance Programs, Selected Industrialized Countries 44

2.3 Government Expenditures on Labor Market Programs, Selected Industrialized Countries, 1988–1990 45

2.4 Training Programs in Selected Industrialized Countries, 1988–1990 46

4.1 The World's 500 Largest MNEs 99

4.2 Outward Stocks of Triad FDI 99

4.3 Direction of Canada's Trade, by Flows 102

4.4 Direction of Canada's FDI, by Stocks 102

Figures

1.1 Alternative Measures of Relative Size 5

1.2 Alternative Measures of Income per Capita 6

1.3 Direction of Trade, 1989 7

1.4 Real Exchange Rate Index, Mexican/U.S. Goods 16

1.5 Growth Rate of Population in Mexico, the United States, and Spain, 1930–1990 19

1.6 Foreign Direct Investment as Percentage of GDP, 1990 22

1.7 Per Capita Foreign Direct Investment, 1990 23

4.1 Global Flows of Trade in the Triad, 1990, Exports Only 100

4.2 Global Stocks of FDI in the Triad, 1990 101

4.3 Globalization and Sovereignty 105

Preface

The negotiations for a North American Free Trade Agreement (NAFTA) displayed unique features that, from the outset, distinguished them from all previous trade discussions. The negotiations started with the United States, Mexico, and Canada pursuing a comprehensive trade and investment arrangement, emphasizing the removal of classic trade barriers such as tariffs and quotas as well as newer themes such as trade in services and protection of intellectual property. The political debate surrounding the negotiations, however, quickly expanded the negotiations to include three other issue areas, which the three governments at first resisted. First, nongovernmental organizations (NGOs) insisted on including nontraditional issues such as the environment and labor standards in the negotiating agenda. Second, although not part of the negotiations, questions of human rights were raised, as were other social issues such as the cost of health care. Third, and most sensitive, questions regarding the impact of economic integration between low-wage and high wage countries led to the comparison of NAFTA with other regional models such as the European Community; this led to anxieties in all three countries about a compromise of sovereignty. More broadly, the debate assumed a watershed character, defining whether the United States was to move toward a neoisolationist and neoprotectionist mode.

It was in this context that we asked the contributors to this volume to explore these frontier issues of trade in the North American region.

The NAFTA negotiations have changed the definition of what is encompassed in a "trade" negotiation. Thus, Howard Rosen looks at the history of U.S. labor-adjustment assistance programs and proposes solutions for North America in Chapter 2. In Chapter 3, Jan Gilbreath and John Benjamin Tonra address how environmental questions can be handled in the context of a trade negotiation, drawing on both European and North American experiences. The boundaries between trade and ancillary issues are likely to foster political tension for years to come, a theme that is reviewed in Howard J. Wiarda's look at the politics of NAFTA in the United States (Chapter 5). The theme of the relationship between commercial integration and political democratization in Mexico is explored by authors M. Delal Baer and Sidney Weintraub (Chapter 7).

This volume was also inspired by the questions that NAFTA has posed regarding the limits of national sovereignty in all three countries. Soul-searching regarding national sovereignty and cultural identity has been especially notable in Canada and Mexico, both of which harbor historical apprehensions regarding their colossal neighbor. A profound transformation of the suspicion-laden attitudes and defensive nationalism that constrained intergovernmental relations in North America should be a significant by-product of free trade. Chapters 4 and 6, by Alan M. Rugman and Soledad Loaeza, respectively, are attempts to come to grips with the delicate counterpoint between national autonomy and economic integration. Both authors explore the trade-offs between the traditional attachment to earlier notions of sovereignty and the enhanced economic well-being represented by economic integration. In the United States especially, there are concerns about the preservation of environmental standards and social policy in the face of heightened North American integration. Thus, the meaning of sovereignty is being revamped to accommodate the new realities of intensified regional and global interdependence.

The forces of regional economic integration are proceeding simultaneously in Europe, with the follow-on to Maastricht; in Asia, with stepped-up intraregional investment; and in North America. These regional integration movements display commonalities and contrasts and invite comparative analysis. The North American experiment might profit from the mistakes and successes of regional initiatives elsewhere. The contributors to this volume were asked to make an effort to include a comparative dimension in their analyses wherever relevant. Valuable insights regarding the impact of integrating lower-wage countries into a high-wage region are offered in Chapter 1, with Timothy J. Kehoe's rigorous comparison of the accession of Spain and Greece into the European Community. Rosen (Chapter 2) introduces a comparison of U.S. labor market policy with the European experience in his examination of adjustment mechanisms and policies. This dimension is most notable in Gilbreath and Tonra's superb comparison of the European and North American handling of environmental issues (Chapter 3).

The studies in this volume were commissioned before all the details of the NAFTA agreement itself and the side agreements on the environment and labor were complete. A detailed analysis of the various texts was never the objective of the endeavor. Rather, these chapters were designed to chart a path for understanding the agenda of new issues that are emerging in North American political and economic relations. This new agenda is driven by the multiplying linkages among previously distinct issue areas, which suggest a continuing need for greater interdisciplinary research in the future. In particular, closer collaboration among trade specialists and environmental experts is vital to resolving many of the policy dilemmas posed by the emerging global economy. New opportunities for collaboration in the field of political economy are also opened up by the intriguing relationships implied by the twin global processes of economic and political reform. Finally, comparative regional analysis holds promise as powerful forces of integration push nations toward new exercises in regional institution-building and policy-setting.

Special thanks are due to the Ford Foundation, whose financial support made this volume possible. Thanks are also extended to the contributors, who have graciously updated their chapters to keep up with fast-breaking events, and to CSIS Americas Program's Joyce Hocbing, whose help was invaluable in the final editing of the book.

M. Delal Baer
Sidney Weintraub

Part 1

The Economic and Social Dimensions of NAFTA

1

Assessing the Economic Impact of North American Free Trade

Timothy J. Kehoe

In June 1990, the president of Mexico, Carlos Salinas de Gortari, and the president of the United States, George Bush, announced their intention to negotiate a free trade agreement between their countries. In February 1991, Canada joined the process, and in June 1991, formal negotiations on a North American Free Trade Agreement (NAFTA) began.

The prospect of NAFTA generated a large amount of economic research analyzing its possible impacts on the three countries involved. The tool of choice for this sort of analysis has been the applied general equilibrium model, which traces its roots to the work of L. Johansen and to the work of J. S. Shoven and J. Whalley.[1] Applications of this type of model to analyze NAFTA tend to find small but favorable overall impacts of such an agreement on each of the three countries. The intuition behind these findings is, as we shall see, fairly obvious. Furthermore, differences in the detailed results are easily explained in terms of differences in the underlying assumptions of the different models.

The models that have been used to analyze NAFTA tend to focus on the static gains and losses from trade liberalization. These are the effects that are felt after relative prices have had time to adjust and such resources as labor and capital have had time to move from one sector to another in response to this adjustment. To adequately capture these static effects, we need to model the interactions of a large number of sectors in the economies involved. Comparing the results of a static applied general equilibrium analysis of Spain's entry into the European Community (EC) in 1986 with later data on Spain suggests that this sort of model can do a good job in analyzing and, to some extent, predicting these effects.

Although the overall impact of NAFTA is expected to be favorable for each of the three countries, some sectors are sure to benefit more than the average. Also, some sectors are likely to suffer in terms of losses of output and employment. Because applied general equilibrium models are designed to analyze the impact of policy changes like trade liberalization on

Unless otherwise noted, "dollars" refers to U.S. dollars.

relative prices and resource allocation over a period of several years, they can help us to identify those sectors of an economy where extra care is needed in structuring the transition mechanisms that will be built into the treaty.

In addition to the static effects captured by these models, there are dynamic effects, such as the impact of NAFTA on capital flows and growth rates, that involve the evolution of the Canadian, Mexican, and U.S. economies over time. Spanish data suggest that the dynamic impact of trade liberalization can be more significant than the static effects. To adequately capture these dynamic effects, we need to model the intertemporal decisionmaking processes of the agents in the model. We want to be able to capture, for example, the effect of NAFTA on savings and investment decisions. To be sure, many models of NAFTA analyze the effect of a higher level of capital stock in Mexico, but the increase in capital stock is imposed exogenously on the model rather than being modeled as the result of the agreement.

Mixing together some recent economic theory, recent data for Mexico, and empirical work on the determinants of growth rates across countries and then performing some crude calculations, we can develop rough estimates of the capital accumulation and productivity growth in Mexico that could result from NAFTA. These estimates reveal a favorable impact that dwarfs the static impact found by more conventional analyses. Although NAFTA would also be expected to have a favorable dynamic impact on Canada and the United States, we would expect this impact to be smaller given the sizes, levels of economic development, and current degrees of economic openness of these two countries relative to Mexico. In fact, the most significant dynamic impact of NAFTA on Canada and the United States could be the feedback of Mexican growth in providing favorable investment opportunities and markets for exports.

North America and NAFTA

Simply comparing the relative sizes and levels of economic development of the three North American economies goes a long way toward providing intuition for many of the predictions about the impact of NAFTA. Figure 1.1 presents several indicators of the relative sizes of Canada, Mexico, and the United States. All three countries have large land areas and are rich in natural resources. The United States is roughly ten times as large as Canada both in terms of population and in terms of gross domestic product (GDP). Although the United States has only about three times as many people as Mexico, it had more than twenty-seven times as much national income in 1988.

The disparity in this latter set of comparisons is explained by noting that Mexican income per capita, measured in 1988 dollars, was only about

Figure 1.1 Alternative Measures of Relative Size

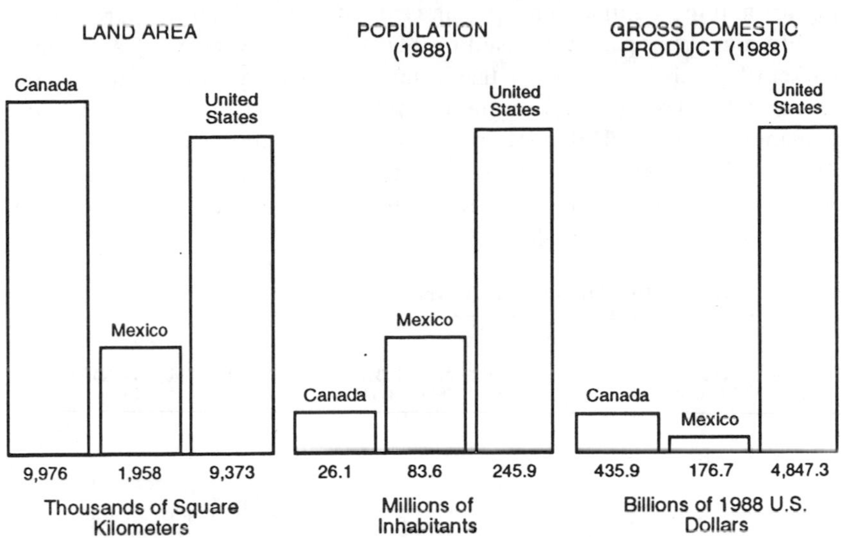

Source: World Bank, *World Development Report* (New York: Oxford University Press, 1990); and R. Summers and A. Heston, "The Penn World Table (Mark 5): An Expanded Set of International Comparisons, 1950–88," *Quarterly Journal of Economics,* 106 (1991), 327–368.

one-ninth of that in the United States. This figure must be treated with care because it uses exchange rates to convert an income figure measured in pesos per capita into a dollars-per-capita figure. The real exchange rate, which measures the value of the peso versus that of the dollar in terms of purchasing power, has had wide swings over the past decade. These swings can unduly influence income comparisons using exchange rate conversions. In 1991, for example, Mexican income per capita was about $3,400. The 62 percent increase in income since 1988 can be roughly broken down as a 7 percent increase in terms of 1988 pesos, a 12 percent increase due to inflation in the dollar, a 36 percent increase due to a real appreciation in the value of the peso versus the dollar, and a 7 percent increase due to compounding of these various effects. Looked at another way, the U.S. dollar appreciated far less against the peso in nominal terms than would have been justified by the differences in the rates of inflation in Mexico and the United States. In another illustration of the perils of using comparisons based on exchange rate conversions, we can calculate that real U.S. income per capita fell by more than 34 percent between 1985 and 1988 when measured in 1985 Spanish pesetas; it rose by almost 8 percent over the same period when measured in terms of 1985 dollars.

Measuring different countries' incomes in terms of one country's currency can be useful for thinking about some trade issues, but it is misleading for making comparisons of standards of living. For this purpose, we should make comparisons based on real incomes in terms of a common basket of goods, comparisons that assume purchasing-power parity in exchange rates. Using data from the UN International Comparison Program, R. Summers and A. Heston have constructed such numbers.[2] As shown in Figure 1.2, they find levels of income per capita in the United States and Mexico that differ by a factor of less than four, rather than a factor of nine.

Figure 1.2 Alternative Measures of Income per Capita

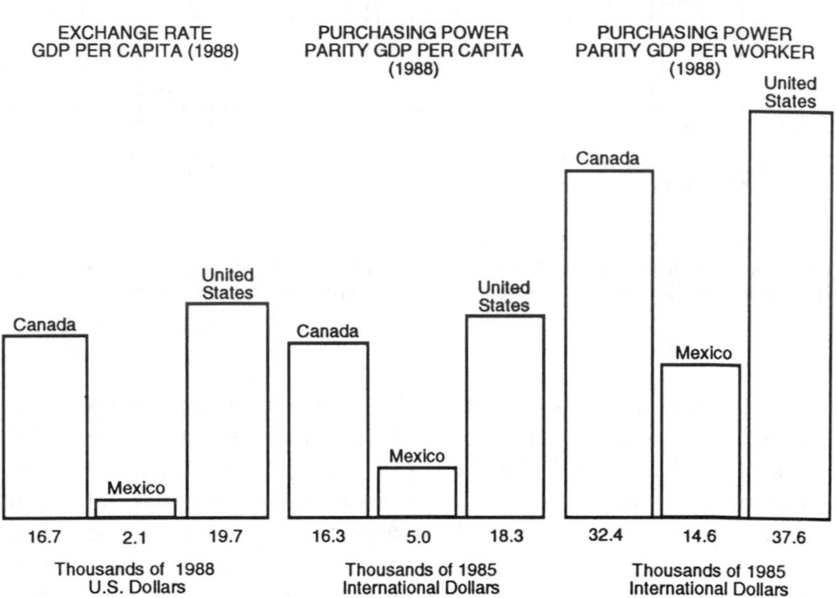

Source: World Bank, *World Development Report* (New York: Oxford University Press, 1990); and R. Summers and A. Heston, "The Penn World Table (Mark 5): An Expanded Set of International Comparisons, 1950–88," *Quarterly Journal of Economics,* 106 (1991), 327–368.

But even these purchasing-power parity incomes per capita are misleading if we are interested in comparing productivity levels across countries. Because Mexico has a higher rate of population growth, a larger fraction of its population is very young and consequently not in the labor force, as compared to the U.S. population. When we calculate purchasing-power parity outputs per worker, we see that those in the United States and Mexico differ by a factor of less than three.

Such statistics portray the Mexican and Canadian economies as much smaller than the U.S. economy and Mexico as much poorer than either Canada or the United States. This suggests that NAFTA would have much larger impacts on Canada and particularly on Mexico than it would on the United States. Another set of statistics that suggests the same conclusion are the data on the direction of trade, reported in Figure 1.3. Although Canada is the number one trading partner of the United States, and Mexico is number three after Japan, the United States conducts only about one-quarter of its trade with its two North American neighbors. In contrast, more than two-thirds of foreign trade in both Canada and Mexico is with the United States. They have very little direct trade with each other. Put bluntly and somewhat simplistically, foreign trade for Canada and for Mexico means trade with the United States.

Table 1.1 reports the composition of that trade by sector. Although all three countries are large agricultural producers, there was relatively little North American trade in agricultural goods, other than wood products, in

Figure 1.3 Direction of Trade, 1989 (millions of 1989 U.S. dollars)

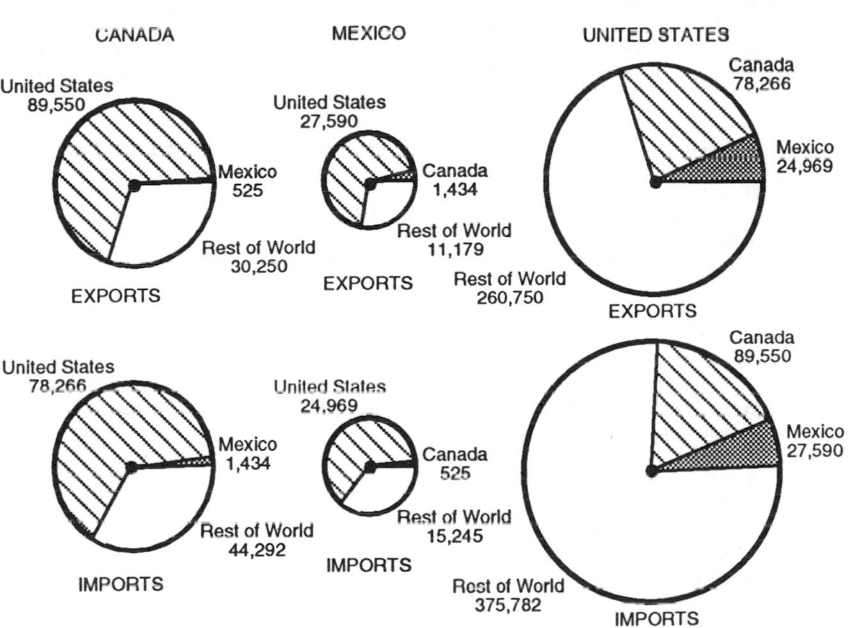

Source: International Monetary Fund, *Direction of Trade Statistics Yearbook* (Washington, DC: IMF, 1990).

Table 1.1 U.S. Merchandise Trade by Commodity, 1989 (millions of U.S. dollars)

SITC Code Number[a]	Merchandise	Exports			Imports		
		World	Canada	Mexico	World	Canada	Mexico
0	Food and live animals	29,425	1,903	1,990	22,497	3,567	2,446
03	Fish-related products	2,299	198	22	5,711	1,226	397
04	Cereals	15,457	209	976	1,017	417	27
05	Vegetables and fruits	3,808	738	140	5,686	260	1,095
1	Beverages and tobacco	5,510	83	19	4,690	583	258
2	Crude materials except fuels	26,947	2,288	1,493	16,524	8,339	675
22	Oil seeds	4,362	127	358	186	122	27
24	Cork and wood	4,965	439	143	3,733	3,333	103
25	Pulp and waste paper	4,343	184	362	3,164	2,748	8
28	Metal ores and scrap	5,313	819	225	4,205	1,257	178
3	Mineral fuels, related products	9,865	1,678	712	56,094	8,053	4,457
33	Petroleum, related products	4,828	656	518	52,411	5,126	4,359
4	Animal and vegetable fats, oils	1,350	47	143	785	91	21
5	Chemicals, related products	36,485	4,210	2,195	21,768	4,087	600
51	Organic chemicals	10,609	941	680	7,330	625	162
52	Inorganic chemicals	4,323	483	206	3,464	1,284	215
6	Manufacturing by material	27,243	5,865	2,961	65,055	16,989	2,769
64	Paper, related products	4,195	738	616	8,926	6,391	380
65	Textiles, related products	3,897	696	387	6,417	372	186
67	Iron and steel	3,278	633	451	11,376	1,678	315
68	Nonferrous metals	4,699	1,068	308	11,042	4,782	710
7	Machinery, transport equipment	148,800	33,194	10,813	210,810	39,293	12,213
71	Power-generating machinery	14,166	2,915	852	14,488	2,865	1,214
72	Specialized machinery	13,644	2,446	711	13,390	1,564	151
74	General industrial machinery	13,095	2,745	1,228	14,974	1,742	728
75	Office machines, computers	2,318	2,572	691	26,251	1,704	776
76	Telecommunications	7,669	803	1,161	23,607	953	2,675
77	Electrical machinery	23,921	3,572	3,477	33,034	2,453	4,211
78	Road vehicles	25,480	15,891	2,080	73,843	25,830	2,405
79	Other transport equipment	25,038	1,669	406	7,217	1,920	45
8	Miscellaneous manufacturing	32,637	4,326	2,469	80,470	3,637	2,766

Table 1.1 (continued)

82	Furniture	1,006	277	236	5,278	1,187	533
84	Apparel, clothing	2,087	109	375	26,026	262	596
87	Scientific instruments	10,924	1,201	656	5,964	472	471
9	Not classified elsewhere	28,388	21,011	1,222	12,820	3,909	1,237
	Total[b]	346,650	74,605	24,017	491,513	88,548	27,442

Source: Organisation for Economic Cooperation and Development, *Foreign Trade by Commodities, Series C* (Paris: OECD, 1990).

Notes: [a] Standard International Trade Classification (Revision 3), one-digit and selected two-digit. [b] Total is the sum of major SITC categories 0, 1, 2, 3, 4, 5, 6, 7, 8, and 9.

1989. Canada exports significant amounts of wood, paper products, and nonferrous metals to the United States. This pattern reveals Canada's comparative advantage in raw materials compared to the United States, which itself exports large amounts of these sorts of goods to the rest of the world. Both Canada and Mexico export large amounts of petroleum to the United States. By far the biggest category of trade among North American countries, however, is machinery and transport equipment. The largest category of Canadian exports to the United States, at the two-digit Standard International Trade Classification (SITC) level, is road vehicles and parts; this is also the largest category of exports from the United States to Canada. The largest two categories of U.S. exports to Mexico are electrical machinery and road vehicles and parts; these are also the second and third largest categories of exports from Mexico to the United States, after petroleum and petrochemicals.

NAFTA would eliminate most tariffs on trade among the three countries, it would substantially reduce nontariff barriers to trade (NTBs), and it would ensure the free flow of capital throughout the region. Unlike the European Community, NAFTA would ensure neither common trade barriers against the rest of the world nor the free flow of labor. Although it would establish a dispute resolution mechanism, there are no plans to create central North American government bodies like the European Parliament and the EC bureaucracy. Neither is there serious talk about a common currency system in NAFTA like that of the EC, although both Canadian and Mexican monetary authorities carefully manage their currencies' exchange rates with the U.S. dollar.

Applied General Equilibrium Analyses of NAFTA

In 1991, Mexican tariffs on imports from the United States averaged about 11 percent when weighted by value imported; U.S. tariffs on imports from

Mexico averaged about 4 percent. There are no tariffs on most of the trade between the United States and Canada as a result of their own free trade agreement (FTA), which went into effect in 1989. Nontariff barriers are expected to be reduced substantially by NAFTA, although, given the experience of the U.S.-Canada Free Trade Agreement, we should not expect them to be completely eliminated. Currently, there are significant NTBs on agricultural imports in all three countries. There are also NTBs on imports of processed foods, particularly meat, dairy products, and sugar in the United States and Canada. The United States has significant NTBs on imports of textiles and apparel, and Mexico has NTBs on imports of chemicals. All three countries have significant NTBs on imports of automobiles and automotive parts.[3] NTBs usually take the form of import quotas, phytosanitary regulations, and licensing regulations. At present, there are few restrictions on capital flows in North America. The obvious exceptions are in Mexico, and they consist of laws prohibiting private ownership, foreign or domestic, in the petroleum industry and some parts of the petrochemical industry; laws restricting foreign ownership of banks; and laws institutionalizing ownership of much of the agricultural land—the *ejido* system, a communal form of land ownership unique to Mexico.

There are many applied general equilibrium analyses of the impacts of eliminating these barriers to trade. Although all employ multisectoral general equilibrium models, the emphasis differs across models. Brown, Deardorff, and Stern model the general impact on all three countries.[4] Bachrach and Mizrahi, who constructed their model for KPMG Peat Marwick, concentrate on liberalizing Mexican-U.S. trade.[5] Cox and Harris focus on the impact of NAFTA on Canada; Sobarzo focuses on Mexico.[6] Roland-Holst, Reinert, and Shiells pay special attention to modeling the reduction of NTBs; Hinojosa and Robinson look at modeling labor markets and migration from the rural sector to the urban sector in Mexico and migration from Mexico to the United States.[7] Hunter, Markusen, and Rutherford concentrate on the impact on the automobile industry; Trela and Whalley concentrate on textiles, apparel, and steel; and Levy and van Wijnbergen and Robinson, Burfisher, Hinojosa-Ojeda, and Thierfelder focus on agriculture.[8] Young and McCleery analyze some of the dynamic impacts of NAFTA, although neither of their models explicitly models intertemporal savings and investment decisions.[9]

It is worth noting that all these models are calibrated to pre-1989 data. In general, the policy simulations include the trade liberalization that was part of the U.S.-Canada FTA and at least some of the liberalization that has occurred in Mexico since 1985. In 1985, Mexico was one of the most closed economies in the world, with tariffs as high as 100 percent, licenses required to import all goods, and laws that prohibited foreigners from investing in the stock market or, with a few exceptions, from owning more than 49 percent of any business or private property.

Table 1.2 summarizes the overall effects of NAFTA on welfare in the Brown, Deardorff, and Stern model.[10] These results are fairly typical of those found in these models: The impact of NAFTA as a percentage of GDP is largest in Mexico and smallest in the United States, with Canada falling in between, even though the absolute gain may be largest in the United States. It makes little difference to Canada whether Mexico joins U.S.-Canada Free Trade Association. What these results also have in common with those of many of the other models is that the biggest impact of NAFTA occurs if capital is allowed to flow to Mexico from the United States or from the rest of the world. In all these models, such capital flows are exogenously imposed, either to increase Mexican capital by a fixed amount or to lower the marginal product of capital to a fixed level.

Table 1.2 Changes in Economic Welfare in Different Applied General Equilibrium Simulations of NAFTA

	Canada		Mexico		United States	
Simulation	Total[a] (%)	GDP (%)	Total[a] (%)	GDP (%)	Total[a] (%)	GDP (%)
NAFTA: Tariffs, NTBs	3.51	0.7	1.98	1.6	6.43	0.1
NAFTA: Tariffs, NTBs, Foreign investment	3.66	0.7	6.30	5.0	13.23	0.3
U.S.-Mexico: Tariffs, NTBs	0.08	0.0	1.93	1.5	3.66	0.1
U.S.-Mexico: Tariffs, NTBs, Foreign investment	0.23	0.0	6.26	4.9	10.65	0.2
U.S.-Canada	3.36	0.6	0.04	0.0	2.87	0.1

Source: D. K. Brown, A. V. Deardorff, and R. H. Stern, "A North American Free Trade Agreement: Analytical Issues and a Computational Assessment," manuscript, University of Michigan, 1991.

Note: [a]Billions of U.S. dollars.

The overall size of the impact depends on modeling assumptions. Brown presents an excellent summary and evaluation of the different results.[11] In models with constant returns to scale and perfect competition, such as that of Bachrach and Mizrahi,[12] the effects tend to be small; this is because they only pick up the traditional gains caused by countries expanding the production of goods in which they have comparative advantage and thereby increasing efficiency within North America.

Other models—such as the Brown, Deardorff, and Stern, the Cox and Harris, the Roland-Holst, Reinert, and Shiells, and the Sobarzo models—find larger gains because they model some industries as operating under conditions of increasing returns to scale and imperfect competition.[13] In the Cox and Harris and the Sobarzo models, where domestic producers collude to set prices as high as possible, lowering trade barriers has the maximum possible procompetitive effects, forcing producers to lower prices and produce at a more efficient scale. In these models, there are relatively large gains. Furthermore, in the Cox and Harris model, Canada benefits significantly from NAFTA, over and beyond the benefits that it reaps from the U.S.-Canada FTA, because the threat of competition from Mexico forces Canadian producers to operate more efficiently, even though there may be few Mexican exports to Canada under NAFTA. The Brown, Deardorff, and Stern model treats producers as monopolistically competitive, and it obtains a lesser procompetitive effect than do the Cox and Harris and the Sobarzo models. Roland-Holst, Reinert, and Shiells model markets as contestable, which is the closest possible assumption to perfect competition in models with increasing returns. Here, the procompetitive effects are even smaller, and the results are similar to those in models with perfect competition.

The models with enough detail for this purpose point to some obvious winners and losers among the different sectors. There should be an overall expansion in agricultural trade, with grain and oil seed production expanding in Canada and the United States and contracting in Mexico. Conversely, fruit and vegetable production should expand in Mexico at the expense of that in the United States. This is obviously an area where care is needed in structuring the transition, given the large numbers of poor farmers engaged in growing corn in Mexico and of migrant farm workers engaged in picking fruits and vegetables in the United States. Sugar and apparel producers in the United States also seem likely to lose significant market shares to Mexican producers, although this depends on how far NTBs in these sectors are actually lowered by NAFTA. Effects in industries such as textiles, automobiles, and automotive parts are ambiguous. It is possible that the U.S. textile industry will expand by acting as a supplier to Mexican apparel producers. Similarly, Mexican and U.S. automobile and automotive parts producers could engage in production-sharing relations, taking advantage of the comparative advantages of each country and becoming more competitive with producers from East Asia and Europe. In cases like these, much depends on the domestic content provisions written into the treaty.

An applied general equilibrium analysis of this sort becomes even more useful when the agreement is on the table. It can then be used to evaluate the different NTBs left in place by the treaty as well as the transition mechanisms included in it.

The Spanish Experience

Although large amounts of energy and resources have gone into constructing applied general equilibrium models and using them to perform policy analyses over the past two decades, it is surprising how little effort has been made in evaluating the performance of such models after such policy changes have actually taken place. Only by showing that a model can replicate and, to some extent, predict the principal developments that occur in the economic system that it intends to represent can we justify putting confidence into the results of such models. In this chapter, I compare modeling NAFTA to modeling Spain's entry into the EC in 1986, in order to evaluate the performance of these models. Spain's recent economic experience also serves as a possible indication of what would happen in Mexico as a result of NAFTA.

One approach to empirically validating a model is to investigate how well it performs in tracking the impact of policy changes and exogenous shocks after these shocks have occurred. Such exercises have been performed by Dervis, de Melo, and Robinson; Devarajan and Sierra; and Parmenter, Meagher, McDonald, and Adams.[14] Another approach is to compare predictions with actual outcomes. The problem with this approach is that the actual data can be significantly affected by unforeseen exogenous shocks that happen concurrently with the foreseen policy change. Applied general equilibrium modelers of the U.S.-Canada FTA complain, for example, that it is difficult to compare their predictions with the economic experience of the last several years because of the recessions in both countries. Because applied general equilibrium models have very explicit structures, however, it should be possible to disentangle the impacts of different shocks and policy changes by using the model.

Kehoe, Polo, and Sancho take a step in this direction.[15] They assess the performance of a model of the Spanish economy built in 1984–1985 to analyze Spain's 1986 entry into the EC. The first column of Table 1.3 shows the percentage changes in relative prices that actually took place in Spain between 1985 and 1986. The second column shows the model predictions. In each case, the prices have been deflated by an appropriate index so that a consumption-weighted average of the changes sums to zero: These sorts of models are designed to predict changes in relative prices, not in price levels. Notice that the model fares particularly badly in predicting the changes in the food and nonalcoholic beverages sector and in the transportation sector. There are obvious historical explanations for these failings: In 1986, the international price of petroleum fell sharply, and poor weather caused an exceptionally bad harvest in Spain. Incorporating these two exogenous shocks into the model yields the results in the third column in Table 1.3, which correspond remarkably well to the actual changes.

Kehoe, Polo, and Sancho perform similar exercises comparing model results, both with and without the exogenous shocks, with the actual data

Table 1.3 Comparison of Spanish Model's Prediction with the Data by Sector (percentage change in relative price[a])

Sector	Actual 1985–1986	Model	Adjusted Model
1. Food and nonalcoholic beverages	1.8	–2.3	1.7
2. Tobacco and alcoholic beverages	3.9	2.5	5.8
3. Clothing	2.1	5.6	6.6
4. Housing	–3.2	–2.2	–4.8
5. Household articles	0.1	2.2	2.9
6. Medical services	–0.7	–4.8	–4.2
7. Transportation	–4.0	2.6	–6.6
8. Recreation	–1.4	–1.3	0.1
9. Other services	2.9	1.1	2.8
Weighted correlation with 1985–1986[b]	1.000	–0.079	0.936

Source: T. J. Kehoe, C. Polo, and F. Sancho, "An Evaluation of the Performance of an Applied General Equilibrium Model of the Spanish Economy," Working Paper 480, Federal Reserve Bank of Minneapolis, 1992.

Notes: [a] Change in sectoral price index deflated by appropriate aggregate price index.
[b] Weighted correlation coefficients with actual changes 1985–1986. The weights used are (1) 0.2540, (2) 0.0242, (3) 0.0800, (4) 0.1636, (5) 0.0772, (6) 0.0376, (7) 0.1342, (8) 0.0675, (9) 0.1617; these are the consumption shares in the model's benchmark year, 1980.

for changes in industrial prices, production levels, returns to factors of production, and major components of GDP. In general, the unadjusted model does somewhat better in predicting the actual changes in these variables than it does in predicting those in relative prices of consumption goods; the adjusted model does somewhat worse. Overall, however, the exercise shows that this sort of model can do a good job of predicting the changes in relative prices and resource allocation that result from a major policy change.

To be sure, the major policy change that occurred in Spain in 1986 was a tax reform that converted most indirect taxes to a value-added tax, in accordance with EC requirements. The process of trade liberalization began in 1986 and is captured in the model. Unlike the modeling exercises discussed in the previous section, however, the work on Spain did not concentrate on trade issues. Consequently, the results from the Spanish model do not help us much in discriminating among the model structures utilized in the various models for analyzing NAFTA.

One way to evaluate these different modeling strategies would be to modify the Spanish model, incorporating alternative assumptions about product differentiation, returns to scale, and market structure. Alternative versions of the model could then be used to "predict" the impact of the trade liberalization that has occurred in Spain in recent years, and the results could be compared with the data. Similarly and more to the point, the different models used to analyze the impact of NAFTA could be evaluated by using them to "predict" the impact of the policy changes and exogenous shocks that have buffeted the three North American economies over the past decade.

If NAFTA is implemented, it will be possible, in less than a decade, to go back and see which models performed better in predicting its effects. One difficulty with doing this involves comparing sectoral disaggregations across models. Modelers have an obligation to provide a correspondence between the sectors in their models and accessible statistical sources. The consumption goods sectors in the Spanish model, for example, correspond to those in the consumer price index published by the Spanish government, and the industrial sectors correspond to those in the national income accounts. Furthermore, details on this correspondence have been published; see Kehoe, Manresa, Polo, and Sancho.[16]

Spanish experience also indicates that real exchange rate movements can swamp the effects of lowering tariffs. Table 1.4 recounts the history of the real exchange rates of Mexico, Spain, and the United States over the past twelve years. The real exchange rate is an index of the rate at which a domestic basket of goods trades for an international basket of goods. A large number indicates a high price of foreign goods relative to domestic goods; this would tend to encourage exports and discourage imports. Notice in Table 1.4 how Spain's real exchange rate appreciated up to 1991 after that country joined the EC. A similar phenomenon already seems to be taking place in Mexico.

Table 1.4 Real Exchange Rate Indices[a] (1980 = 100): 1980–1991

	Mexico	Spain	United States
1980	100.0	100.0	100.0
1981	84.2	110.6	81.9
1982	115.2	112.4	82.9
1983	125.4	130.4	80.1
1984	102.9	127.1	74.3
1985	99.1	125.3	72.7
1986	144.6	108.3	81.5
1987	157.5	100.4	87.0
1988	130.1	97.8	90.3
1989	118.3	93.6	86.7
1990	114.5	80.9	88.1
1991	109.9	94.4	102.5

Source: Data from Banco de México, Mexico; Instituto Nacional de Estadística and Banco de España, Spain; and Department of Commerce, Bureau of Economic Analysis, United States.

Note: [a] The real exchange rate of country i is defined as:

$$Q_i = (P^*/P_i) \times (E_i/E^*) \times 100$$

where P^* is an international price index, expressed in units of a basket of currencies of 133 countries, per an international basket of goods; P_i is the domestic consumer price index expressed in domestic currency per domestic basket of goods; E_i is the exchange rate in domestic currency per dollar; and E^* is an international exchange rate in baskets of currencies per dollar. Q_i is therefore expressed in units of domestic baskets of goods per international basket of goods.

Figure 1.4 illustrates the large swings in the real peso–U.S. dollar exchange rate (obtained by dividing the figures in the first column of Table 1.4 by those in the third column and multiplying by 100). Notice that the movements in this exchange rate overwhelm the reduction of the existing tariffs to zero. A glance at these sorts of numbers explains why efforts to establish a common currency have made so much progress in Europe. It is hard not to speculate about the pressures that will build up in North America to at least smooth out fluctuations like those pictured in Figure 1.4.

One obvious explanation for the sharp real appreciations of the Mexican peso and the Spanish peseta, captured by the statistics in Table 1.4, is the large amount of foreign investment flowing into each country as trade liberalization has taken effect. In each case, investment in the stock market has expanded more rapidly than direct investment (see Table 1.5).

As Kehoe stresses, the dynamic impact of NAFTA is likely to dwarf the static impact analyzed by most applied general equilibrium models.[17] Perhaps the major impact that entry into the EC has had on the Spanish economy has been the sharp increase in foreign investment, shown in Table 1.5. This foreign investment is closely related to increases in GDP and imports. From 1980 to 1985, investment in Spain actually fell by 1 percent per year, as shown in Table 1.6. In contrast, since Spain's entry into the EC in

Figure 1.4 Real Exchange Rate Index, Mexican/U.S. Goods

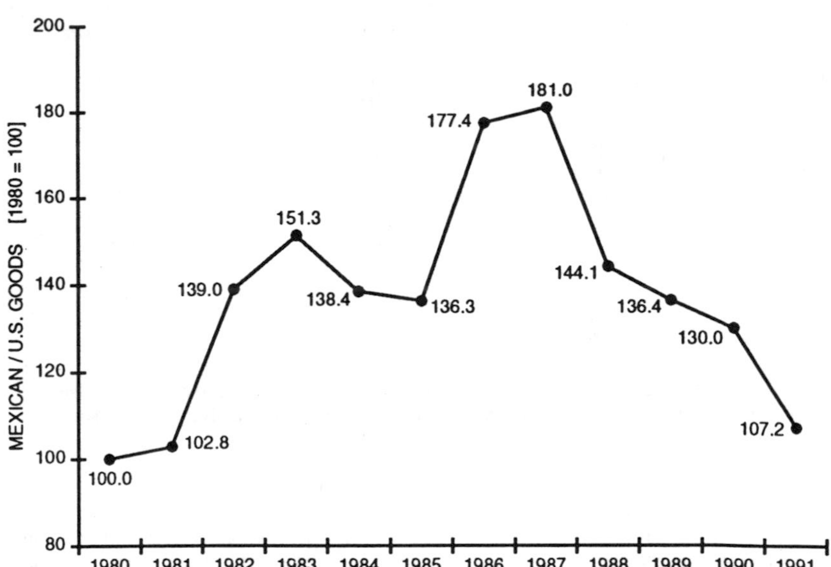

Source: Data from Banco de México and U.S. Department of Commerce, Bureau of Economic Analysis.

Table 1.5 Foreign Investment[a] in Mexico and Spain, 1980–1991 (millions of U.S. dollars)

	Mexico			Spain		
	Direct Investment	Portfolio Investment	Total	Direct Investment	Portfolio Investment	Total
1980	2,155	—[b]	2,155	1,182	—	1,182
1981	3,836	—	3,836	1,436	103	1,539
1982	1,657	—	1,657	1,272	–68	1,204
1983	461	—	461	1,379	42	1,421
1984	391	—	391	1,523	54	1,577
1985	491	—	491	1,718	232	1,950
1986	1,522	—	1,522	3,073	1,228	4,301
1987	3,248	—	3,248	3,825	3,799	7,624
1988	2,595	—	2,595	5,786	2,291	8,077
1989	3,037	493	3,530	6,955	7,989	14,944
1990	2,633	1,995	4,628	10,904	5,368	16,265
1991	4,762	7,540	12,302	5,721[c]	19,385[c]	25,106[c]

Source: Data from Banco de México and IMF, International Financial Statistics.
Notes: [a] Does not include investment in real estate. [b] — indicates no investments.
[c] Preliminary estimates.

Table 1.6 Growth Rates of GDP and Various Components in Mexico and Spain, 1980–1991 (real change in percent per year)

	Mexico				Spain			
	GDP	Investment	Exports	Imports	GDP	Investment	Exports	Imports
1980	8.3	14.9	6.1	31.9	1.5	1.3	0.6	3.8
1981	8.8	16.2	11.6	17.7	–0.2	–3.3	8.4	–4.2
1982	–0.6	–16.8	21.8	–37.9	1.2	0.5	4.8	3.9
1983	–4.2	–28.3	13.6	–33.8	1.8	–2.5	10.1	–0.6
1984	3.6	6.4	5.7	17.8	1.8	–5.8	11.7	–1.0
1985	2.6	7.9	–4.5	11.0	2.3	4.1	2.7	6.2
1986	–3.8	–11.8	5.3	–12.4	3.3	10.0	1.3	16.5
1987	1.7	0.1	10.1	2.0	5.6	14.0	6.1	20.2
1988	1.4	5.8	5.0	37.6	5.2	14.0	5.1	14.4
1989	3.1	6.5	3.0	19.0	4.8	13.8	3.0	17.2
1990	3.9	13.4	5.2	22.9	3.6	6.9	3.2	7.8
1991	3.6	8.5	5.1	16.6	2.4	1.6	8.4	9.4

Sources: Data from Instituto Nacional de Estadística Geografía e Informática, Mexico, and Instituto Nacional de Estadística, Spain.

1986, investment has grown by 10 percent per year on average. Similarly, GDP growth has increased from a 1.4 percent yearly average in 1980–1985 to 4.1 percent in 1986–1991, and import growth has increased from 1.3 percent to 14.2 percent. A similar pattern has emerged in Mexico with the *apertura,* or openness policy, that began to take effect in 1988 and 1989.

NAFTA could be expected to reinforce this pattern, with substantial increases in GDP fueled by foreign and domestic investment and with even more substantial increases in imports leading to large trade deficits. In both Spain and Mexico, many (if not most) of the current discussions of economic openness in the press, among academic analysts, and in policy circles concentrate on the sustainability of these investment booms and the corresponding trade deficits.

There are, of course, many differences between Spain's experience after joining the EC and Mexico's experience in joining NAFTA. Some commentators like to stress the regional development funds that the EC allocates to its poorer members. As a percentage of GDP, however, these numbers are trivial: In 1990, for example, the funds Spain received from the EC amounted to 0.28 percent of GDP for regional policy, 0.11 percent for social policy, and 0.57 percent for agricultural policy. It must be remembered that these funds are generated by member state contributions; Spain's net receipts from the EC in 1990 amounted to only 0.23 percent of GDP. These sorts of numbers are typical for the poorer members of the EC. Rather than regional or social policy, the major component of the EC budget is the Common Agricultural Policy, and the principal beneficiary of this policy is France, one of the richer members.

A far more significant difference between the Spanish experience and the Mexican experience is the lack of labor mobility between the two countries. Table 1.7 shows estimates of workers' remittances from abroad for Mexico, three relatively poor EC countries, and Turkey. Even though the Mexican number is hard to estimate because of illegal immigration and even though it may be underestimated, it is clear that the lack of legal labor mobility would affect Mexico in NAFTA in ways that it has not affected the poorer countries in the EC.

Another area in which Spain's experience differs from Mexico's is in population growth (see Figure 1.5). Table 1.8 reports population growth numbers in Mexico that are astonishing in comparison with those in Spain and the United States. Although this population growth has slowed significantly in recent years, Mexico has been left with a large baby boom

Table 1.7 Net Workers' Remittances, 1990, from Various Immigrant-Sending Countries

	Total[a]	Percent of GDP	Per Capita[b]
Greece	1,775	3.07	175.74
Mexico	2,020	0.85	23.43
Portugal	4,271	7.52	410.67
Spain	1,747	0.36	44.79
Turkey	3,246	3.36	57.86

Source: World Bank, *World Development Report* (New York: Oxford University Press, 1992).
Notes: [a] Millions of U.S. dollars. [b] U.S. dollars.

generation entering into the work force. These new workers must be equipped with capital, both physical and human, if levels of output per worker are to be increased—or even just maintained.

Capital Flows

Lack of labor mobility in NAFTA could be largely offset by capital flows. One would expect capital to flow from the relatively capital-rich Canada and the United States to the relatively capital-poor Mexico. Indeed, it is by exogenously imposing a substantial capital flow of this sort that many of the static models are able to show a significant welfare gain to Mexico. Two points about capital flows should be stressed, however. First, differences in capital-labor ratios between Mexico and its northern neighbors cannot be the sole explanation for the large differences in output per worker. Consequently, simply equalizing capital-labor ratios cannot be the solution to the problem of eliminating income differences. Second, when analyzing the savings and investment decisions that determine capital flows, we must take into account the significant differences in the age profiles of populations in Mexico and its neighbors.

The argument that differences in capital-labor ratios cannot be the sole explanation of differences in output per worker across the three countries

Figure 1.5 Growth Rate of Population in Mexico, the United States, and Spain, 1930–1990

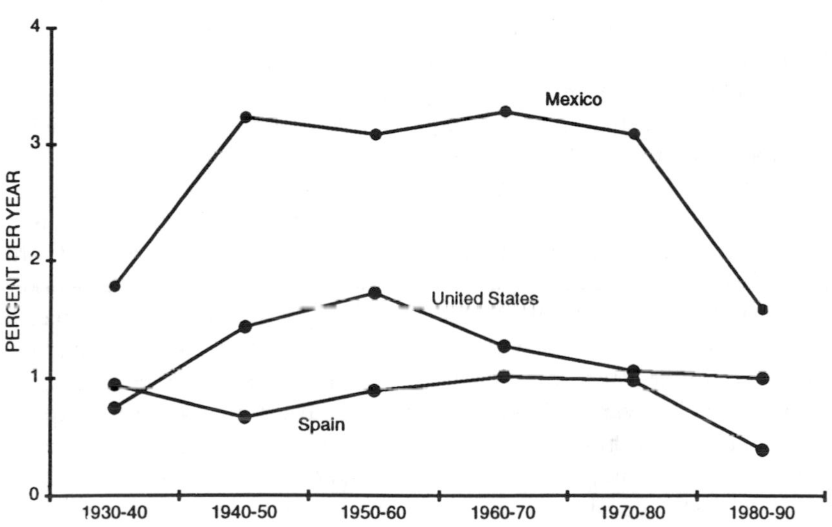

Source: Data from Nacional Financiera, *La Economía Mexicana en Cifras* (Mexico: Nacional Financiera, 1991); Instituto Nacional de Estadística; and U.S. Department of Commerce, Bureau of the Census.

Table 1.8 Total Population of Mexico, Spain, and the United States, 1930–1990 (population in millions and average yearly growth rate per decade)

	Mexico		Spain		United States	
Decade	Total	Growth Rate	Total	Growth Rate	Total	Growth Rate
1930	16.7	—	24.0	—	122.7	—
1940	19.9	1.78	26.4	0.94	132.1	0.74
1950	27.4	3.23	28.2	0.66	152.3	1.43
1960	37.1	3.08	30.8	0.89	180.7	1.72
1970	51.2	3.28	34.0	1.01	205.1	1.27
1980	69.4	3.09	37.5	0.98	227.8	1.06
1990	81.3	1.59	39.0	0.39	251.5	1.00

Source: Data from National Financiera, *La Economía Mexicana en Cifras* (Mexico: Nacional Financiera, 1991); Instituto Nacional de Estadística, Spain; and Department of Commerce, Bureau of the Census, United States.

Note: — indicates no data for the decade from 1920 to 1930.

of North America is fairly simple: If capital is relatively scarce in Mexico, then its marginal product should be much higher there than in the United States or Canada. Therefore, we should observe much higher real interest rates in Mexico than in the United States or Canada. Based on the output per worker figures of Summers and Heston for Mexico and the United States in 1988, which differ by a factor of 2.6, simple calculations in the Technical Appendix to this chapter show that real interest rates in Mexico should have been more than 86 percent per year.[18] During the period 1988–1990, the real return on bank equity in Mexico (and banks are the major source of private capital there) averaged 28.2 percent per year, as compared to 4.7 percent in the United States.[19] Because 28 percent is far lower than the 86 percent that we would expect if differences in capital-labor ratios were the principal determinants of the differences in output per worker between Mexico and its neighbors, we must look elsewhere for an explanation.

A more general point is that differences in capital per worker cannot be the sole explanation of differences in output per worker across countries. This is supported both by historical evidence, such as that of Clark, and by even more extreme examples of differences in output per worker: According to Summers and Heston, for example, real GDP per worker in Haiti in 1988 was 4.9 percent of that in the United States.[20] Calculations like those in the Technical Appendix would suggest that interest rates in Haiti should be over 11,000 percent per year if differences in the capital-labor ratio were the sole explanation of the differences in output per worker. Furthermore, historical evidence indicates that Mexico has not always been starved of funds for investment. The problem has often been that investments abroad, particularly in the United States, have been more attractive. Between 1977 and 1982, for example, $17.8 billion of private investment flowed into Mexico, and $18.7 billion flowed out.[21]

Although capital flows cannot provide all the answers to Mexico's problems, they are important. If capital flows could lower the net interest rate in Mexico from 28 percent to 5 percent per year, we would estimate that the capital-labor ratio in Mexico would increase by a factor of about 5.5 (see Technical Appendix for details). This would increase Mexican output per worker to about $24,300, which would close the current gap with the U.S. level by about 42 percent.

Some of the current high return on capital in Mexico can be accounted for by an inefficient and oligopolistic financial services sector. NAFTA might increase the efficiency of this sector. Even more significantly, NAFTA would create a stable economic environment that would encourage private investment in Mexico. It would do this in at least two ways. First, it would lock the Mexican government into the free trade policy and the liberal policy toward foreign direct investment that it is currently pursuing unilaterally. Second, it would shield Mexican producers from protectionist tendencies in the United States, which fluctuate with the business cycle and are sensitive to a variety of special interest groups. Direct foreign investment in Mexico has increased dramatically in recent years, as seen in Table 1.5. Some of this increase had been due to the liberalization of Mexican laws regarding such investments, and some has undoubtedly resulted from improvements in the expectations for Mexico's economic future.

One point to be stressed about capital flows into Mexico is that they are now—and probably will be in the future—tiny in comparison with capital flows into the United States over the past decade: In 1989, for example, the United States absorbed $71.9 billion in foreign direct investment, $59.2 billion in investment in equities, $35.0 billion in investment in corporate bond purchases, and $128.2 billion in government bond purchases.[22] Mexico still has a long way to go in terms of receiving foreign direct investment before it becomes a major recipient by international standards (see Figures 1.6 and 1.7).

A sensible analysis of capital flows must model consumer savings decisions. In this instance, we must take into account demographic differences between the countries of North America. To illustrate the importance of demographic differences, I note that half the population of Mexico is currently under the age of twenty, but the populations of Canada and the United States are currently aging as the postwar baby boom generation reaches middle age; see Table 1.9. These differences would be very important in an overlapping-generations context in which life-cycle consumers dissave when young and build up human capital; save during the middle years of their lives; and dissave again when old, during retirement. An example of an applied general equilibrium model with overlapping generations is provided by A. J. Auerbach and L. J. Kotlikoff.[23] Modeling demographic differences in an overlapping-generations framework would

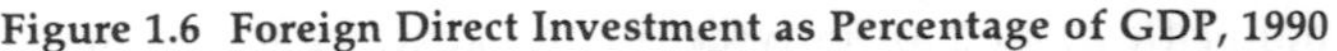

Figure 1.6 Foreign Direct Investment as Percentage of GDP, 1990

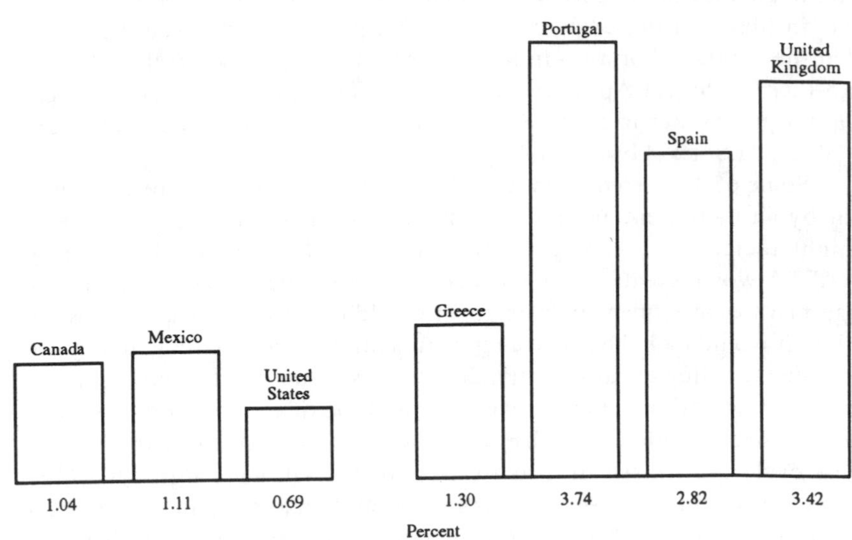

Source: World Bank, *Global Economic Prospects and the Developing Countries* (Washington, DC: World Bank, 1992), and World Bank, *World Development Report* (New York: Oxford University Press, 1992).

be especially important in a model in which the accumulation of both human and physical capital plays an important role.

Productivity Growth

As we have seen, a low capital-labor ratio cannot be the only factor in explaining the low level of output per worker in Mexico compared to that in a country like the United States. It is in this area that the new, endogenous growth literature, which follows P. M. Romer and R. E. Lucas and focuses on endogenous technical change, may provide potential answers.[24] This literature is still at a tentative, mostly theoretical level. In this section, I use preliminary empirical work at an aggregate level to estimate the impact of free trade on growth rates in Mexico.

Although my calculations are fairly crude, they suggest that the dynamic impact of NAFTA could dwarf the static effects found by more conventional applied general equilibrium models. R. Baldwin has done similar kinds of suggestive calculations to estimate the dynamic gains from the European Community's 1992 Program.[25] Unlike Baldwin's analysis, however, the results presented here are based on theories and empirical

Figure 1.7 Per Capita Foreign Direct Investment, 1990

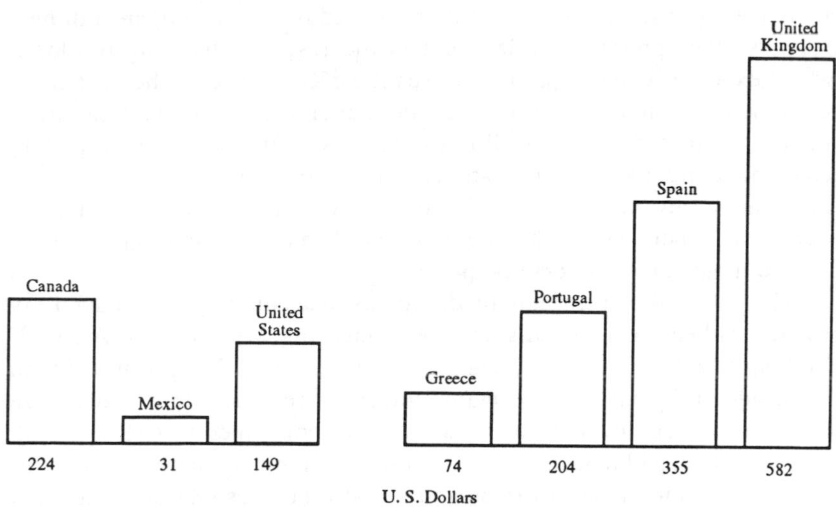

Source: World Bank, *Global Economic Prospects and the Developing Countries* (Washington, DC: World Bank, 1992), and World Bank, *World Development Report* (New York: Oxford University Press, 1992).

Table 1.9 Population of Mexico, Spain, and the United States by Age Groups, 1990 (percentage)

Age	Mexico	Spain	United States
0–15	41.0	21.4	23.2
16–24	19.2	15.2	13.0
25–64	35.6	50.0	51.2
65 and over	4.2	13.4	12.6

Source: Data from Instituto Nacional de Estadística Geografía e Informática, Mexico; Instituto Nacional de Estadística, Spain; and Department of Commerce, Bureau of the Census, United States.

estimates that deal with trade directly. Baldwin obtains his numbers by multiplying estimates of static gains from trade obtained by other researchers by a multiplier derived from a highly aggregated growth model with dynamic increasing returns but without any explicit role for trade. Neither Baldwin's analysis nor that presented here takes into account phenomena like unemployment or underutilization of capacity. It is possible that a free trade agreement would provide dynamic gains based on a more traditional macroeconomic analysis; S. Fischer has some suggestive results in this regard.[26]

Although endogenous growth literature is still at a tentative stage, the intuition behind it is fairly simple. Increased openness can alter the growth rate in clear ways: Economic growth is spurred by the development of new products. New product development is the result of learning by doing (where experience in one product makes it easier to develop the next product in the line) and of direct research and development. On the final product side, increased openness allows a country to increase specialization, achieving a larger scale of operations in those industries in which it has a comparative advantage. On the input side, increased openness allows a country to import, rather than develop itself, many technologically specialized inputs to the production process.

The potential that learning by doing has in accounting for productivity growth has been recognized since the pioneering work of K. J. Arrow.[27] The long history of micro-evidence goes back to T. P. Wright, who found that productivity in airframe manufacturing increased with cumulative output at the firm level.[28] Later studies have confirmed this relationship at both the firm and industry level. Recent research that incorporates learning by doing into models of trade and growth includes that of Stokey and Young.[29]

Consider the following simple framework, as presented by D. K. Backus, P. J. Kehoe, and T. J. Kehoe. Output in an industry in some country depends on inputs of labor and capital, country- and industry-specific factors, and an experience factor that depends, in turn, on previous experience and output of that industry in the prior period.[30] Keeping constant the rates of growth of inputs, the crucial factor in determining the rate of growth of output per worker is the rate of growth of the experience factor. Output per worker grows faster in industries in which this experience factor is higher. The level of growth of output per worker nationwide is a weighted average of the rates of growth across industries. One way increased openness promotes growth is by allowing a country to specialize in certain product lines and attain more experience in related industries.

Modeling dynamic increasing returns as the result of learning by doing is a reduced form specification for a very complex microeconomic process. It captures the effects of the learning curve documented by industrial engineers and, to some extent, the adoption of more efficient production techniques from abroad and from other domestic industries. The learning that takes place is not solely related to physical production techniques but also to the development of complex financial and economic arrangements between producers of primary and intermediate goods and producers of final goods. The ability of a country to benefit from learning by doing depends on the educational level of the work force. It also depends on whether a country is at the frontier of development of new products and production techniques or if it can import these from abroad: It is easier to play catch-up than to be the technological leader.

Increased openness also allows a country to import more specialized inputs to the production process. Stokey and Young have proposed models in which new product development is still the result of learning by doing but in which the primary impact of learning by doing is in the development of new, more specialized inputs.[31] Trade allows a country to import these inputs without developing them itself. P. Aghion and P. Howitt, G. M. Grossman and E. Helpman, L. Rivera-Batiz and P. M. Romer, and others have proposed similar models in which it is research and development that leads to the development of new products.[32] (Here, of course, the relationship of trade and growth is more complicated if one country can reap the benefits of technological progress in another country by importing the technology itself without importing the products that embody it.)

The most interesting aspect of this theory, however, is the perspective it gives us on trade and growth. The natural interpretation of the theory that emphasizes specialization in final products is that technology is embodied in people and is not tradeable. Trade may influence the pattern of production, including both the scale of production and the pattern of specialization, and in this way, it affects growth. In the model with specialized inputs, technology is embodied in product variety, and there is a more subtle interaction between trade and growth. Recall that increases in the number of varieties of intermediate goods raise output. Therefore, if these varieties are freely traded, a country can either produce them itself or purchase them from other countries. By importing these products, a small country can grow as fast as a large one. When there is less than perfectly free trade in differentiated products, we might expect to find that both scale and trade in differentiated products are positively related to growth.

Using cross-country data from a large number of nations over the period 1970–1985, Backus, Kehoe, and Kehoe analyze the determinants of growth.[33] Various other researchers have used similar cross-country data sets to estimate the parameters of endogenous growth models; R. Levine and D. Renelt offer a survey of this work.[34] Typically, researchers in this area find that their results are very sensitive to the exact specifications of the model and the inclusion or exclusion of seemingly irrelevant variables. Backus, Kehoe, and Kehoe find, however, that in explaining rates of growth of output per worker in manufacturing, results related to the theory sketched out in this section are remarkably robust. Using their methodology, we can estimate some parameters for a model in which both specialization in final output and the ability to import specialized inputs foster growth. The results of this estimation are found in the Technical Appendix. In terms of trade policy, the crucial variables in this analysis are a measure of specialization in exports and a measure of the extent to which a country is open to trade in highly specialized inputs. For the first measure, I use a specialization index for exports, and for the second, I use the

Grubel-Lloyd index, a common measure of intraindustry trade; both are described in the Technical Appendix.[35]

My results indicate that changes in the manufacturing productivity growth rate correspond to changes in these two measures given by the following formula:

$$g' - g = 0.309 \log\left(\frac{ES'}{ES}\right) + 0.890 \log\left(\frac{GL'}{GL}\right)$$

Here, g' and g are the new and the old productivity growth rates measured in percent per year, ES' and ES are the new and the old export specialization indices, and GL' and GL are the new and the old Grubel-Lloyd indices.

To illustrate the dramatic impact of trade liberalization possible in a dynamic model that contains the endogenous growth features discussed in this section, let us suppose that NAFTA allowed Mexico to increase its level of specialization in production of final manufactured goods and imports of specialized inputs. The average values over 1970–1985 of the specialization indices and Grubel-Lloyd indices for the three North American countries follow. The values of the same indices for South Korea, a country with about the same output per worker as Mexico, are also included for comparison.

	Export Specialization Index	Grubel-Lloyd Index
Canada	7.10×10^{-2}	0.638
Mexico	5.93×10^{-4}	0.321
United States	1.92×10^{-3}	0.597
Korea	5.43×10^{-2}	0.362

Suppose that free trade allows Mexico to increase its specialization index to 1.0×10^{-2} and its Grubel-Lloyd index to 0.6. Dramatic increases of this sort are possible: In 1970, for example, Ireland had a Grubel-Lloyd index for manufactured goods of 0.150; in 1980, seven years after joining the European Community, this index was 0.642.

Using that relationship, we would estimate the increase in the growth rate of manufacturing output per worker of 1.43 percent per year:

$$1.430 = 0.309 \log\left(\frac{1.00\times10^{-2}}{5.93\times10^{-4}}\right) + 0.890 \log\left(\frac{0.600}{0.321}\right) = 0.873 + 0.557$$

It is clear that much is at stake in the issues discussed here. Suppose that Mexico is able to increase its growth rate of output per worker by an additional 1.43 percent per year by taking advantage of both specialization and increased imports of specialized intermediate and capital goods. After thirty years, its level of output per worker would be more than 50 percent higher than it would otherwise have been. By way of comparison, if Mexico's output per worker had been 50 percent higher in 1988 than it actually was, then Mexico's output per worker would be about the same as Spain's.[36] My earlier calculations suggested that Mexico could increase its output per worker by about 66 percent by increasing its capital per worker until the rate of return on capital is equal to that in the United States. Admittedly, these calculations are very crude, but they suggest that increased openness has a significant impact on growth through dynamic increasing returns. Furthermore, the dynamic benefits of increased openness dwarf the static benefits found by more conventional applied general equilibrium models.

Obviously, this is an area that requires more research, and even a crude disaggregated dynamic general equilibrium model of North American economic integration would make a substantial contribution. More empirical work also needs to be done. Notice, for example, that the Grubel-Lloyd indices reported earlier fail to capture the observation that Korea is fairly closed in final goods markets but open to imports of intermediate and capital goods.

My analysis therefore suggests that Mexico has more to gain from free trade than either Canada or the United States. Both of the latter countries are already fairly open economies, and the United States is big enough to exploit its dynamic scale economies. Mexico, however, has a smaller internal market. To follow an export-led growth strategy, it must look to the United States, as the trade statistics in Figure 1.3 indicate.

Notes

I would like to thank Karine Moe at the University of Minnesota and Patricia Bravo at the Secretaría de Comercio y Fomento Industrial for their help in gathering the data.

1. See L. Johansen, *A Multi-Sectoral Study of Economic Growth* (Amsterdam: North-Holland, 1960), and J.S. Shoven and J. Whalley, "A General Equilibrium Calculation of the Effects of Differential Taxation of Income from Capital in the U.S.," *Journal of Public Economics* 1 (1972):281–321.

2. R. Summers and A. Heston, "The Penn World Table (Mark 5): An Expanded Set of International Comparisons, 1950–1988," *Quarterly Journal of Economics* 106 (1991):327–368.

3. For a summary of these barriers, see U.S. International Trade Commission, *The Likely Impact on the United States of a Free Trade Agreement with Mexico,* Publication 2353 (Washington, DC: ITC, 1991).

4. D.K. Brown, A.V. Deardorff, and R.H. Stern, "A North American Free Trade Agreement: Analytical Issues and a Computational Assessment," manuscript, University of Michigan, 1991.

5. C. Bachrach and L. Mizrahi, "The Economic Impact of a Free Trade Agreement Between the United States and Mexico: A CGE Analysis," manuscript, KPMG Peat Marwick, 1992.

6. D. Cox and R.G. Harris, "North American Free Trade and Its Implications for Canada: Results from a C.G.E. Model of North American Trade," manuscript, University of Waterloo, 1991; H.E. Sobarzo, "A General Equilibrium Analysis of Gains from Trade for the Mexican Economy of a North American Free Trade Agreement," manuscript, El Colegio de México, 1992.

7. D. Roland-Holst, K.A. Reinert, and C.R. Shiells, "North American Trade Liberalization and the Role of Nontariff Barriers," manuscript, U.S. International Trade Commission, 1992; R. Hinojosa-Ojeda and S. Robinson, "Alternative Scenarios of U.S.-Mexico Integration: A Commutable General Equilibrium Approach," Discussion Paper 609, University of California–Berkeley, 1991.

8. L. Hunter, J.R. Markusen, and T.F. Rutherford, "Trade Liberalization in a Multinational-dominated Industry: A Theoretical and Applied General Equilibrium Analysis," manuscript, University of Colorado, 1991; I. Trela and J. Whalley, "Bilateral Trade Liberalization in Quota Restricted Items: U.S. and Mexico in Textiles and Steel," manuscript, University of Western Ontario, 1991; S. Levy and S. van Wijnbergen, "Transition Problems in Economic Reform: Agriculture in the Mexico-U.S. Free Trade Agreement," manuscript, World Bank, 1991; and S. Robinson, M.E. Burfisher, R. Hinojosa-Ojeda, and K.E. Thierfelder, "Agricultural Policies and Migration in a U.S.-Mexico Free Trade Area: A Computable General Equilibrium Analysis," manuscript, Department of Agricultural and Resource Economics, University of California–Berkeley, 1991.

9. A. Young, "Learning by Doing and the Dynamic Effects of International Trade," *Quarterly Journal of Economics* 106 (1991):369–406, and R.K. McCleery, "An Intertemporal, Linked, Macroeconomic CGE Model of the U.S. and Mexico Focussing on Demographic Change and Factor Flows," manuscript, East-West Center, Honolulu, 1992.

10. Brown, Deardorff, and Stern, "A North American Free Trade Agreement."

11. D.K. Brown, "The Impact of a North American Free Trade Agreement: Applied General Equilibrium Models," manuscript, Tufts University, 1992.

12. Bachrach and Mizrahi, "The Economic Impact of a Free Trade Agreement."

13. See Brown, Deardorff, and Stern, "A North American Free Trade Agreement"; Cox and Harris, "North American Free Trade and Its Implications for Canada"; Roland-Holst, Reinert, and Shiells, "North American Trade Liberalization"; and Sobarzo, "A General Equilibrium Analysis."

14. See K. Dervis, J. de Melo, and S. Robinson, *General Equilibrium Models for Development Policy* (Cambridge: Cambridge University Press, 1982), Chapter 10; S. Devarajan and H. Sierra, "Growth Without Adjustment: Thailand, 1973–1982," manuscript, World Bank, 1986; and B.R. Parmenter, G.A. Meagner, D. McDonald, and P.D. Adams, "Structural Change in the 1970s: Historical Simulations with ORANI-F," Institute of Applied Economic and Social Research, University of Melbourne, 1990.

15. T.J. Kehoe, C. Polo, and F. Sancho, "An Evaluation of the Performance of an Applied General Equilibrium Model of the Spanish Economy," Working Paper 480, Federal Reserve Bank of Minneapolis, 1992.

16. T.J. Kehoe, A. Manresa, C. Polo, and F. Sancho, "Una matriz de contabilidad social de la economía española," *Estadística Española* 30 (1988):5–33.

17. T.J. Kehoe, "Towards a Dynamic General Equilibrium Model of North American Free Trade," in Joseph Francois and Clint Shiells, eds., *Modeling Trade*

Policy: Applied General Equilibrium Assessments of North American Free Trade (Cambridge: Cambridge University Press, forthcoming).

18. Summers and Heston, "The Penn World Table (Mark 5)," pp. 327–368.

19. See P.M. Garber and S.R. Weisbrod, "Opening the Financial Services Market in Mexico," manuscript, Brown University, 1991.

20. See G. Clark, "Why Isn't the Whole World Developed? Lessons from the Cotton Mills," *Journal of Economic History* 47 (1987):141–173, and Summers and Heston, "The Penn World Table (Mark 5)," pp. 327–368.

21. P. Garcia-Alba and J. Serra-Puche, *Financial Aspects of Macroeconomic Management in Mexico* (Mexico City: El Colegio de México, 1985), p. 45.

22. See the *Economic Report of the President* (Washington, DC: U.S. Government Printing Office, 1991).

23. A.J. Auerbach and L.J. Kotlikoff, *Dynamic Fiscal Policy* (Cambridge: Cambridge University Press, 1987).

24. See P.M. Romer, "Growth Based on Increasing Returns Due to Specialization," *American Economic Review* 77 (1987):56–62, and R.E. Lucas, "On the Mechanics of Economic Development," *Journal of Monetary Economics* 22 (1988):3–42.

25. R. Baldwin, "Measurable Dynamic Gains from Trade," *Journal of Political Economy* 100 (1992):162–174.

26. S. Fischer, "Growth, Macroeconomics, and Development," *NBER Macroeconomics Annual* 6 (1992):329–364.

27. K.J. Arrow, "The Economic Implications of Learning by Doing," *Review of Economic Studies* 24 (1962):155–173.

28. T.P. Wright, "Factors Affecting the Cost of Airplanes," *Journal of Aeronautical Sciences* 3 (1936):122–128.

29. See N.L. Stokey, "Learning by Doing and the Introduction of New Goods," *Journal of Political Economy* 96 (1988):701–717, and Young, "Learning by Doing."

30. D.K. Backus, P.J. Kehoe, and T.J. Kehoe, "In Search of Scale Effects," *Journal of Economic Theory* 58 (1992):377–409.

31. See Stokey, "Learning by Doing and the Introduction of New Goods," and Young, "Learning by Doing."

32. See P. Aghion and P. Howitt, "A Model of Growth Through Creative Destruction," manuscript, Massachusetts Institute of Technology, 1989; G.M. Grossman and E. Helpman, "Product Development and International Trade," *Journal of Political Economy* 97 (1989):1261–1283; and L. Rivera-Batiz and P.M. Romer, "International Trade with Endogenous Technological Change," manuscript, University of Chicago, 1989.

33. Backus, Kehoe, and Kehoe, "In Search of Scale Effects."

34. R. Levine and D. Renelt, "A Sensitivity Analysis of Cross-Country Growth Regressions," manuscript, World Bank, 1990.

35. See H. Grubel and P.J. Lloyd, *Intra-Industry Trade* (London: Macmillan, 1975).

36. Data for this comparison are from Summers and Heston, "The Penn World Table (Mark 5)."

Technical Appendix

Differences in Output per Worker and Interest Rates

To illustrate the point that differences in capital-labor ratios cannot explain the differences in output per worker that are observed between the United States and Mexico, we can perform calculations similar to those of Lucas (1990). Suppose that each of the two countries has the same production function:

$$Y_j = \gamma N_j^{(1-\alpha)} K_j^{\alpha}$$

where Y_j = GDP
N_j = size of work force
K_j = capital
γ and α = parameters
j = country identification (us = United States and mex = Mexico)

In per capita terms, where $y_j = Y_j/N_j$ and $k_j = K_j/N_j$, this becomes $y_j = \gamma k_j^{\alpha}$. The net return on capital r_j is

$$r_j = \alpha \gamma k_j^{(\alpha-1)} - \delta$$

where δ is the depreciation rate. In 1988, according to Summers and Heston (1991), real GDP per worker was \$14,581 in Mexico and \$37,608 in the United States. Suppose that $\alpha = 0.3$, which is roughly the capital share of income in the United States. Then, to explain this difference in output per worker, we need capital per worker to be larger than that in Mexico by a factor of 23.5,

$$\frac{k_{us}}{k_{mex}} = \left(\frac{y_{us}}{y_{mex}}\right)^{1/\alpha} = \left(\frac{37{,}608}{14{,}581}\right)^{1/0.3} = 23.5$$

Suppose that $\delta = 0.05$ and $r_{us} = 0.05$, which are roughly the numbers obtained from calibration. Then, the net real interest rate in Mexico should be 17.2 times that in the United States,

$$r_{mex} = (r_{us} + \delta)\left(\frac{k_{us}}{k_{mex}}\right)^{1-\alpha} - \delta = 0.10(23.5)^{0.7} - 0.05 = 0.86$$

At least two objections can be raised to the above calculations. First, a comparison based on per capita GDP in U.S. dollars using the exchange rate to convert pesos into dollars would suggest that y_{us}/y_{mex} is much larger, about 7.9. Second, calibrating the capital share parameter using Mexican GDP data would yield a larger value, about 0.5. These two objections work in opposite directions, however, and the calculations can be defended as being in a sensible middle ground: Income comparisons based on exchange rate conversions neglect purchasing-power parity differentials, much of what is classified as net business income in Mexico is actually returned to labor, per capita comparisons rather than per worker comparisons neglect demographic differences, and so on.

If we accept that other factors besides differences in capital-labor ratios must be crucial in explaining differences in output per worker, we must accept that Mexico and the United States have different production technologies. One possibility is that the constant terms differ:

$$Y_j = \gamma N_j^{(1-\alpha)} K_j^{\alpha}$$

This difference could be explained by differences in infrastructure, level of education of the work force, and so on. Using this production function, we can estimate the impact of policies that would result in an inflow of capital into Mexico that lower the net real interest from 28 percent to 5 percent per year.

We first estimate the change in the capital-labor ratio:

$$k_{mex} = [\alpha \gamma_{mex}/(r_{mex} + \delta)]^{1/(1-\alpha)}$$

$$\frac{k'_{mex}}{k_{mex}} = \left(\frac{r_{mex} + \delta}{r'_{mex} + \delta}\right)^{1/(1-\alpha)} = \left(\frac{0.28 + 0.05}{0.05 + 0.05}\right)^{1/0.7} - 5.5$$

Plugging this change into the production function, we can estimate the increase in output per worker that would result from this capital inflow:

$$\frac{y'_{mex}}{y_{mex}} = \left(\frac{k'_{mex}}{k_{mex}}\right) = 1.67$$

which implies that output per worker would increase to about $24,300 per year.

Openness to Trade and Productivity Growth

Consider a relationship of the form

$$g(\overline{y}^j) = \alpha + \beta_1 \log \overline{Y}^j + \beta_2 \log \sum_{i=1}^{I} (\overline{X}_i^j/\overline{Y}^j)^2 + \beta_3 \log \overline{GL}^j + \beta_4 \log y^j + \beta_5 \, PRIM^j + \epsilon^j$$

where $g(\bar{y}^j)$ = average yearly growth of manufacturing output per worker in percent form from 1970 to 1985

$\bar{Y}^j$ = 1970 manufacturing output

$\sum_{i=1}^{I} (\bar{X}_i^j/\bar{Y}^j)^2$ = specialization index for exports at the three-digit SITC level

$\overline{GL}^j$ = 1970 Grubel-Lloyd index of intraindustry trade

y^j = 1970 per capita income

$PRIM^j$ = 1970 primary school enrollment

A bar above the variable indicates that the variable deals with the manufacturing sector only; the specialization index and the Grubel-Lloyd index, for example, are computed for manufacturing industries only.

The Grubel-Lloyd (1975) index for country j is

$$GL^j = \frac{\sum_{i=1}^{I} (X_i^j + M_i^j - |X_i^j - M_i^j|)}{X^j + M^j}$$

where X_i^j = exports of industry

M_i^j = imports of industry

X^j = total exports

M^j = total imports

Backus, Kehoe, and Kehoe (1991) find a strong positive relation between the Grubel-Lloyd index for all products at the three-digit SITC level and growth in GDP per capita for a large sample of countries. They also find a strong positive relationship between the Grubel-Lloyd index for manufactured products and growth in manufacturing output per worker. Trade in category 711, nonelectrical machinery, might consist of imports of steam engines (7113) and exports of domestically produced jet engines (7114). Simultaneous imports and exports of these goods provide the country with both and lead to more efficient production.

I include total manufacturing output and the specialization index to account for the impact of specialization in production of final goods. One motivation for using export data is that specialization is most important in the export sector. Another motivation is purely practical: The trade data permit a more detailed breakdown of commodities. Furthermore, the export specialization index can be thought of as a proxy for the total production specialization index: If exports are proportional to outputs, then

$$\overline{X}_i^j = \epsilon \overline{Y}_i^j$$

and

$$\sum_{i=1}^{I} (\overline{X}_i^j / \overline{Y}^j)^2 = \epsilon^2 \sum_{i=1}^{I} (\overline{Y}_i^j / \overline{Y}^j)^2$$

and the two indices are proportional. The Grubel-Lloyd index is included, as I have explained, because it captures, in a loose way, the ability of a country to trade in finely differentiated products, which my theory implies is important for growth. I include initial per capita income and the primary enrollment rate partly because they are widely used by other researchers in this area, such as Barro (1991), and partly because they may be relevant to my theory: The inclusion of per capita income allows for less-developed countries, which are playing catch-up in order to face different technological constraints. The inclusion of the enrollment rate allows for differences in countries' ability to profit from learning by doing because of differences in levels of basic education.

A regression of this relationship yields

$$g(\overline{y}^j) = \underset{(5.686)}{2.602} + \underset{(0.259)}{0.743} \log \overline{Y}^j + \underset{(0.113)}{0.309} \log \sum_{i=1}^{I} (\overline{X}_i^j / \overline{Y}^j)^2$$

$$+ \underset{(0.410)}{0.890} \log \overline{GL}^j - \underset{(0.799)}{0.172} \log y^j + \underset{(2.271)}{2.421} \, PRIM^j$$

$$NOBS = 49 \qquad R^2 = 0.479$$

(The numbers in parentheses are heteroskedasticity-consistent standard errors.) Notice that in this regression, the coefficients all have the expected signs and that the first three variables—total manufacturing output, the specialization index, and the Grubel-Lloyd index—are all statistically significant.

2

Adjustment and Transition Mechanisms for a U.S.-Mexico Free Trade Agreement

Howard Rosen

The North American Free Trade Agreement, although it promises to benefit all the parties involved, will place additional pressure on the U.S. labor market.[1] The adjustment pressures associated with any agreement come against the backdrop of the structural changes in the U.S. labor market that have been taking place over the last two decades. In addition, increased trade resulting from a successful outcome of the multilateral negotiations of the Uruguay Round of the General Agreement on Tariffs and Trade (GATT), strengthening of the internal market under the European Community 1992 Program, and market liberalization in Eastern Europe and the former Soviet republics are certain to intensify competitive pressures facing U.S. producers and workers over the coming years.

The economic gains derived by liberalizing trade are *net* gains—there are both winners and losers. This point has grown in significance as international trade has become more important to the U.S. economy. The benefits of trade liberalization may outweigh their associated costs, as many have argued concerning the U.S.-Mexico free trade agreement. But we cannot ignore the fact that critical segments of the U.S. economy may experience severe dislocation as a result of such liberalization. Experience suggests that these dislocation effects are usually concentrated by industry and region, making the adjustment process even more difficult. Empirical studies suggest that trade-dislocated workers tend to be minorities, women, and older workers.[2] These workers face high barriers to adjustment.

The responsibility to assist those workers adversely affected by changes in international trade can be argued on ethical, economic, and political grounds.[3] It seems only just to help the few who are adversely affected by policies designed to benefit the economy as a whole. Government labor market programs serve as one vehicle for helping reduce the adjustment burden borne by these workers. On the other hand, inadequate programs feed the sense of insecurity that targeted workers experience as they face the prospect of economic change, thus strengthening their opposition to such change and jeopardizing any potentially greater economywide benefits that might result from trade liberalization.

A Brief Survey of U.S. Labor Market Programs

Over the years, the United States has developed an array of programs designed to assist dislocated workers, including those whose jobs are particularly sensitive to changes in international trade (see Table 2.1 for a survey of these programs). The largest and most far-reaching of these programs is unemployment insurance (UI).

Unemployment Insurance

Under the existing unemployment insurance program, unemployed workers on behalf of whom contributions have been made to the UI trust fund are eligible to receive twenty-six weeks of benefits, equal to, on average, between 35 to 40 percent of their previous wages. The program also allows for an additional thirteen weeks of benefits under certain conditions during periods of considerable economic downturn. Workers must show that they are actively searching for work in order to receive benefits.

Reflecting the public's dislike of large government-supported income maintenance programs, the benefits of the U.S. unemployment insurance program are less generous and of shorter duration than those of similar programs in other industrialized countries. On the one hand, some claim that this has reduced long-term unemployment in the United States relative to Europe, where unemployed workers receive benefits for longer periods. On the other hand, recent reports suggest that possibly only one-third of all unemployed workers collect benefits under the U.S. program due, in large part, to restrictive eligibility criteria. On average over the last decade, only half of the total number of unemployed workers were eligible for these benefits because UI does not cover new entrants, reentrants, and those who leave their jobs voluntarily.

Unemployment insurance aims primarily to offset income loss during unemployment spells. Only limited attention is paid to making job-search assistance available, and there is no training provided under this program. Furthermore, benefits are structured around previous wages and are not sensitive to difficulties that individual workers might experience in finding new jobs, such as those related to age, family status, education level, or location.

Job Training Partnership Act

Other programs offer additional benefits to selected groups of workers, attempting to address some of the inadequacies of UI. In addition to income maintenance payments under the UI program, dislocated workers receive job-search and training assistance under the Job Training Partnership Act (JTPA) and, more recently, under the Economic Dislocation and Worker Adjustment Assistance (EDWAA) program. The Reagan administration proposed JTPA in 1982 as a replacement for the Comprehensive Employment and Training Act (CETA). JTPA encompasses many of the same activities that were available under CETA, except for public service employment, but JTPA funding is substantially lower than that of CETA. Following the Reagan era policy of "new federalism," the new law decentralized the program, providing states with increased responsibility for benefit delivery and oversight. JTPA covers training services for economically disadvantaged youth and adults (Title II-A), the summer youth employment and training program (Title II-B), employment and training services for dislocated workers (Title III), employment and training services for Native Americans and migrant and seasonal farm workers (Title IV-A), the Job Corps (Title IV-B), and veterans' employment and training programs (Title IV-C).

Title III of JTPA authorized state programs to provide job-search assistance, classroom training, on-the-job training, relocation assistance, and pre-layoff assistance to dislocated workers, defined as individuals who were laid off and unlikely to return to their previous industries or occupations. This included workers who lost their jobs as a result of permanent plant closings as well as the long-term unemployed who had substantial barriers to employment, such as advanced age or lack of skills. States received three-quarters of the Title III funds according to a formula based on the magnitude and character of unemployment.

In addition to decentralizing the distribution of the program's benefits, the federal government also delegated data collection and program monitoring activities to the states, making it more difficult to evaluate the program's effectiveness. An early review of JTPA by the U.S. General Accounting Office (GAO) suggested that less than 10 percent of the eligible displaced workers received benefits under Title III in the first three years of the program.[4] Another early evaluation indicated that older workers and those with modest educations are less likely to be served by JTPA than would be expected based on their representation in the population of displaced workers. Such findings suggest that those individuals who are most in need of assistance are actually least likely to receive it under JTPA programs for displaced workers.[5]

Economic Dislocation and Worker Adjustment Assistance Act

Two important developments relating to JTPA occurred in 1988. First, the Worker Adjustment and Retraining Notification Act (WARN) was enacted in July, requiring certain firms to provide sixty days' advance notice to

Table 2.1 U.S. Labor Market Adjustment Programs

Program	Eligibility	Benefits	Financing	Coverage
Unemployment insurance	Involuntary unemployment.	Income maintenance payments, at 35–40 percent of previous wages for 26 weeks, with possible 13-week extension.	UI trust fund financed by employer payments; $20.2 billion in FY 1990 and $28.3 billion in FY 1991.	2.5 million in 1990, 37 percent of unemployed workers (larger number for 1991).
Job Training Partnership Act/ Economic Dislocation and Worker Adjustment Assistance	Dislocated workers, defined as those who have little possibility of returning to their previous jobs.	Job-search assistance, training, and relocation benefits. Possibility of needs payments if enrolled in training. All benefits are determined and distributed at the state and local levels.	Federal share is budgetary outlay by congressional appropriation. Three-fourths of funds are allocated to states based on matching formula, of which 60 percent must be further distributed to substate level. Half of all JTPA/EDWAA funds must be allocated for training; $425 million in FY 1990 and $500 million in FY 1991.	150,000 average per year between 1984 and 1989; less than 10 percent of eligible workers.

Trade Adjustment Assistance	Workers previously employed by firms that have been certified by U.S. Department of Labor as being hurt by imports.	Income maintenance payments set at UI level for up to 52 weeks (inclusive of regular UI benefits) and may be extended for an additional 26 weeks. Payments conditioned on enrollment in training. Job-search assistance, training, and relocation benefits available.	Financed entirely through budgetary outlay by congressional appropriation; $160 million in FY 1990 and $240 million in FY 1991.	In 1989, 90 000 workers were certified, 24,000 received payments, and 17,000 enrolled in training. (Certification dropped significantly in 1990.)
Clean Air Act	Workers adversely affected by implementation of acid rain regulations.	Same as JTPA. Needs-related payments are conditioned on training.	$50 million additional congressional appropriation to JTPA for FY 1990.	Not yet implemented.
Defense Conversion Act	Workers displaced by cutbacks in defense programs.	Same as JTPA.	$150 million additional congressional appropriation to JTPA for FY 1991.	Not yet implemented.

workers prior to a mass layoff or plant closing. Second, Congress enacted significant changes in Title III of JTPA under the Economic Dislocation and Worker Adjustment Assistance Act, which was passed as part of the Omnibus Trade and Competitiveness Act. According to these changes: (1) state rapid-response units are to be created; (2) states are to pass on at least 60 percent of JTPA/EDWAA funds to substate areas, and (3) half of those substate funds are to be spent on training rather than job-search assistance and related activities.

Under JTPA/EDWAA, the federal government provides most of the program's funding, but benefits are distributed locally. This separation of responsibilities reflects recent evidence that local programs are better suited for reaching targeted populations. Yet it is difficult to measure JTPA/EDWAA's true effectiveness at helping workers adjust because only a small percentage of eligible workers participate in the program. The number of people who took part in JTPA between 1985 and 1989 represented only 18 percent of the total number of dislocated workers during that period.[6] Thus, although this program may be successful in assisting those workers who participate, it appears to be much too small to make a difference in addressing any overall adjustment pressures in the economy at large.[7]

Trade Adjustment Assistance

The third labor market instrument of U.S. adjustment policy is the Trade Adjustment Assistance (TAA) program. Created in 1962, TAA was an attempt to garner labor support for the Trade Expansion Act of 1962, authorizing U.S. participation in the Kennedy Round of GATT negotiations. Under TAA, workers who had lost their jobs because of trade concessions could apply for income maintenance payments and training benefits. However, a strict interpretation of eligibility requirements prevented anyone from receiving benefits under the program until 1969, and even after a more liberal reinterpretation of these requirements, only 46,000 workers received benefits over the following five years.

Congress made significant program changes in the Trade Act of 1974, once again as a means to gain support for another round of trade negotiations, this time the Tokyo Round. Eligibility requirements were liberalized, and the benefit package was enriched. A worker no longer had to prove that his or her job loss was due to a trade concession but only that increased imports "contributed importantly" to that loss. Income maintenance payments (trade readjustment allowances, or TRAs) were set at 70 percent of the worker's previous wage but could not be more than the national average wage in manufacturing. TRA payments were made in addition to regular UI payments, although both benefits together were capped at 80 percent of the worker's previous wage. The eligibility period remained fifty-two weeks, with a possible twenty-six-week extension for workers over sixty or enrolled in a training program. Workers could also be compensated for 80 percent of their job-search and relocation costs, up to a maximum of $500.

After eligibility requirements were made less restrictive and after merchandise imports more than doubled between 1974 and 1980, there was a significant increase in petitions for TAA benefits. The number of workers receiving TRA grew from 62,000 in 1976 to over 500,000 in 1980. Likewise, TRA outlays grew from $71 million in 1976 to $1.6 billion in 1980.[8] However, the number of workers who received training under this program never rose above 5 percent of all workers receiving TRA payments. Coupled with administrative problems, which resulted in many workers receiving lump-sum benefits after they had found new jobs or returned to their old jobs, these figures indicated that TAA was not contributing to long-run labor market adjustment.

This criticism, together with the administration's efforts at reducing nonmilitary government expenditures, led President Reagan to recommend abolishing TAA in 1981. The administration argued against maintaining a separate program for trade-impacted workers and instead supported a revised, although smaller, economywide training program.[9] Congress accepted JTPA but also insisted on maintaining TAA, albeit with certain revisions. As a result of the Omnibus Budget Reconciliation Act of 1981, TRA payments were reduced, and the emphasis of TAA shifted from income maintenance to training and other reemployment benefits. TRA payments were reduced to the same level as standard UI benefits, and payment could begin only after workers exhausted their UI benefits. UI and TRA payments were capped at fifty-two weeks; if a worker was enrolled in training, benefits could continue for another twenty-six weeks.

Following the 1981 changes, there was a noticeable decline in the number of TAA petitions received and approved and, accordingly, a decline in the amount of government outlays under the program.[10] Even so, the Reagan administration continued its efforts to abolish the program and bring these workers under the umbrella of JTPA. Congress rejected every attempt, although it agreed to several program changes. The Consolidated Omnibus Budget Reconciliation Act of 1985, which extended the life of TAA, required a worker to be enrolled in a job-search program as a condition for receiving TRA benefits. Under the Omnibus Trade and Competitiveness Act of 1988, TAA was further extended to September 30, 1993, and eligibility was expanded for a one-time inclusion of workers engaged in oil exploration and drilling. Injury determination criteria and the benefit package were left intact, although the requirement that workers be enrolled in training as a condition for receiving TRA payments was strengthened.

The number of workers certified for TAA remained quite low between 1981 and 1985 but rose rather sharply in fiscal years (FYs) 1986 and 1987, probably in response to the worsening trade situation. The number of certified workers declined in FY 1988, as the traded goods sector began adjusting to the depreciation of the dollar. Over 116,000 workers were certified for TAA benefits during the two years following the program changes enacted in the Omnibus Trade and Competitiveness Act of 1988; more than 40 percent were from the oil and gas industry.[11] Another 41 percent of the certified workers were from the apparel and automobile industries.[12]

The training component of TAA remains rather small, with expenditures equaling only one-fifth of the amount allocated for TRA payments. Outlays for job-search assistance and relocation benefits are even smaller. For the most part, TAA's primary function remains income maintenance, even after several attempts to change the program's focus.

Overall, U.S. labor adjustment policies during the 1980s had three characteristics: (1) general economywide programs were emphasized, (2) responsibility for benefit delivery and evaluation was passed to the states, and (3) heavy emphasis was placed on training rather than income maintenance as the programs' main objective. The creation of JTPA and EDWAA and repeated attempts by the administration to cancel TAA reflected these policy objectives. TAA survived the decade—although in a drastically reduced form—due to continued congressional support for the program.

The TAA program that existed between 1977 and 1981 provided more generous benefits than the current JTPA program, and not surprisingly, participation rates were much higher. Between 1977 and 1981, when TAA was most active, a little more than 1 million workers received TRA benefits, or approximately 7 percent of the total number of workers who involuntarily lost their jobs during that period. By contrast, less than 1 million workers participated in JTPA between 1984 and 1989, approximately 4 percent of the number of involuntarily unemployed during that period, in spite of the fact that JTPA eligibility requirements are much more liberal and the pool of potential workers is much wider than under TAA.[13] The most important distinction between JTPA/EDWAA and TAA is that TAA is an entitlement, similar to unemployment insurance. As an entitlement, it guarantees workers the benefits mandated under the program. In contrast, benefits provided under JTPA/EDWAA are discretionary and, as a result, vary by state. Furthermore, the absence of any incentive to spend funds budgeted for JTPA/EDWAA has contributed to low participation rates.

Nonetheless, evaluations of TAA prior to 1981 do not provide any clear evidence that participation led to more efficient or more rapid labor market adjustment, despite the program's generous benefits and relatively large enrollment. In addition, it is difficult to argue that TAA and any effect it may have had in helping workers to adjust to changes in international trade significantly offset protectionist pressures in the United States. Almost two-thirds of the workers certified for TRA benefits between April

1975 and September 1989 were employed in the automobile, textile and apparel, and steel industries, which also were protected by formal or voluntary export agreements negotiated or extended during the same period.

Several recent congressional actions suggest that U.S. labor market policies continue to undergo change. In both the Clean Air Act of 1990 and the Defense Conversion Act of 1990, Congress insisted on including adjustment programs in order to secure approval. Under the Clean Air Act, Congress allocated to JTPA an additional $50 million per year for five years to assist coal miners who might lose their jobs as a result of the act's acid rain provisions. In addition to the basic training and other job-search assistance benefits available under JTPA/EDWAA, extended financial assistance will be available to workers if they are enrolled in qualified training programs and have exhausted their UI benefits. Likewise, the 1990 Defense Department Reauthorization Bill provides compensation for people who lose their jobs due to base closings or reorganizations. The important thing to note in this regard is that Congress remains sensitive to the needs of workers adversely affected by changes in economic conditions and government policies.

International Comparisons

Based on a review of labor market programs in the industrialized countries, it appears that in both absolute and relative terms, U.S. programs are embarrassingly limited in scope.[14] The United States provides the lowest benefits package for the shortest period of all the major industrialized countries (Table 2.2). Under the UI program, workers can receive between 35 to 40 percent of previous earnings for up to twenty-six weeks, compared to 60 percent in Canada, 30 to 75 percent in France, over 60 percent in Germany, and between 60 to 80 percent (for up to one year) in Japan.

Moreover, public expenditures on unemployment insurance as a percent of gross domestic product in the United States are approximately one-third of those in the United Kingdom and one-quarter of those in Canada, France, and Germany (Table 2.3). Relative U.S. expenditures on all labor market programs are lower than in most other industrialized countries, and they are only marginally higher than in Japan. In terms of expenditures, benefits, and participation, U.S. efforts to train workers are also quite small in relation to GDP (Table 2.4). U.S. government expenditures for training, about one-third of 1 percent of GDP, are significantly smaller than similar expenditures in Canada, France, Germany, and the United Kingdom. It is estimated that the United States spends approximately $1,800 per participant on training, one-fourth of the amount Germany allocates. The participation rate for U.S. training programs is also the lowest among the five countries reviewed, at 1 percent of the labor force.

Table 2.2 International Comparison of Unemployment Insurance Programs, Selected Industrialized Countries

Country	Eligibility	Benefits	Financing
United States	Varies by state.	Income maintenance payments average 35 to 40 percent of previous year's wages for 26 weeks. Benefits can be extended for 13 weeks in cases of severe economic downturn. Some job-search assistance is available. Training provided under JTPA (EDWAA).	Employer contributions vary by state.
Canada	Minimum of 10 weeks of work, with contributions.	60 percent of previous earnings, up to $680 per week. Term of coverage depends on employment history and regional unemployment level. No possibility of extension. Some training available.	Employer and employee contributions. Employer contribution is 140 percent of employee contribution.
France	Minimum employment of 3 months, with contributions.	Benefits based on length of previous employment, ranging from 30 to 75 percent of previous wages. Training and job counseling also available.	Employer and employee contributions. Employer contributions are between 150 and 180 percent of employee contributions.
Germany	Must be employed for at least 1 year over a 3-year period.	Benefits range from 63 to 68 percent of previous earnings, depending on family status. Benefit term depends on days worked, with a minimum of 22 weeks, and age.	Equal employer and employee contributions.
Japan	Must be employed for 6 months prior to layoff.	Benefits range from 60 to 80 percent of previous wages for 90 to 300 days, depending on worker's age and length of contribution to insurance fund.	Employer and employee contributions.
United Kingdom	Must be employed for at least 1 full year, with contributions.	Benefits based on marital and family status, not linked to previous earnings. Can receive benefits for up to 1 year. No extensions are available. Job counseling and training are available.	Employers contribute between 5 and 10 percent of wages, and employees contribute between 7 and 9 percent of wages.

Table 2.3 Government Expenditures on Labor Market Programs, Selected Industrialized Countries, 1988–1990 (as a percent of GDP)

Country	Training	Unemployment Compensation	Total Labor Market Programs
Canada	0.22	1.58	2.09
France	0.28	1.34	2.87
Germany	0.23	1.30	2.32
Japan	NA	0.36	0.52
United Kingdom	0.22	0.94	1.62
United States[a]	0.10	0.38	0.62

Source: Organization for Economic Cooperation and Development, *Labor Market Policies for the 1990s* (Paris: OECD, 1990), pp. 52–53.
Note: [a] U.S. data include Perkins Act vocational training.

Proposed Changes in Trade Adjustment Assistance

Proposals for changes in the existing TAA program can be grouped into three areas: eligibility, benefits, and financing. In the area of eligibility, recent debate has focused on targeted versus general labor programs. Changes in labor market programs during the Reagan administration shifted the emphasis away from special programs (TAA) and toward general, economywide programs (JTPA). Recent initiatives concerned with workers adversely affected by the Clean Air Act and the Defense Conversion Act have shifted this emphasis once again back to programs for selected groups of workers.

As already suggested, workers whose job loss is related to changes in international trade differ from dislocated workers as a whole; therefore, some special attention to their adjustment needs is warranted. But limiting a program to cover only those workers adversely affected by changes in U.S.-Mexican trade would be too restrictive. The difficulties that already exist in identifying trade-impacted workers would be exacerbated by confining certification to workers affected by U.S.-Mexican trade. The result would probably be a return to the conditions that typified the period between 1962 and 1969, when no workers were certified for TAA benefits because of strict eligibility criteria. In addition, this kind of program would overlook dislocation that resulted from third-market trade effects under the U.S.-Mexico free trade agreement.

Another set of questions concerning eligibility involves secondary workers. The existing TAA program does not include workers in industries that provide inputs for trade-sensitive sectors or service workers in communities that experience trade-related dislocation. It is hard to defend a policy of providing assistance to the final producers and not to other workers who experience similar adjustment pressures. Short of improving and

Table 2.4 Training Programs in Selected Industrialized Countries, 1988–1990

Country	Participation (percent of labor force)	Average Duration (months)	Total Expenditures (percent of GDP)	Expenditures per Participant (U.S. $)	Expenditures per Participant (percent of average income)
Canada	1.1	6.0	0.22	7,000	37
France	2.3	2.5	0.28	4,600	27
Germany	1.5	8.0	0.25	7,200	37
United Kingdom	1.4	NA	0.22	5,000	31
United States	1.0	3.5	0.05	1,800	9

Source: Organization for Economic Cooperation and Development, *Labor Market Policies for the 1990s* (Paris: OECD, 1990), p. 35.

strengthening economywide adjustment programs, matching the benefit levels of TAA, the best alternative would be to extend TAA to secondary workers.

Eligibility for TAA is currently determined by industry certification, which is prompted by a petition filed by a group of firms or workers. An alternative trigger might be a regional determination. This method could address two important facts of trade-related dislocation: First, trade-related dislocation tends to be highly concentrated by region; second, it is more difficult to find a new job in an area experiencing high unemployment. Workers in a region might become eligible for TAA when unemployment rises above a certain level and if the region's employment is highly reliant on international trade, as determined by trade as a percentage of the local economy or by an indicator of a change in import penetration.[15] This method would also take into account the broader definition of secondary workers.

The second area for possible program reform concerns the actual benefit package. Under the current TAA program, workers are eligible for income maintenance payments, training, relocation allowances, and job-search assistance. The most important aspect of the program's benefit structure is that it is an entitlement, which means that all eligible workers are guaranteed the benefits upon request, regardless of the number of people seeking benefits or any budgetary ceiling. The entitlement aspect of the program should be preserved so that workers can truly depend on the availability of benefits when they need them.

One problem with the existing benefit package is that there is no incentive to enroll in training until after unemployment insurance benefits are exhausted (that is, twenty-six weeks after separation). The program should be changed to encourage people who have little possibility of returning to their previous job or who do not have a high level of skills to enroll in training while they receive their unemployment insurance payments. These payments should not be seen as "compensation" for losing a job but rather as income maintenance during a period of transition.

Better coordination of the various U.S. labor market programs is needed. Enrollment in TAA or EDWAA should not be exclusive; workers who are eligible for TAA should also be able to receive benefits under EDWAA if relevant. In addition, individual efforts at adjustment should be encouraged. The U.S. tax code should be changed to allow workers to deduct expenditures incurred in training for a *new* job. Unemployed workers should also be able to borrow against their pensions and individual retirement accounts (IRAs) during periods of dislocation to help pay for retraining and relocation, if necessary. Alternatively, people should be able to contribute to "individual training accounts" (ITAs), which would operate much like IRAs but for the sole purpose of helping workers make transitions during their professional careers. Unused funds could be treated like IRAs or other pension disbursements upon retirement.

The last area of program reform concerns financing. Currently, TAA is financed by direct government expenditures, with no revenue offset. One option might be to continue financing the program through general government expenditures while offsetting the cost by adding a small payroll tax. This method is used for unemployment insurance and extended benefits.

Another financing method could be designed along the lines of the "user fee" concept. For example, TAA might be financed by earmarking tariff revenues or an import surcharge or fee.[16] The Omnibus Trade and Competitiveness Act of 1988 directed U.S. trade representatives to negotiate GATT acceptance of an import fee, but they were not successful. As an alternative, the program might be financed through general tariff revenues, which are currently estimated at $17 billion and expected to rise at a rate of 5 percent per year. A portion of the total tariff revenue or simply the value of the annual increase might be used to finance TAA expenditures. The mechanism for such a process already exists because the original TAA was supposed to be financed by a Trade Adjustment Assistance Trust Fund, made up of tariff revenues.[17] The trust fund was never established, primarily as a result of the Office of Management and Budget's (OMB's) opposition to earmarked trust funds.

The original proposed trust fund suggests that the creators of TAA saw a link between industry relief and adjustment. This link could be resuscitated by designating revenue from tariffs granted under new industry petitions for relief or through earmarking the resulting revenue from converting quantitative restrictions to tariffs or auctioning quota rights. Such a conversion would provide additional benefits to the U.S. trade policy as a whole, and it would also create enough money to fund a generous adjustment program in the United States.

The third possibility would be to finance TAA through the use of the extended benefit trust fund. Given the changes in criteria for receiving extended unemployment insurance benefits and a payroll tax surcharge to replenish the fund following the 1982–1983 recession, the trust fund currently has close to $8 billion. One recent congressional proposal to expand extended benefits is estimated to cost slightly more than $5 billion. Thus, there would still be sufficient funds to finance, in part or in full, the TAA program. In addition to the fact that the resources are already allocated in a trust fund, TAA serves as a sort of extended unemployment insurance program in itself. And the adjustment burden under the U.S.-Mexico free trade agreement would be expected to decline as the amount of trade liberalization diminishes, thereby allowing time for the fund to be replenished in case of an economywide downturn.

Conclusion

The U.S. labor market must be flexible to meet the economic challenges on the horizon. The government should therefore maintain policies that enhance the U.S. competitive position abroad, and it must continue to work toward opening foreign markets to goods and services produced by U.S. workers. It must also provide adequate programs to help workers adjust to changing economic conditions at home and abroad. Existing U.S. labor market programs are inadequate to meet these challenges.

Such programs are currently too shortsighted. Unemployment insurance benefits are relatively small and are available for only a short period of time. This short-run orientation, according to two analysts, forces people to settle for lower-wage jobs and forego necessary retraining, thereby postponing any serious adjustment for the future.[18] In addition, workers must have a more secure income base if they are to undergo a serious retraining effort. Any adjustment program must provide adequate income maintenance to enable workers to undertake the kind of retraining they need to fully adjust to the changes currently taking place in the U.S. labor market.

Training is critical to the flexibility of any labor force. The transition between jobs is especially difficult for workers who lack basic skills, but a modest investment in training could significantly alter the income loss and reemployment hurdles they face. The movement from manufacturing to service jobs requires further retraining in different skills and appreciation for new technologies. Although training has received more attention in U.S. programs over the last few years, this attention has not translated into adequate funding. In fact, the current level of spending barely covers the costs of one class at the secondary-education level.

Regardless of the net effect of the U.S.-Mexico free trade agreement, increased trade between the two countries will most likely contribute to the adjustment pressures that already exist in the U.S. labor market. To preserve the greater benefits that will come to the economy as a whole through further trade liberalization, it is reasonable to address the needs of the few who will bear the burden. Improvement in the existing Trade Adjustment Assistance program, as outlined earlier, is the first step that should be taken.

Notes

1. See Gary C. Hufbauer and Jeffrey Schott, *North American Free Trade* (Washington, DC: Institute for International Economics, 1992).

2. See Michael C. Aho and James Orr, "Demographic and Occupational Characteristics of Workers in Trade-sensitive Industries," Economic Discussion Paper

2, Bureau of International Labor Affairs, U.S. Department of Labor, April 1980, and, more recently, Robert W. Bednarzik, "Trade-sensitive U.S. Industries: Employment Trends and Worker Characteristics," Economic Discussion Paper 37, Bureau of International Labor Affairs, U.S. Department of Labor, July 1990.

3. For a more complete discussion of the rationale behind adjustment programs, see Gary C. Hufbauer and Howard Rosen, "Trade Policy for Troubled Industries," *Policy Analyses in International Economics* 15 (Washington, DC: Institute for International Economics, March 1986), pp. 29–41.

4. U.S. General Accounting Office, *Dislocated Workers: Local Programs and Outcomes Under the Job Training Partnership Act*, GAO/HRD 87-41 (Washington, DC: GAO, 1987).

5. Margaret Simms, "The Effectiveness of Government Training Programs" (Paper prepared for the U.S. Department of Labor, Commission on Workforce Quality and Labor Market Efficiency).

6. See U.S. Department of Labor, "Summary of Title III Program Performance for Program Year 1989," mimeo, and Diane Herz, "Worker Displacement Still Common in the Late 1980's," *Monthly Labor Review* 114, no. 5 (May 1991):3–9.

7. The administration points to a survey that suggests that approximately 70 percent of JTPA participants found new jobs. But given the different nature of JTPA, it is difficult to compare this success rate with those of other programs. JTPA covers a broader population of workers—from manufacturing to services sectors, from unskilled blue-collar workers to highly educated white-collar professionals. In addition, the reemployment rate applies to all workers who receive any JTPA benefits, not just training.

8. Some critics claim that the Carter administration used TAA in an attempt to win the support of unions and other labor segments in its 1980 reelection bid, resulting in a large increase in benefit outlays in that election year.

9. See the previous discussion concerning the JTPA and its replacement of CETA.

10. When the percentage of petitions certified for benefits fell below 10 percent in 1981, some charged that the Department of Labor was being more restrictive in its certification process. This criticism was never proven, and the percentage of petition approvals since 1983 has returned to pre-1980 levels.

11. Under the law, workers from the oil and gas industry were given a limited period during which they were eligible to receive TAA benefits. This allowance added almost 50,000 people to the number of workers certified to receive TAA benefits after October 1988. Without these oil and gas workers, the number of certified workers would probably have been closer to 69,000 between October 1988 and August 1990.

12. This includes workers certified between October 1988 and August 1990. After subtracting the oil and gas workers from the total number of certified workers, apparel and automobile workers constituted almost three-quarters of all workers certified to receive TAA benefits between October 1988 and August 1990.

13. Again, the use of all involuntarily unemployed as the denominator results in an understatement of the percent of eligible workers who receive JTPA benefits, although it still provides some idea of the order of magnitude.

14. See Howard Rosen, "Recent Initiatives in Adjustment Policy: New Ideas or Old Habits?" (Paper prepared for the United Nations Conference on Trade and Development, January 1991).

15. Japan already employs such a trigger for its adjustment programs.

16. For a fuller discussion of these proposals, see Hufbauer and Rosen, "Trade Policy for Troubled Industries," and C. Fred Bergsten, Kimberly Ann Elliott, Jeffrey J. Schott, and Wendy E. Takacs, "Auction Quotas and US Trade Policy," *Policy Analyses in International Economics* 19 (Washington, DC: Institute for International Economics, September 1987).

17. This fund was to be established in accordance with Section 245 of the Trade Act of 1974.

18. Adam Seitchik and Jeffrey Zornitsky, *From One Job to the Next* (Kalamazoo, MI: W.E. Upjohn Institute for Employment Research, 1989).

3

The Environment: Unwelcome Guest at the Free Trade Party

Jan Gilbreath and John Benjamin Tonra

Perhaps the most startling development in the North American Free Trade Agreement debate was the emergence of the environment as an issue on the negotiating agenda. The mobilization of the powerful environmental lobby took U.S. and Mexican policymakers by surprise early in the negotiating process. Even after negotiations were complete, unresolved environmental questions still threatened the accord's ratification by the U.S. Congress and created deep divisions within the Democratic Party. And by fall 1993, the accord had been successfully challenged, at least temporarily, in the U.S. federal courts on the basis that it required an environmental impact statement (EIS).

A loose coalition of Canadian, U.S., and Mexican environmental groups had been able to press their governments for unprecedented environmental concessions in the creation of a trade instrument. The fruit of their labors was the successful negotiation, in August 1993, of a parallel environmental agreement to accompany NAFTA. Among other things, the agreement created a Commission for Environmental Cooperation with some authority to screen and arbitrate environmental disputes. The establishment of the commission broke new ground in linking international trade to environmental concerns through the mechanism of an international agreement. By pushing for a trilateral body with a far broader mandate than North American border commissions had previously enjoyed, environmentalists were successful in institutionalizing their concerns in a way that is likely to be repeated in a future round of the General Agreement on Tariffs and Trade. The commission, which is authorized to monitor environmental programs in NAFTA countries, is also likely to spur some concern among other Latin American nations that hope to sign on to the NAFTA accord in the near future.

Ironically, although the environmental lobby was forceful and successful in NAFTA trade negotiations, it had been splintered throughout the negotiating process.[1] Some differences surfaced after the Sierra Club, Friends of the Earth, and Public Citizen pursued their lawsuit to force an environmental impact statement on NAFTA, thereby threatening a lengthy delay or even the demise of the trade accord. Most leading U.S. environmental groups, particularly those that had set up offices in Mexico and undertaken cooperative programs with the Mexican government, were disturbed by the federal district court ruling for a NAFTA-related EIS. (This ruling was later overturned on appeal.) Other groups argued that Mexican underdevelopment would leave it prey to the depredations of international capital seeking an environmental free ride.

Many trade specialists and economists looked at the environmentalists' intervention as aberrant and part of an ideologically driven campaign. Others recognized that legitimate environmental issues were at stake but insisted that it would be technically impossible and politically unwise to muddy the waters of a free trade agreement with extraneous considerations. The U.S. administration overcame an initially dismissive response to the environmental community's demands and built a congressional coalition in favor of NAFTA. Indeed, public policy toward the environmentalists changed dramatically under the Clinton administration because the new president had campaigned on the promise that strong environmental and labor protections would be built into parallel accords to NAFTA.

Mexico's government asserted that criticisms of Mexican policy and enforcement were unfair and that most problems in these areas ultimately would be resolved by economic growth derived from a successful agreement. Worried, however, that the accord would be lost in the U.S. Congress and having invested so much of his own political capital in negotiating an accord, Mexican President Salinas agreed to the U.S. proposal for stronger environmental controls.

Initially, Canadian officials were the most sanguine. They had successfully dismissed the concerns of environmentalists in the debate over the U.S.-Canada Free Trade Agreement and expected to do so again. But when the issue of trade sanctions or tariffs for environmental protection arose, the Canadians were forced to deal with an unpleasant reality. Government leaders, under a new prime minister facing her first general election, were determined not to be seen as caving in to U.S. demands. Kim Campbell refused to go along with a tentative U.S.-Mexican agreement providing for environmental tariffs and sanctions. From the Canadian officials' perspective, trade disputes under the 1988 U.S.-Canada FTA, particularly the ones on softwood lumber, lobsters, and rules of origin on automobile parts, had resulted in protracted legal battles that cost the Canadian treasury and industry dearly. Consequently, the Canadian government—vigorously supported by industrial and business leaders—balked at the idea of giving U.S. negotiators one more tool with which to bludgeon them in trade disputes.

The debate over the environment and NAFTA clearly mirrors a larger debate in multilateral trading arrangements. At the same time that North

American trade negotiators were dealing with this issue, the GATT itself had revived a long-defunct working group on environmental matters. And the European Community has encountered a number of political roadblocks in dealing with its environmental issues. To understand why NAFTA became such an environmental battleground, it is helpful to take a closer look at how these other trade groups deal with environmental concerns and how the three North American countries dealt with their transboundary environmental disputes before NAFTA.

Linking Trade and the Environment

Concern over the environmental effects of trade predates NAFTA by at least twenty years, and the attention given to the issue has intensified with the changing patterns of global investment. At the global level, fewer and fewer companies exist within a national context. Multinationals now enter into joint ventures and subcontracting, licensing, and other interfirm relationships with companies throughout the world. Similarly, decisions to set up research and development, processing, manufacturing, and sales and marketing units are made in an international context, factoring in the comparative advantage of each country for every stage in the production process. Such economic integration, whether international or regional, forces national decisionmakers to face two environmental implications. The first is the fact that environmental and natural resource issues related to trade and the economy have moved beyond the effective control of nation-states. The second is the realization that political boundaries offer no protection from environmental damage caused by poor planning or poor regulation in another jurisdiction.

Environmentalists have discussed a number of ways in which a liberalized trading regime may undermine environmental quality and resource management.[2] Free trade by definition limits the ability of states to regulate their borders. To eliminate qualitative trade restrictions, divergent national standards need to be addressed. If the labeling, packaging, content, sanitary, or manufacturing regulations differ between markets, then trade is hindered as producers struggle to meet sometimes contradictory requirements. Thus, without some level of coordination or harmonization of standards, many significant welfare gains associated with free trade may be lost.

Eliminating border controls also may have an effect on capital and investment flows. In deciding where to locate an industrial facility, producers will want to assess the costs of production—including environmental costs—in various locations available to them. This may lead to industrial migration—producers leaving a strict, high-cost regulatory environment for a permissive, low-cost one—and thereby create pollution havens. In traditional economic terms, the low-cost jurisdiction is simply enjoying the fruits of its comparative advantage. In environmental terms, however, the costs of that advantage are borne not only by the host jurisdiction but also by its neighbors (as in the Chernobyl disaster) or in some even more extreme cases (such as ozone depletion), by the planet as a whole.

A liberalized trade system may also run counter to environmental principles through its dispute mechanisms, designed to settle allegations of unfair trading practices. Environmentalists often advocate the insertion of environmental escape clauses in dispute settlement mechanisms, but trade specialists argue strongly that such clauses would enable governments to bypass free trade through a plethora of spurious environmental restrictions. A government, for example, may claim that discriminatory trade practices are in its national interest for environmental, health, or consumer protection reasons. But the legitimacy of environmental standards often will be challenged, and the question of whether or not such standards have scientific justification frequently becomes a key issue.[3] Moreover, applying strict scientific criteria to environmental standards has been condemned by many in the environmental community as a smoke screen for deregulation and lowered standards. They point out that valid environmental regulations can fall because it is often difficult to determine with certainty the cause-and-effect linkages in environmental matters. In addition, many path-breaking standards are based less on scientific proof than on political demands following a unique local tragedy, a single piece of research, or perhaps simply national taste. Such standards would usually not pass a rigorous scientific-proof test.

Finally, the question of sustainable development is becoming more urgent. Free or liberalized trade may mean that commodities such as petroleum, minerals, or timber are exploited more rapidly because market forces, not national policy, will determine rates of consumption. This has obvious implications for environmental policy in terms of resource conservation, habitat preservation, and the development of renewable resources and alternative technologies.

Increased economic growth from a free or liberalized trading regime creates additional environmental challenges. The Mexican *maquiladoras* ("in-bond assembly plants") on the U.S.-Mexican border have created enormous strains on the region's public infrastructure. They have also worsened atmospheric pollution, generated substantial volumes of industrial waste, and resulted in groundwater contamination. A European Community report on the environmental impact of the single integrated market highlighted similar difficulties. The report estimated that two atmospheric pollutants, sulphur dioxide and nitrous oxide, will increase by 9 percent and 13 percent, respectively, as a result of a 6 percent increase in economic activity generated by the single market. An August 1993 report commissioned by the provincial government in Ontario and prepared by

Canadian environmental groups also drew attention to the environmental consequences of trade and growth.

These issues of sustainable development have drawn environmentalists into the trade arena, with some understandable resistance from trade economists. However, the linkages between trade and environment have also been addressed within the economic debate itself. Trade impinges on public health and safety under the economic rubric of externalities. Simply put, externalities are the costs associated with production that are not paid by the producer but carried by the society as a whole. A good whose production, sale, or consumption imposes an environmental burden is said to cost more than the price the market sets for it. This, in effect, represents a subsidy. To eliminate that subsidy, economists will usually call for a tax equal to the differential between the producer's cost and society's cost—the "polluter pays" principle.[4] Many environmentalists, however, argue that it is far better to prohibit pollution in the first place, rather than to allow companies to pay for destroying the environment or to trade in pollution rights. Instead, they call for heavy financial penalties to enforce strict compliance standards and to fund research into new technologies. This command-and-control model is the one most often used in environmental policy.

The World Trading System

Much of the world's trading system now functions within the context of the GATT. But the GATT has been criticized for its handling of environmental issues. Such issues are covered in Article XX of the GATT, which permits signatory states to make trade-restrictive regulations, "necessary to protect human, animal, plant life, or health," on a nondiscriminatory basis. The article is worded in narrow terms and specifically excludes any action that is "a disguised restriction on international trade."

These narrow terms are the subject of increasing debate in the international discussion of trade and environment. They figured prominently at the June 1992 United Nations Conference on Environment and Development. And Agenda 21, an 800-page document detailing the objectives and activities outlined in the Rio Declaration on Environment and Development, specifically discusses the importance of the GATT's role in fostering international cooperation that would accelerate sustainable development, particularly in developing countries.[5]

Despite the UN's sense of an urgent mission for the GATT, a number of the GATT Council decisions support the contention that trade restrictions must be very narrowly based if they are to stand up as environmental provisions within the context of the GATT. Proposed changes to GATT provisions outlined in the so-called Dunkel draft do little to widen the scope of environmental issues. Traditionally, GATT Council decisions have applied only to multilateral accords banning the import of specific goods: ivory, sealskins, whale products, leopard skins, and so on. Attempts to expand their application have been unsuccessful.

A GATT signatory state may apply extraordinary tariffs to goods that the state has determined are being deliberately dumped (i.e., sold below cost). Proposed alterations to these provisions that have emerged in the United States would permit costs associated with environmentally sound production to be included in the calculation of a good's total cost of production. If a comparative advantage could be attributed to the fact that a good was produced without reference to appropriate environmental standards, then a proportionate tax could be applied. However, these ideas have not been tested before a GATT arbitration panel.

GATT's multilateral and intergovernmental nature is another stumbling block to effective environmental regulation. GATT attempts to harmonize food standards, for example, ran into serious opposition, and the issue is still far from resolved. Industrialized member states complained that the proposals, based on standards set by the UN Codex Alimentarius Commission, were too weak and permitted harmful residues of pesticides. Developing states argued that the pesticides at issue were often produced for export by companies based in the industrialized world and that regulations banning their residue on produce were simply attempts to protect domestic agricultural markets against cheaper imports.

Attempts by GATT to improve its handling of environmental and trade linkages also have been stymied. Although a trade and environment working group was established more than twenty years ago, it was inactive until October 1991 when the United States withdrew its objections at the GATT governing council. The mandate of this group is to review existing international environmental treaties pertaining to trade, such as the Montreal Protocol on ozone depletion, the Washington Convention on trade in endangered species, and the Basel Convention on the transportation of hazardous wastes and the transparency of national environmental regulations affecting trade, packaging, and labeling requirements. This agenda is far narrower than that proposed by environmental groups or the United Nations.

Environmentalists have repeatedly called upon the GATT Council and ministers to deal with environmental matters in a more coherent and consistent way. They propose that a so-called green round of trade talks be held, making the environment a central component of the trade agenda by setting rules on standards, production processes, and natural resource exploitation that would promote sustainable development. The complexity of such an endeavor is enormous given the diversity of world standards and the absence of any consensus on what constitutes scientific proof for environmental safeguards.

Environment-friendly market-entry thresholds in Europe and North America would exclude many of the developing world's manufactured and agricultural exports. At the same time, fears of global warming and deforestation have prompted demands that the developing world minimize the rapid exploitation of its commodities and natural resources. Consequently, developing states are exceedingly reluctant to admit environmental factors into the multilateral trade debate and thereby worsen their ability to export.

A Note on GATT Dispute Resolution

Environmentalists view GATT's ruling in the 1991 tuna-dolphin conflict between the United States and Mexico as a prime example of why the GATT dispute resolution mechanism must be changed to take into account the environmental impacts of trade rulings. Specifically, the tuna-dolphin case questions the need to revise antidumping and countervailing duty laws in light of environmental issues. The dispute began when environmentalists brought suit in U.S. district court under the Marine Mammal Protection Act, which prevents the import of tuna caught with purse seines (nets) unless a foreign country can demonstrate that it has a dolphin protection program similar to that of the United States and a comparable average incidental dolphin kill rate.

In 1990, the district court restricted tuna imports from Mexico and several other countries. Mexico protested to the GATT, and in October 1991, a GATT panel ruled that U.S. tuna import restrictions violated the GATT's equal-treatment provisions. The United States did not disagree with Mexico's contention that U.S. law imposed quantitative restrictions on tuna imports, but it contended the restrictions were necessary to protect animal life. The GATT panel ruled that although the United States could apply such measures in its own jurisdiction, it could not manipulate production outside of the United States. Mexico subsequently reduced the dolphin mortality rate from yellowfin tuna fishing by about 85 percent in the eastern Pacific. But U.S. government officials say that the language of the Marine Mammal Protection Act is so specific that a single dolphin kill per tuna shoal in the eastern Pacific can throw the Mexicans out of compliance with U.S. law. Therefore, the embargo continues.

As far as Mexican officials are concerned, the United States is simply trying to keep Mexico out of the U.S. tuna market for economic reasons (two earlier U.S. tuna embargoes against Mexico were clearly based on economic considerations), and the continuing embargo is seen as one more example of militant U.S. environmentalism aimed at forcing wide ranging changes in Mexican public policy.

Canadian-U.S. Environmental Relations

The environmental relationship between the United States and Canada has been based upon asymmetries: inequalities of interest, commitment, and accountability that have ebbed and flowed over time. As a result of disputes over water contamination at the turn of the century, the Boundary Waters Treaty was signed in 1909. This treaty covered what were defined simply as "boundary waters" and stipulated that such resources "shall not be polluted on either side to the injury of health or property on the other."[6] To give effect to this blanket prohibition, the International Joint Commission (IJC) was established to make largely nonbinding judgments on transboundary water issues.

From 1925 to 1941, Canada and the United States were involved in what came to be known as the Trail Smelter Arbitration. In this case, residents of Washington State were adversely affected by sulphur dioxide fumes from a Canadian smelter. Both sides eventually submitted to binding arbitration, in which they agreed that "no state had the right to use or permit the use of its territory in such a manner as to cause injury by fumes in or to the territory of another or to the properties or persons therein."[7]

The second phase of the Canadian-U.S. relationship began with the environmental crisis of conscience in the late 1960s and 1970s. Global overpopulation and famine, coupled with air and water pollution, were seen as imminent dangers to human survival. In the United States, this agenda was picked up by the popular media and adopted by the political establishment. As a result, the United States soon instituted a comprehensive legislative package for environmental protection. In Canada, with its relatively small population and vast untapped resources, the concerns were somewhat more muted. Rather than adopt the absolutist approach of the United States and insist upon low emissions, Canadian regulators took a more utilitarian view. They set standards for emissions to a level that, they calculated, could be supported by the medium (air or water) in which they were emitted.

This divergence in standards was exacerbated by political differences. As the United States suffered a crisis of confidence regarding its environmental future, Canadians were in the midst of a period of national renewal, marked by a vibrant sense of Canadian identity, optimism for the future, and confidence in economic growth. Canadian officials at the provincial and national levels designed new resource exploitation schemes in timber, paper and pulp, energy, petrochemicals, and hydro resources to support this national advance. Meanwhile, on the U.S. side of the border, such initiatives were viewed with alarm. A vista of new pollution sources emerging from Canada was feared, just as progress was beginning to be made on limiting and reducing pollution in the United States. Furthermore, two very different regulatory regimes were being developed in the United States and Canada: Washington called the shots on U.S. environmental policy, but the confederal compromise of the Canadian constitution meant that most aspects of environmental policy—including resource exploitation—were left in the hands of the provincial governments.

These differences led to a difficult period in Canadian-U.S. environmental relations. The tension was broken only by the signing of the 1972 Great Lakes Water Quality Agreement (amended in 1978 and twice subsequently). Canadian proposals for power plants (Aikokan in Ontario, Poplar in Saskatchewan) and water diversion or dam projects in both the United States and Canada (at Richelieu-Champlain in Quebec, Skagit-Ross in Washington State, and the Garrison Diversion project in North Dakota) provoked vigorous and sometimes bitter cross-national exchanges.

Acid rain became the environmental cause célèbre of the early 1980s, marking a third significant phase in bilateral environmental relations between the United States and Canada. U.S. officials say Canadians became obsessed with acid rain abatement, but the Canadian media and political elites again and again hammered home the message that U.S. industrial emissions were returning to earth in the form of acid rain over Canada. Today, Canadians believe acid rain has endangered some 48,000 lakes, cost billions of dollars in tourism and sport fishing annually, and damaged the nation's forests, which support a $14-billion-per-year industry and provide about 10 percent of Canadian jobs.

Canadians were now in the role of environmental demanders, insisting that the United States pursue a comprehensive program to radically reduce the presence of acidifying gases (sulphur dioxide and nitrogen oxide) in U.S. industrial emissions. Unfortunately for Canada, the United States was in the process of turning its back on just this type of centralized regulation.

Canada and the United States signed the 1980 Acid Rain Memorandum of Intent in the closing months of the Carter administration. The memorandum mandated a series of negotiations that were to lead to an acid rain reduction agreement. With the advent of the Reagan administration, however, the prospects for such an agreement steadily diminished. All that was eventually achieved was a 1987 agreement providing for the binational study of airborne pollution and its implications; no attempt was made to reduce the elements identified as harmful. Not until 1990 did the Clear Air Restoration and Standards Attainment Act finally emerge from the U.S. Congress, with a goal of reducing sulfur dioxide emissions by 10 million tons.

The Great Lakes

One long-standing transborder environmental issue has been the pollution of the five Great Lakes, which, combined with the St. Lawrence River, are the source of drinking water for 25 million people in North America. The final cost for a complete Great Lakes cleanup has been estimated at about $100 billion.[8] Despite several water quality agreements between the United States and Canada, sewage pollution has been a problem in the lakes since the early 1900s, when people on both sides of the border began dying from typhoid and cholera (waterborne diseases). In response to these problems, the 1909 Boundary Waters Treaty set up the IJC, which concluded from a 1912 study that contaminants from untreated sewage, mostly from the United States, were the source of much of the pollution in the lower Great Lakes.[9]

In 1985, after a number of studies, the IJC decided that water quality in the lakes had improved substantially, particularly in Lakes Superior, Huron, and Michigan. Nevertheless, toxic pollution continued to be a problem, even though both Canada and the United States had prohibited the production of compounds containing chlorinated hydrocarbons (as in dichloro-diphenyl-trichloro-ethane, or DDT) and mercury by 1972. Today, the lakes' water quality problems continue. As Alan M. Schwartz points out in his recent analysis, "Even with the best of coordinated efforts and strong funding commitments [both of which are highly uncertain] the best hope for the future of the Great Lakes system will be regulations and enforcement to prevent new problems. Existing problems such as leaking waste disposal areas from practices discontinued over a decade ago will be with us for a long time."[10]

Transborder Sewage and Garbage Pollution

Other localized transboundary pollution problems normally associated with rapid economic development also plague the Canadian-U.S. relationship. Although the vast majority of the sewage pollution in the Great Lakes has come from U.S. communities, the city of Victoria, British Columbia, discharges some 20 million gallons of raw sewage into international waters, which then flows to the northwest coastline of Washington State. U.S. officials complain that they have spent billions of dollars to clean up sewage problems on their side of the border, and they expect Canadians to do the same.

In another case, changing environmental regulations in Canada are creating problems with transboundary garbage transfers. When Ontario began looking for funds to finance a recycling program, tipping fees to local garbage dumps rose to $150 a metric ton (from $18 in 1987).[11] The increase prompted Canadian haulers to begin an exodus into New York, where tipping fees are only about $35. U.S. officials estimate that as much as 500,000 tons of garbage entered the United States from Canada in 1991, aggravating a severe U.S. shortage of landfill space.

U.S.-Canada Free Trade Agreement

The conservative government of Brian Mulroney took office in 1984. At that time, signs of increased protectionism in the U.S. Congress led many Canadian policymakers to advocate a free trade agreement to get guaranteed and secure access to the vast U.S. market. In addition, Canadian manufacturers were concerned that slow progress in the GATT negotiations, coupled with faster progress in European integration, could leave Canadian industry out in a multilateral wilderness, without liberal access to significant export markets. This position was strongly endorsed by the Canadian Royal Commission on Economic Prospects, which, in 1985, came out in favor of a free trade agreement with the United States. Negotiations were initiated in the same year, and the U.S.-Canada Free Trade Agreement went into effect on January 1, 1989.

Because the two nations enjoyed a rough parity in levels of economic development, environmental standards, and labor laws, no serious thought was given to linkages between economic integration and environmental protection. As Peter Morici notes, "In the U.S.-Canada talks, environmental and workplace safety issues did not come up because the United States and Canada already have comparable laws and are engaged in continuous processes to resolve transborder problems."[12]

Nevertheless, there were environmental concerns, prompted, for the most part, by those who opposed a free trade deal in principle. Throughout the Canadian debate over ratification of the accord, the Mulroney government steadfastly insisted that the trade agreement had no adverse implications for Canada's environment. Opponents of the trade agreement, however, used environmental issues as a battering ram with which to attack the agreement as a betrayal of Canadian independence and sovereignty. The prospect of voracious U.S. entrepreneurs pillaging Canadian natural resources was a constant theme.

Although both governments succeeded in keeping the environment off the bilateral trade agenda, a number of trade-related environmental issues have since arisen, and they have forced negotiators to expand their agenda in the context of the NAFTA debate.

Energy Policy

Research on the relationship between liberalized trade, a consequent increase in economic growth and output, and the additional pollution arising from greater energy use was carried out by the European Commission in the context of the EC 1992 Program.[13] The basic question at hand was whether the emission of greenhouse gases would increase at a slower or faster rate than the estimated increases in economic activity. The study's conclusions came as a great surprise to the Commission. Additional economic activity deriving from the 1992 Program had been forecast to be between 4.5 percent to 7 percent of the EC's GDP. The Commission's environmental study found that

> in the absence of any change in policies or technologies, there would be increases in pollution and in threats to the environment. . . . It is unlikely that environmental damage would increase uniformly pro rata with

> economic growth: the outcome would depend upon the types of economic activity which are stimulated . . . the nature and extent of their environmental impacts and the spatial distribution of these impacts.[14]

The report used a modeling exercise on sulphur dioxide and nitrogen oxide to illustrate the point. Using an economic growth rate of 6 percent, the study concluded that under the new, single integrated market regime, sulphur dioxide levels would increase by 8 percent to 9 percent and nitrogen oxide levels would rise by 12 percent to 14 percent. A report issued in late summer 1993 by the Ontario provincial government, which opposes the free trade agreement, made similar predictions about increases in overall pollution levels. This was, however, partly based on an assumption that changes in the structure of local industry under a new FTA would be environmentally damaging.

Federal and provincial policymakers have long looked to Canada's resource base as a source of economic activity and wealth. Despite criticism of their low value-added content, timber, mining, and other extractive industries have played an important part in Canadian economic development. One area of significant importance is energy. With a relatively small population and rich energy reserves, Canada has the potential to be a crucial supplier to the voracious U.S. energy market (only Canada exceeds the United States in per capita energy consumption). Indeed, the match between Canadian supplies and U.S. demand has proved irresistible to Canadian utilities, who have lined up to build new plants in the belief that sales to the U.S. market will be an integral part of their economic viability in the years ahead.

The Canadian James Bay–Great Whale project illustrates this emerging debate on the economic and environmental consequences of trade in energy. The Hydro-Quebec utility plans to construct a massive hydroelectric facility in northeastern Quebec, which will divert the Nottaway and Rupert rivers into seven new reservoirs and eleven massive powerhouses. The project will flood thousands of acres of virgin Arctic wilderness and eventually have a capacity of more than 26,000 megawatts of electricity. Though a significant part of the economic rationale for the project had been provided by a twenty-year, $20-billion electricity supply contract with the state of New York, the cancellation of that contract has not preempted Hydro-Quebec's plans. Opponents of free trade point to the environmental consequences of this massive public works project as indicative of the adverse impact of the free trade accord. Supporters insist that the region will benefit economically from the development and operation of the plant as well as from the downstream ancillary services.

Harmonization Issues

During the trade talks, divergent environmental standards were not a central concern because Canada and the United States have similar levels of economic and industrial development. Nonetheless, harmonization of standards has been and continues to be a difficult issue for both the United States and Canada. Without any recognition of environmental principles, however, this issue has been treated strictly in the context of trade, with no reference to its wider implications.

The U.S.-Canada agreement discusses harmonization in vague terms. On pesticides, for example, it mandates both sides to "work toward equivalent guidelines, technical regulations, standards, and test methods." No other information is given.

Despite the many similarities between the two countries, pesticide control and harmonization continue to be very confusing issues. Due to limited domestic research facilities, Canada has largely had to adopt the substance of U.S. pesticide regulations. However, an important qualification should be made. Canadian regulations require that new pesticides be field-tested in Canada before their sale is approved. This has resulted in about 20 percent fewer pesticide approvals in Canada than in the United States. But this does not mean that Canadian regulations are tougher; in several instances, it simply means that manufacturers will not pay for the requisite tests in Canada to gain access to a relatively small market.[15]

Pesticide restrictions between the two countries also vary in stringency. Canada has a significantly smaller regulatory staff, with about 70 people, compared to the U.S. staff of more than 700.[16] The greater resources devoted to U.S. pesticide regulation means, then, that Canada frequently finds itself emulating U.S. actions. In terms of reevaluating existing pesticides, the United States and Canada have taken similar actions over the past twenty years, but in the case of residue limits in foods, Canadian regulation tends to be more stringent.

The U.S.-Canada agreement also failed to resolve the issue of divergent local, state, or provincial standards. It offers no guidance as to whether, in the context of bilateral standards harmonization or through a trade dispute mechanism, the higher environmental standards of a local community are to be overturned or sustained.

Under the current U.S.-Canada free trade agreement procedures, complaints about violations of environmental or work standards in either country are made by interested parties or by governments, and these, under certain circumstances, are referred to arbitration panels. Although the panelists can call on environmental experts for advice on technical matters, environmentalists are not included on the roster of prospective panelists.

Because the system is not set up to specifically address environmental disputes, those issues get little consideration, and most cases with an environmental component are actually disputed on other grounds. One of the most significant cases, involving the size of Canadian lobsters, had an environmental component to it, as did the recently settled case of punitive U.S. taxes imposed on beer from the Province of Ontario in retaliation for the province's imposition of a tax on aluminum beer cans.

European Community Environmental Policy

The 1985 Single European Act (SEA) and the 1992 Treaty on European Union signed in Maastricht provide the European Community with the constitutional basis and regulatory tools to pursue effective environmental regulation. What is less clear is whether the Community and its member states have the political will to see effective environmental regulation managed from Brussels rather than the national capitals.

Though citizens and environmental groups increasingly look to Brussels for the initiation, application, and enforcement of environmental standards, the EC itself is suffering from a crisis of confidence. The bruising ratification procedure of the 1992 Maastricht Treaty has led to calls for less central interventionism and greater latitude for the member states. Simultaneously, the decision of the United Kingdom's government to "opt out" of the treaty's tougher labor and social standards has been pointed to as an indication of future "competitive devaluations" in environmental and social policies.

Other important limitations to EC policy also exist. First, the Community is not a sovereign state, and its legislative process is slow, complex, and, of necessity, a matter of exquisite compromise. Second, the legislation that finally emerges must often be translated into national statutes—a task that is not always successfully completed. Indeed, the enactment of EC laws continues to be delayed or blocked by member states' failure to draw up and enforce required national legislation. Third, the EC's enforcement mechanisms are weak. Finally, the essential policy nature of decisionmaking between twelve states and EC institutions means that provisions are frequently reduced to lowest-common-denominator norms.

Primacy of EC Law

Although Ottawa, Mexico City, and Washington are confronted with many of the same issues that the EC has faced, an important difference remains: European Community law predominates over national legislation, and citizens have the right of direct appeal to Community institutions to protest the actions of their national governments, local authorities, or businesses. NAFTA, on the other hand, is strictly an intergovernmental arrangement. This difference is crucial when assessing ways of tackling similar problems. Whereas the member states of the Community may assign tasks to EC institutions and give them ultimate decisionmaking authority, the parties to the North American trade talks are restricted to designing trilateral mechanisms for cooperation.

No provision exists for environmental policy in the text of the EC's founding treaties. The Community's environmental law effectively dates from the 1972 Paris summit of EC heads of state and government. At that conference, the member states made environmental protection an EC goal—a decision precipitated by concerns expressed at the Club of Rome and UN's Stockholm Conference on the Human Environment in 1972. EC environmental action plans were subsequently created in 1973, 1977, 1983, and 1987. The Fifth Action Programme for the Environment, covering the years 1993–2000, was agreed upon in May 1992.

The EC's right to legislate on the environment was initially limited for it was based on a residual powers clause of the Treaty of Rome. The 1985 Single European Act, which amended the EC's founding treaties, regularized the right of the EC to legislate on environmental matters and set out the objectives of an EC environment policy: to preserve and protect environmental quality, to ensure the rational use of natural resources, and to protect human health. The 1992 Treaty on European Union strengthened the Community's legislative power by placing a new reliance upon qualified majority voting rather than unanimity.[17]

Principles, Mechanisms, and Policies

The environmental principles underlying EC regulations stipulate that action should be precautionary and preventive rather than reactive in nature, that pollution should be rectified at its source, that the polluter must pay, and that environmental implications should be integrated into all Community decisionmaking.

EC law consists of regulations, directives, decisions, and opinions. Regulations are directly applicable in all member states and have binding legal effect. Directives are binding statutes setting overall policy goals, which must be implemented through national legislation within a specific time frame. Decisions are binding upon the individual, company, or member state to which they are addressed. All these may be enforced through national courts or the European Court of Justice, and some recent cases exemplify this judicial power. A July 1993 Court of Justice ruling, for example, mandated that the United Kingdom comply with EC hygiene standards on all its beaches (at present, 25 percent of all beaches in the United Kingdom fail to meet these standards). The EC Commission has also threatened to bring the United Kingdom to court again for failing to meet drinking water standards. And a March 1993 Commission discussion paper suggested the use of liability law to pursue polluters. (Interestingly, the U.S. superfund is specifically mentioned as a legal model that should *not* be followed in this context.)

EC environmental policy is usually established through directives, initiated by the European Commission after consultation with other EC institutions. After the directives are reviewed by the European Parliament, which may pursue amendments to the legislation, the Council of Ministers (in this case, made up of the twelve national environment ministers) makes the final decision. The appropriate article determines if a particular decision can be made by a qualified majority vote or if it must be unanimous within the Council.

EC directives are implemented through national legislation, and there are ample remedies to counteract weak execution. If a member state fails to enact or enforce EC standards, then the European Commission, at its own initiative or pursuant to a petition from a community citizen, may pursue the issue through the European Court of Justice. Remedies under Article 171 of the Union Treaty now include fines against a member state for failing to implement an EC directive. In addition, Community citizens or interest groups have the legal right to demand EC investigation of alleged infractions of Community-based environmental laws. In 1991, nearly 500 such petitions were submitted to the Commission for action. To date, the Commission, having passed approximately 200 measures, has lodged more than 45 legal cases against member states for failure to properly enact and enforce environmental legislation.

EC environmental legislation covers four main policy areas: air pollution, water quality, waste management, and dangerous substances. Air pollution legislation has established Community-wide norms and standards for emissions from automobiles, power stations, and certain industrial plants; prior authorization is required for construction of power stations and plants; and there are regulations for carbon and suspended particulate pollution, leaded gasoline, and chlorofluorocarbons, among other substances. Like all other Community directives, these legally binding limits are enforced by national authorities in the first instance; if those authorities fail to act, the Commission can compel them to take enforcement action.

Water quality directives have been issued to cover standards for drinking water, swimming water, freshwater supporting fish life, groundwater, sewage treatment plants, and marine dumping. The Community also has established maximum limits for dangerous substances such as cadmium and mercury.

A series of new directives mandate catalytic converters on new autos by 1994 and lower emissions standards by January 1996, which will place EC emission standards among the world's lowest. Another directive on gasoline storage and distribution aims to reduce levels of evaporation. It has an escape clause to allow higher standards in local or national areas at the behest of member states.

Community directives dating to 1975 address hazardous waste and its disposal and supervision. Other directives in this category address discharge limits, procedures, surveillance, and monitoring of a range of toxic wastes such as polychlorinated biphenals (PCBs) and waste from titanium dioxides. Other legislation covers the shipment of wastes across internal Community frontiers.

Community law also covers the use of certain dangerous chemicals and substances. Directives have established labeling, notification, packaging, and classification requirements and have also set limits on the use of some substances, such as asbestos and benzene. Any proposed new chemical substance is subject to Community scrutiny before it can be sold in any member state as part of the European Inventory of Existing Commercial Chemical Substances.

As of March 1993, companies also became subject to published environmental audits sponsored by the EC. Reports include full descriptions of on-site activities; summaries of emissions, waste production, and resource consumption; and information on noise pollution.

The environmental impact assessment (EIA) of major EC construction projects is an increasingly important addition to the EC's legal armory. Planning applications for oil refineries, power stations, radioactive waste sites, chemical plants, and most infrastructure projects must now include environmental impact studies submitted to the appropriate local or national authority. If such a study is not submitted or if its conclusions are not taken into account, the Commission may intervene and halt further work on any project.

The Commission has taken a number of high-profile actions in recent years to underline its commitment to this process, including legal steps against ten member governments for infractions of the EIA process. However, since the turmoil surrounding the ratification of the 1992 Union Treaty, the Commission has clearly taken a more "sensitive" line vis-à-vis the member states and has been anxious to avoid confrontations. But judging by past experience, this reticence is likely to be a temporary phenomenon rather than a fundamental shift of policy.

EC Trade and the Environment

The European Community was established with an explicit set of goals involving the free movement of people, goods, services, and capital throughout the member states. A 1988 European Commission study—the Cecchini Report—estimated, however, that more than 190 billion European Currency Units (ECUs) were being lost each year in the absence of a single integrated EC market. By eliminating these costs, the Community GDP could realize a potential gain of 4.5 percent to 6 percent.[18] This was the basis of the EC 1992 Program—the creation of the single internal market.

The harmonization of national standards and regulations is a central part of such a single market program, and it had been the subject of ongoing Community attention since the Treaty of Rome was signed. The harmonization of divergent national standards on the content, production, packaging, and safety of goods was understood to be a key element of any attempt at trade liberalization, whether in the context of a free trade agreement, a customs union, or a single market. Article 30 of the treaty prohibits all "quantitative restrictions and all measures having equivalent effect." Exceptions to this provision—that is, derogations from Community law—may be made under Article 36 of the treaty on the grounds of public health, safety, or environmental protection. In 1988, it was estimated that divergent national standards represented 80 percent of all remaining nonfiscal barriers to trade within the Community.[19]

In 1979, the European Court of Justice radically expanded and strengthened the application and effect of Article 30. In the "Cassis de Dijon" decision, it ruled that any product legally sold in one member state must be permitted access to the markets of all other member states, unless it was proved that the product contravened "essential requirements" of health, safety, or environmental policy under the terms of Article 36.[20] This principle of presumptive access would later become the basis of Community policy.

Article 100 of the Treaty of Rome gave the Community powers to harmonize standards to a single norm through directives. The process, which required unanimity within the Council of Ministers, was frustratingly slow, tedious, and ultimately counterproductive. It also left the initiative for new technical standards to national governments, permitting them to create new regulations faster than the Community was able to harmonize old ones.

In May 1985, the Council of Ministers adopted the New Approach, based on the Cassis de Dijon principle. As a result, the European Commission was able to introduce a dual-track system of harmonization. First, only the essential requirements covering health, safety, and environmental protection standards under Article 36 would be harmonized by directives. Community standards would then be set by specialized Community agencies, such as the European Committee for Standardization, the European Committee for Electrotechnical Standardization, and the European Telecommunications Standards Institute. In the absence of fully harmonized EC standards, all national standards would be mutually recognized across the Community. An information network was established through which all member states were required to notify the Commission and other member states of proposed new standards. Either the Commission or a member state could demand a judgment on whether that standard established a new barrier to trade. More than forty such proposals have been blocked to date.

The 1985 Single European Act permitted the use of qualified majority voting in the Council of Ministers for all measures "which have as their object the establishment and functioning of the internal market (Article 100a/1)." This new voting procedure sparked fears that more stringent national standards would be undermined by lower Community norms. At the insistence of the Danish government, supported by Germany and the

Netherlands, the SEA balanced this provision with a demand that proposals for standardization under the single market program be made on the basis of "high levels of protection (Article 100a/3)." A specific opt-out clause also was introduced. After a harmonization measure is adopted by qualified majority vote, a member state may notify the Commission that it is applying for a higher national standard (Article 130t). If the Commission argues that this measure is a "disguised restriction on trade," the member state may bring the matter to the European Court of Justice for a final decision.

Where environmental measures are not part of the single market program, Article 130s applies. The 1992 Union Treaty introduced qualified majority voting for all environmental legislation except that involving fiscal matters (e.g., taxation), urban and rural planning (e.g., zoning regulations), and the structure of energy supplies (e.g., the nuclear choice). As with national standards described previously, states that are defending higher national standards from a lower Community norm may again rely upon Article 130t.

Legislative protection for higher standards also has been buttressed by some European Court of Justice case law. In a 1988 case, the Court ruled that a Danish regulation on returnable bottles could be justified on the basis of environmental prerogatives. In a significant qualification, however, it also ruled that the trade-restrictive effects of such measures had to be proportionate to the environmental objective; the adjudication of proportionality would be made on a case-by-case basis.

Using the new directive process, the Community has instituted more than 2,000 European standards on consumer health, safety, and environmental issues. Products conforming to these new standards are then granted the Community "CE" (Communauté Européenne) mark. Regulations on the labeling and packing of processed foods and a uniform system of labeling food additives have been introduced. The Community also has established basic norms for pesticides, hormones, slaughterhouse sanitation, health control of third-country imports, and food irradiation. For nonfood goods, the Community has established standards on medicinal products, motor vehicles, cosmetics, medical equipment, building products, pressure vessels, and toys. It also has initiated a Community-wide notification system for dangerous consumer products.

One concern with the New Approach of mutual recognition and fast-track harmonization has involved the potential for national standards erosion and deregulation. The standards-creating bodies, such as the European Standards Committee (CEN) and Cenelec (a division of CEN that deals with technical electrical standards), comprise the national standards organizations of the EC and the European Free Trade Association countries. These organizations largely rely upon the technical expertise and judgment of the major national organizations, such as the German Standards Institution

(DIN) and the British Standards Institution (BSI). But the power of producers within these organizations has led to allegations that the system does not adequately protect the health, safety, and environmental interests of consumers.[21]

Critics have also underlined the divergent approach of EC member states, which frustrates attempts to set available standards to the highest existing norm in the Community. Producers from less-developed Community regions argue that to insist on standardization to the highest possible levels reduces the consumer's ability to purchase lower-quality, lower-priced goods. Meanwhile, high-standard countries are understandably concerned that their standards should not be lowered.

Finally, the inevitable bureaucratization of centralized standards generates public criticism. Multinational standards do not respect national idiosyncrasies. Thus, the Commission periodically comes under passionate attack for attempting to redefine, reformulate, or outright ban peculiar localized products. The British sausage, local French cheeses, and Irish jams and preserves have all allegedly been threatened with EC extinction. In most cases, suitable adjustments to the standards have resolved difficulties, but these leave a residue of dissatisfaction with the Community's "mania" for common standards.

EC Environmental Policy and Industrial Migration

Deregulated borders in the Community have tremendous impacts on capital and investment flows. But available evidence suggests that EC companies do not base their investment decisions on the differing environmental frameworks of the member states. First, only in exceptional cases, such as the petrochemical or pulp and paper industries, do pollution abatement costs amount to a substantial proportion of the total cost structure.[22] Second, in some industrial sectors where pollution costs are a significant element, the EC has already established Community-wide norms and standards. Third, because these facilities usually involve large-scale capital investment, their mobility is limited.[23] Fourth, because studies suggest that once an operation is in place, the regulatory environment gets tougher, most producers base their own cost projections on mid-to-high environmental compliance.[24] And fifth, some studies suggest that in the absence of higher local norms, many industrial concerns bring their own higher domestic standards with them.[25] This is not always the case, however, between First and Third World countries, as the Mexican-U.S. experience has indicated.

These studies do not suggest that uniform treatment exists within the Community. As in the United States, industrial development agencies—regionally and among the member states—compete for international capital. They seek to attract facilities to their jurisdictions through tax, grant, and infrastructure incentives. Many of these agencies, primarily in the European periphery of Greece, Spain, Portugal, Ireland, southern Italy, Wales, and Scotland, would use a business-friendly climate as an enticement to attract industry: low levels of unionization, reduced labor costs, and lower corporate taxation. The state of environmental regulation may be an element in such a package, but thus far, studies have not found that this is a significant factor in industrial location decisions within the Community.[26]

Future EC Policy Direction

The Fifth Action Programme for the Environment suggests that the Community is moving further in the direction of favoring market mechanisms. The EC is complementing its traditional policy instruments of regulatory restrictions and prohibitions with fiscal measures like tax allowances, penalties, and grants. The aim is to involve all economic sectors in the formulation of environmental legislation, to set long- and medium-term policy goals, and to expand the range of legal instruments at the Community's disposal.

The Commission has drawn up proposals for an integrated pollution control program, with the objective of moving away from smokestack regulation to improved production processes. The Commission has suggested applying financial levies on pollution emissions above those that might be achieved using the best available technology—essentially an environmental tariff. These charges would be set on a sectoral basis for a number of priority substances. The Commission has also proposed that the money generated in this way be recycled back into the industry for environmental development and research.

In April 1992, the Commission established an environmental audit program. Sectors like electricity and gas production, pulp and paper, textiles, industrial equipment, food processing, and petrochemicals are invited to apply for a special environmental "seal of approval" from the Commission. To qualify, businesses have to establish comprehensive environmental protection procedures and regularly publish information on their compliance levels. These procedures and compliance levels are monitored by EC environmental inspectors. The system has been compared to annual financial audits.

The Commission also has indicated that greater use will be made of the Community's structural development funds to promote positive environmental action. A modest 1.2 billion ECUs were set aside in the 1989–1993 period to fund reclamation projects, clean-technology promotion, and programs to combat air and water pollution in less-developed regions of the Community. This principle has been extended in the new Union Treaty with the establishment of a formal environmental cohesion fund for poorer Community states. Its objective will be to provide resources for environmental investment where member states are faced with "costs deemed disproportionate for the public authorities of a member state" arising from EC environmental legislation.

Other funding for EC environmental initiatives may be forthcoming. A temporary EC fund established on April 1, 1993, will underwrite environmental and transport infrastructure developments in "southern tier" countries. This fund, which will increase to 2,600 million ECUs (at 1992 prices) by the end of 1996, will take the place of the environmental cohesion fund, which was delayed with ratification of the Maastricht Treaty.

The long-debated EC carbon tax is still on the agenda as well. A June 1993 ministerial summit sought a declaration favoring the principle of an energy tax, as outlined under a Commission proposal. But debate over a carbon tax has created such internal dissention that the EC has been unable to ratify the Rio Accords. The United Kingdom opposes the carbon tax in principle, preferring a national regulatory framework. EC heads of state and government have agreed to "fiscal measures" but have not specified whether these should be EC or national measures; to become an EC measure, such fiscal proposals would require unanimity in the Council of Ministers. Southern tier countries—such as Spain, Portugal, Greece, and Ireland—fear negative employment and industrial impacts on their developing economies and also oppose the measure. They argue that richer northern countries should take a disproportionate hit. Meanwhile, an internal EC report has suggested that the Community will not meet its own targets for carbon dioxide emission stabilization.

Evolution of Mexican-U.S. Environmental Issues

The United States and Mexico began addressing their transboundary environmental disputes more than a century ago and established the International Boundary Commission in 1889. This commission was replaced by the International Boundary and Water Commission under the terms of the 1944 water treaty between the two countries. The treaty, which was signed after decades of difficult negotiations, apportioned the waters of the lower Rio Grande–Rio Bravo and the Colorado River and provided an international framework in which to carry out negotiations on water pollution in transboundary surface water.

Even as the water treaty was signed, other natural resource issues were developing along the U.S.-Mexican border. Economic boundaries between Mexico and the United States began to break down after World War II, to be quickly replaced with pockets of industrial integration throughout the nearly 2,000-mile border region. With the end of the bracero guest worker program in 1964, the Mexican government initiated the maquiladora program, aimed at drawing U.S. corporations into northern Mexico for manufacturing and assembly operations that would employ large numbers of unskilled workers. The popularity of this program sparked a major buildup of industry in the border region. Economic integration in the border region further escalated during the 1980s, as Mexico entered GATT and liberalized its import market. The industrial integration that has resulted from these activities, in turn, created a need for strong binational programs and organizations to resolve issues involving the resulting transboundary pollution and resource depletion.

In 1983, the two governments responded with their first comprehensive border pollution accord, signed at La Paz, Baja California Sur, Mexico. The La Paz agreement primarily addressed the pollution problems generated by the rapidly spreading maquiladoras and the environmental impact of the ever-increasing dynamism of the northern Mexico economy. These developments also drew growing numbers of people to both sides of the border region. From 1970 to 1980, the urban population of the border grew by about 50 percent, from 4.36 million in 1970 to 6.49 million in 1980. The growth is expected to increase at least another 42 percent by 2000, up to 9.24 million.[27]

For many years, Mexican-U.S. environmental differences centered on the border region not only because of the burgeoning integration but also because the region represents a special case in transboundary environmental development. It is the world's longest border between a developed, First World country and a less-developed, Third World country. Thus, the opportunity for clashes and the need for cooperation increases as industries migrate to the region. And indeed, the ability of the Mexican and U.S. governments to adequately address their transboundary environmental concerns has been limited by a number of factors: lack of political priority, uneven natural resource policies among the U.S. border states, the special tariff treatment given to the maquiladoras in Mexico, the differences in the assimilative capacities of each country to deal with natural resource threats, and differing levels of environmental consciousness within each nation.

The U.S.-Mexican differences are clearly reflected in the levels of environmental regulatory development of each country. The U.S. government imposed national environmental standards on its state governments in the early 1970s, and the push for the nationalization of environmental policy was internally driven. Washington also established both the Council on Environmental Quality and the Environmental Protection Agency (EPA) and began implementing sweeping amendments to the federal Clean Air Act in 1970.[28] In contrast, Mexico's initial experiment with environmental policymaking, the 1971 Federal Law for the Prevention and Control of Environmental Contamination, was a direct response to international pressure for environmental change, and it represented little more than the establishment of administrative regulatory power under the central government.[29]

It was not until 1988 that the Mexican government placed environmental protection on the domestic political agenda, with the enactment of the General Law for Ecological Equilibrium and Environmental Protection. This law more specifically defined environmental regulation in Mexico, as well as the relations among government agencies that deal with environmental issues. It provided for environmental impact assessments for all federal public works projects, called for technical norms in several areas, and gave the Secretaría de Desarrollo Urbano y Ecología (SEDUE) the authority to shut down polluting industries and to assess substantial penalties to violators. It also gave state and local governments the power to develop their own environmental regulations. Unlike U.S. federal law, Mexico's omnibus act includes both environmental protection and natural resource conservation. It covers air, water, hazardous waste pollution, pesticides, and toxics. The law is not as detailed as U.S. laws, however, and it did not address the cleanup of abandoned hazardous waste sites, restrictions on land disposal of hazardous waste, and regulation of leaking underground storage tanks.[30] On the subjects that it does cover, the Mexican law does not yet have the related regulations and technical norms that will make it comparable to U.S. law. However, throughout 1993, the Secretaría de Desarrollo Social (SEDESOL), which replaced SEDUE in 1992, revamped its technical regulations, with the goal of issuing 151 new rules by year's end.

By the 1980s, population and industrial growth had depleted natural resources to the point that a crisis was brewing in the twin-city metropolitan regions of the border. Freshwater was in short supply in what is mostly a semiarid region. Unregulated industrial growth had contributed to a growing pollution problem in remaining water supplies, fish and wildlife species were becoming extinct in growing numbers, and air pollution was becoming a problem in large urban complexes like El Paso–Ciudad Juárez, the copper smelter regions of Arizona and Sonora, and in the Tijuana–San Diego area.

Although the La Paz agreement fostered a working relationship between the U.S. and Mexican environmental agencies, most environmental policymakers now concede that the agreement had a number of shortfalls. It was vaguely worded and possibly more significant for the international dialogue that it generated than for its value as a tool for fighting border pollution. It did not address the border region's growing shortage of freshwater, and many of its provisions could not be enforced. It also failed to address public infrastructure problems that contributed to environmental deterioration, and it did not cover the financial resource shortages in Mexico that inhibited the nation's ability to deal with industrial and municipal wastes.

However, the five annexes to the La Paz agreement addressed, for the first time, some of the most contentious transboundary pollution issues.

Annex 1 involved construction of Tijuana–San Diego wastewater treatment facilities; Annex 2 addressed joint U.S.-Mexican contingency planning for hazardous substance spills and authorized the establishment of the Inland Joint Response Team for emergency actions; Annex 3 addressed the transboundary shipment of hazardous wastes and substances between the two countries; Annex 4 required copper smelters in Arizona, New Mexico, Texas, and Sonora, Mexico, to comply with emissions limits; and Annex 5 provided for air emissions inventories, air modeling analysis, and other programs aimed at controlling urban air pollution in U.S.-Mexican border cities.

Annex 3 is frequently cited for its failure to resolve one of the most serious transboundary pollution problems: the illegal dumping of toxic and hazardous waste, generated primarily by U.S. companies operating in Mexico. The writers of the annex recognized that Mexico did not have the capacity to store, process, or recycle these wastes. Their goal was to make a corporation that generated them responsible for disposal by requiring that the wastes be transported to the corporation's home country. But the annex left a number of loopholes through which border industries could avoid the costly transport of toxic and hazardous wastes back to their country of origin, which, in more than 90 percent of the cases, is the United States.

Annex 3's failures quickly became evident with the rise of anecdotal evidence of illegal waste dumping in the deserts of the border region and the concomitant rise of certain rare types of cancers and other medical conditions within the region. For example, a cluster of anencephalic babies and higher-than-average leukemia rates have been reported in the region of Brownsville, Texas. Speculation arose that illegal dumping was compromising groundwater integrity in a number of border areas, but because the testing of groundwater supplies for industrial wastes and heavy metals is so expensive, few cases have been documented outside a local study for an area near Nogales, Arizona.

As criticism of the La Paz agreement mounted, border communities, local and state officials, and nongovernment organizations with environmental mandates began searching for an alternative method for dealing with environmental deterioration and natural resource depletion in the border region. The mechanism for tackling these issues became NAFTA, an agreement that promised to bring additional economic activity in the border region and to provide a forum in which joint economic issues could be resolved.

Environment and the North American Free Trade Agreement

Some of NAFTA's opponents have a protectionist trade philosophy, but many of the environmentalists and public policy specialists who entered the debate sought to balance the expanding international trade relationship with sustainable economic growth and rational natural resource use. This had been a growing priority for U.S. environmental groups in the final stages of the Uruguay Round of GATT, and their concerns were reflected in the powerful support that the U.S. Congress gave to linking environment to NAFTA. U.S. environmentalists wanted to use NAFTA's environmental provisions as a blueprint for linking trade and environment in future U.S. trade agreements in Latin America and elsewhere. U.S. Representative Richard Gephardt, who spearheaded much of the congressional expression of concern during trade negotiations, cosponsored a resolution promising that Congress will approve neither NAFTA nor the Uruguay Round of GATT if these agreements jeopardize U.S. labor, environmental, public health, or consumer safety standards. By July 1992, a majority of the House members had signed this resolution.

President Salinas took the U.S. political rumblings seriously, and starting in 1991, he undertook one of the world's most rapid transformations of environmental policy. His policy initiatives resulted in the overhauling of a government department (replacing the Secretaría de Desarrollo Urbano y Ecología with the Secretaría de Desarrollo Social, or Social Welfare Secretariat) in 1992, and the launching of an ambitious new multinational loan program for Mexico's environmental programs. They also led to a costly decision to shut down a refinery in Mexico City, a new and potentially far-reaching crackdown on U.S. and domestic industries operating in Mexico, and new promises to shore up the ailing public infrastructure of the U.S.-Mexican border region.

In March 1992, President Salinas announced that any new industry seeking to open a plant in Mexico must conduct an environmental impact study.[31] He also gave the 220 biggest polluters in Mexico City eighteen months to reduce emissions by 70 percent. The results of this program are not yet available.

Mexico's newly created Social Welfare Secretariat (SEDESOL) includes a new office of environmental attorney general, which has begun a substantial campaign to crack down on industrial polluters. More than 1,000 industrial inspections were conducted along the U.S.-Mexican border from June 1991 to June 1992[32]—a substantial increase from the almost nonexistent enforcement program of 1989. From January 1992 through April 1993, more than 11,000 inspections of industries operating in Mexico were conducted.[33]

Although many environmentalists have commended President Salinas for his progress, nagging doubts continue about Mexico's political will to keep up its substantial progress. Several factors are disturbing:

- During trade negotiations, the Mexican government instituted a policy of requiring performance bonds from certain U.S. and domestic companies to guarantee compliance with Mexican environmental law. However, no records on this program have been made public.[34]

- SEDESOL is delegating substantial responsibilities to state governments in Mexico that are ill equipped at present budget and staff levels to deal with environmental enforcement. In 1991, the EPA reported that eighteen of the thirty-one Mexican states had only recently adopted their own environmental statutes under Mexico's general ecology law.[35] As of June 1992, two states still had no environmental statutes.[36]
- Local governments have resisted the new national program for environmental enforcement. SEDESOL officials have found that some local agencies will not lend their files on industrial plants or otherwise cooperate.
- Although SEDESOL has completed an unprecedented number of inspections for environmental compliance, much information on sanctions that resulted from these inspections, such as the amount of monetary fines, has not been publicized.
- Hundreds of new environmental inspectors have been assigned to the border region from 1991 to the present, and all undergo EPA-sponsored training. But news reports indicate that inspectors sometimes go without pay for months.[37]
- In August 1993, the Mexican government was accused of trying to cover up the environmental damage caused by a tanker that leaked 4,000 tons of sulfuric acid onto Mexico's Pacific coast near Lázaro Cárdenas.[38] Mexican environmental groups criticized the incident as proof that environmental policy was not evolving quickly enough to meet the challenge of disasters.
- Toxic waste disposal and hazardous waste recycling facilities in Mexico are in short supply, environmental services in Mexico are still rare, and little follow-up exists on the required transport of hazardous wastes from maquiladoras to the country of origin. As a result, industrial wastes frequently go into sewer systems for lack of another alternative.[39]
- Public disclosure about environmental practices is practically nonexistent.

Closer trade relations has meant considerable pressure on Mexico to continue its rapid transition in environmental policy. The pressures come from both individual members of the U.S. Congress and from the terms of the environmental accord itself. In a July 27, 1992, speech, U.S. Representative Gephardt asked the Mexican government to establish community right-to-know laws similar to U.S. laws, within a 100-kilometer area of the U.S.-Mexican border.[40] Furthermore, the environmental accord, as negotiated, required all three NAFTA countries to open their environmental programs to additional international scrutiny, which is likely to require some changes to Mexican law. Objectives of the new accord include guaranteeing citizens in NAFTA countries access to national courts to petition for enforcement actions, securing open judicial and administrative proceedings for the creation of environmental laws and regulations, and obliging signatory states to regularly report on the state of their environments.

Categorizing NAFTA Environmental Debate

NAFTA's environmental debate evolved into several categories of issues. These include (1) border pollution, infrastructure, and overall binational management; (2) revenue-raising measures for binational pollution prevention and control; (3) harmonization of health, safety, and environmental standards; (4) industrial migration of dirty U.S. industries; and (5) environmental dispute settlement.

Border Pollution, Infrastructure, and Binational Management

In February 1992, the U.S. Trade Representative's office issued a review of U.S.-Mexican environmental issues. Although the environmental review acknowledged the link between expanded trade and environmental degradation, it is most notable for the fact that it was compiled long before trade negotiations had produced any tangible results; thus, it could not have taken into account the environmental impact of increased trade with Mexico. Much of it focused on border issues, which were reviewed separately in the Mexican-U.S. Integrated Border Environmental Plan. The review was also criticized for its lack of specific information or recommendations on dealing with these binational issues.

The more important document was the Mexican-U.S. Integrated Border Environmental Plan, issued in February 1992.[41] But two years after the plan's implementation, the U.S. government's lack of financial commitment to it rendered it virtually useless, and the plan's hazy provisions failed to gain it credibility from either the border communities or the state governments. The litany of complaints against the plan was endless. Much of the funding promised by both federal governments in the border plan came from existing federal and state programs. The plan also relied heavily on border state financing and placed too little emphasis on contributions that industry could make for environmental programs. Moreover, the plan's provisions were not legally binding, and they did not address the vastly different procedures used to regulate industry in the United States and Mexico. Nor did the plan address the specific environmental impacts of a free trade agreement or guarantee Mexicans access to the kinds of information they sought in the border hearings.

Even as border communities pronounced the first Mexican-U.S. border plan a flop, however, its creation had some beneficial effects. First, it included aspects of border problems not addressed in the La Paz agreement of 1983. Second, it focused some long-needed federal attention on the deteriorating natural resource base of the region. Third, it represented the first comprehensive attempt to integrate the planning and environmental strategies used by the two federal governments. Yet even with federal attention and a fully functional border environmental plan, the problems associated with the lack of water in the semiarid border region will continue to grow to crisis levels. Furthermore, the U.S. border states have vastly differing water use laws, conservation plans on one side of the border are not binding on the other, underground aquifers are drying up or being polluted, and the population throughout the region is growing rapidly.

Revenue-Raising Measures

A portion of the environmental debate on NAFTA centered on infrastructure improvements in Mexico. Public infrastructure has several links to trade: Goods and services do not pass between the two countries without the necessary road system to facilitate their flow, the customs agents to inspect the goods, the computer systems to make the entire system run smoothly, and the municipal services that keep border cities functioning.

But infrastructure improvement is also an environmental and health issue. Implicit within trade negotiations is a U.S. demand that Mexico upgrade its environmental programs to U.S. standards to minimize both the loss of transboundary resources and the health and safety impediments to the increased flow of agricultural products and other commodities and consumer goods. The lack of public services like wastewater treatment adversely affects the supply of natural resources, and infrastructure becomes a health issue when failure to deliver potable water and other necessities generates an increase in infectious diseases.

Infrastructure and environmental neglect already have contributed to serious deficiencies in water delivery systems, wastewater treatment, road paving, public transportation, energy and delivery systems, electrical services, telecommunications, hazardous waste disposal, water conservation and reclamation, pollution control, housing, education, and health care. Such infrastructure deficits within a given region increase the indirect cost of labor and thus the cost of doing business, as well as the overall risk factors associated with making a financial investment within that region.

Mexico will have trouble finding the money to build up its urban border infrastructure to U.S. standards under the trade agreement. By one estimate, the Mexican infrastructure budgets allocated for the northern states lag behind employment creation by as much as ten years; for environmental protection, the delay is even longer.[42] The government has already indicated it will count on foreign investors to finance needed improvements to a deteriorating infrastructure.

Additionally, the country's public infrastructure and educational systems have been substantially neglected since the onset of the financial crisis in 1982, and the population is significantly younger than the U.S. population, thus creating a disproportionate need for social services like education. All these factors, as well as Mexico's relative poverty in comparison with the United States and Canada, will mean that it will be relatively more expensive for Mexico to integrate its environmental standards with those of the other NAFTA members.

In the environmental accord, U.S. Trade Representative Mickey Kantor and Mexican Secretary of Trade and Industrial Development Jaime Serra Puche took these issues into account, agreeing in principle to additional negotiations to establish coordinating and financing mechanisms for environmental infrastructure projects in their border region. They outlined a new border development bank that could provide a border environmental financing facility; generate grants, loans, and financial guarantees from federal, state, and local governments; and harness other resources from the private sector. These funds generated by the border development bank would then be leveraged in international bond markets. The border development bank would be just one source of direct loans and partial guarantees for environmental infrastructure projects. Initially, these would be wastewater treatment and water pollution control projects. Trade negotiators anticipated that any bond debt would be serviced, in part, with user fees paid by border industries or pollution taxes in the region.

Border communities have reacted cautiously to this and previous proposals. They point out that numerous border funding schemes have been advanced since the fast-track debate of 1991. They want funding that can be easily controlled at the local, rather than the federal, level.

In the long term, Mexico cannot be excluded from making its own financial investments in infrastructure. As its economy grows under free trade, so, too, will its opportunities to increase its revenues and earmark portions of them for infrastructure investment.

States and local governments on both sides of the border will need increased levels of funding from their national governments to deliver services as well. But these government units currently face several impediments to enhancing their revenue sources. On the Mexican side of the border, states do not have much ability to tax: Most revenues are collected and disbursed directly from the federal level. By one estimate, for every dollar equivalent of revenue collected by the federal government, only 30 to 40 cents is returned for public services.[43]

Harmonization

U.S. and Mexican health, safety, and environmental practices differ sharply, and these differences are likely to be exacerbated by increased trade, particularly in key sectors like agriculture. In 1992, U.S. Trade Representative Carla Hills vowed that under NAFTA rules, any of the three signatories could bar imports that failed to meet health or environmental standards. She also said that state standards higher than U.S. standards would not be altered by the trade agreement.[44] "If the state of California wants to bar something that has one part per trillion of a residue and even though the rest of the world says one part per billion is good enough, we won't quarrel with the science so long as a scientific methodology has been used to develop the standards," she told the *New York Times*.[45] However, no one, from the U.S. Supreme Court justices on down, has yet offered a definitive explanation of "scientific methodology."

Agriculture is particularly important because of the large volume of Mexican exports to the United States in this sector. Mexico currently supplies the United States with one-half of its winter fruits and vegetables, and the U.S. International Trade Commission has indicated that a trade agreement could increase Mexican agricultural exports to the United States significantly.

But the two countries are not yet prepared for this increased level of agricultural trade. A 1992 study by the U.S. General Accounting Office indicated that Mexico and the United States, even in the absence of a trade agreement, are struggling with unequal pesticide standards and that the Mexican government has a limited capacity for pesticide monitoring.[46] The two countries have differences in terms of (1) tolerances for pesticide usage (and in Mexico, these tolerances extend to commodities for which the United States has no tolerances), (2) pesticides that are allowed in Mexico but not in the United States, and (3) levels of pesticide residues. The parallel accord, as negotiated, vaguely addressed the pesticide issue. The three governments simply agreed to work toward limiting trade in toxic substances banned domestically in each country but did not offer a specific forum or time schedule for these discussions.

Mexico's air emissions standards also differ from U.S. standards, and though Mexican toxic and hazardous waste practices are developing rapidly, they still lag behind U.S. standards. Furthermore, the industrial processes used to create manufactures in Mexico have fewer safeguards for the environment than similar processes in the United States. In light of these discrepancies, the U.S. government has lent some support to upward harmonization. The *Review of U.S.-Mexican Environmental Issues* included among its recommendation to trade negotiators the "right to impose and enforce through trade restrictions product standards and technical regulations that are more stringent than international standards."[47]

Environmentalists believe that NAFTA parties can impose environmental requirements on other signatory countries as long as those requirements are consistent with investment provisions outlined in the trade agreement. In May 1993, a coalition of large U.S. environmental groups drafted a list of demands, which was delivered to the Office of the U.S. Trade Representative.[48]

The group's draft language for NAFTA included provisions allowing a signatory country to maintain sanitary and phytosanitary standards higher than international standards provided that they do not discriminate against imports. This would be consistent with the GATT rules. Another provision would broaden the GATT exemptions to trade rules so that countries could initiate actions to protect natural resources inside their territories and allow exemptions for actions taken outside national boundaries for the same purpose. These are issues that the parallel accord did not address.

Industrial Migration

Industrial surveys—mostly from the 1970s—indicate that lax environmental regulations are not an incentive for industry to relocate. But the cost of pollution abatement in the United States is constantly rising, and this may have led to a shift in industrial decisionmaking. The Bush administration's environmental review of NAFTA acknowledged the increasing cost of pollution abatement in the United States but noted that in more than 85 percent of U.S. industries, pollution abatement represents 2 percent or less of value added. Those industries with high pollution abatement costs generally do not have high tariff protection, according to the report.[49]

Some industries, however, do find environmental inducements for relocating to Mexico. In a 1992 American Chamber of Commerce of Mexico survey of 125 U.S. companies in Mexico, 27 percent of the respondents said comparative environmental protection costs were an incentive to relocate.[50] The survey included questions on the type of technology used to treat industrial wastes. An average of 54 percent said they used Mexican standards, 29 percent used U.S. standards, and 17 percent used the best available technology.

U.S. corporate spending for pollution abatement also is growing in response to increased environmental enforcement in Mexico, the survey concluded. More than 90 percent of the respondents said that the government was enforcing environmental laws more strictly than in past years. The chamber concluded that, on average, 125 U.S. companies operating in Mexico had increased their spending on environmental protection by 85 percent.[51]

Another way of looking at the industrial migration issue is to examine the trends in industrial production of Third World countries. In the case of Mexico, its exports from so-called dirty industries is rising. A 1991 study of Mexico's exports indicated that exports of pollution-intensive products to the United States increased at an average rate of 9 percent annually in the 1980s, compared to 3 percent for all commodities.[52] The study concluded that pollution-intensive products accounted for slightly more than one-tenth of total exports, but it warned that "pollution intensive exports have grown considerably faster than total exports during this period."[53]

Some economists will argue that attempts to impose the costly environmental standards of a developed country on a less-developed country can lead to lower growth, thus exacerbating environmental problems within the less-developed region. Environmental concern is likely to increase as per capita income increases, they reason, because richer societies generally attach more importance to environmental quality. A study by Gene M. Grossman and Alan B. Krueger, of Princeton's Woodrow Wilson School of Public and International Affairs, concluded that air pollution was most severe in countries with an economic output of about $5,000 per person and less severe in richer countries. The study further indicated that Mexico's output is nearing the level that would signal a reduction in pollution. However, Mexico is not included in the study's data base on air pollution—a fact that many news articles failed to acknowledge after the study was released. Environmentalists point to other reasons why this study cannot be applied to Mexico. It did not, for example, take into account many factors unique to Mexico, particularly the adverse effects of too-rapid development on political institutions and those institutions' ability to deal effectively with polluting industries.[54] Another significant factor in environmental degradation is the increase in natural resource consumption as per capita income rises.

Pollution control costs are related to pollution regulation, and the United States and Mexico have different approaches to the enforcement of pollution laws. The U.S. system is based on civil law and due process, including significant civil and criminal litigation of environmental disputes. The U.S. Labor Department and the EPA encourage voluntary compliance but also emphasize workplace inspections to deter violators.

The Mexican system stresses cooperative arrangements between labor and management and between management and the government. In Mexico, though inspections are made, more emphasis is placed on joint labor-management committees to negotiate workplace solutions to problems.[55] Mexico's environmental rulemaking is not yet as encompassing as U.S. rulemaking, and this means that disputes will arise in areas in which there is little common ground.

Mexican environmental enforcement is selective, traditionally sporadic, and highly centralized within the federal government. But in cases where these arrangements fail, the government does not rely on due process to shut down offending industries. Indeed, Sergio Reyes Lujan, one of Mexico's top environmental officials, has stated it takes him only ten minutes to shut down a factory anywhere in the country.[56]

The U.S. system of due process has had its share of problems. Litigation is both expensive and time consuming, and U.S. court decisions give conflicting signals to citizen groups and others who attempt to use the legal system for environmental control. In June 1992, the U.S. Supreme Court, for example, made it harder for environmental groups to sue to enf[illegible] ad by dismissing a lawsuit challenging [illegible] n that U.S. agencies funding developr[illegible] ve to comply with the Endangered Spe[illegible]

[illegible] ruling of U.S. District Judge Charles Ri[illegible] al impact statement for NAFTA sent an [illegible] trading partners. The ruling came at an [illegible] vironmental relations, but it was later overturned on appeal. When the Sierra Club lawsuit was first filed in 1991, it was clear that the Bush administration was not going to deal effectively with the environmental impacts of the trade agreement. But at the time of Judge Richey's ruling, President Salinas had announced that Mexico's expenditures for environmental protection had skyrocketed to 1 percent of GNP—a higher share than France spends and certainly higher than similar expenditures in other developing nations. Much of this was financed with billions of dollars in loans from the World Bank.

Given the level of sacrifice that Mexicans felt they had made to U.S. concerns, the ruling prompted many to question just what measures would assuage the concerns of U.S. environmental groups. The issue was not whether Mexico should continue improving its environmental record but rather how fast a developing country can be expected to do so. Sierra Club spokespeople said their lawsuit was not aimed at Mexico's environmental performance but rather at U.S. trade negotiators who, until August 1993, had made little progress in establishing the kinds of environmental protections for NAFTA that the club had sought for two years.

Other environmentalists not involved in the lawsuit worried that Mexico would be unable to continue cracking down on its own industries much longer without NAFTA as a carrot. President Salinas suffered a backlash generated by domestic industry after he began implementing a broader, stricter environmental policy. In 1993, domestic industry began protesting the costs associated with stronger environmental enforcement, which set off an internal debate within SEDESOL. Environmentalists in Mexico speculated about the political significance of regional demonstrations against environmental enforcement in areas like Querétaro, where the Mexican environmental attorney general shut down public works projects that violated federal law, as well as various private industries guilty of similar offenses.[58] Luis Donaldo Colosio, then head of SEDESOL, underscored this concern when he noted that without free trade, "we wouldn't generate the resources to continue channeling investment to clean the environment and prevent pollution."[59]

Environmental Dispute Resolution

For environmentalists, the experiences of GATT indicated that NAFTA would be better served by an environmental dispute resolution mechanism separate from the one used for trade issues. They reasoned that in trade dispute settlements that do not take into account environmental impacts, environmental and resource conservation measures can be subject to challenge as nontariff trade barriers. They were concerned that if dispute resolution panels do not include environmental specialists, these panels may override U.S. decisions to bar imports without ample scientific evidence that the imports have environmental impacts.

In NAFTA, environmental matters have been separated from other trade disputes with the creation of the Commission for Environmental Cooperation. Under the accord, a governing council under the commission is composed of cabinet-level officers from all three governments or their representatives. Any party can request consultations involving matters affecting the operation of the parallel accord. Specifically, the council can consult on alleged persistent patterns of failure to effectively enforce an environmental law involving the production of goods or services traded within NAFTA.

If consultations fail to resolve a dispute, the complaining party may call a meeting of the council. The council may then use any number of technical advisers to aid in resolving environmental disputes, and it may create working groups to address specific issues.

With a two-thirds vote of the council, an arbitration panel can be established to deal with environmental complaints that cannot be resolved through consultations. Panelists are to be chosen from a previously accepted roster of specialists that include environmentalists. This is a key difference between the NAFTA dispute resolution system and those of both the U.S.-Canada FTA and GATT.

To address the concerns of environmentalists on transparency, a panel's report must be publicly available five days after it is given to the parties involved in the dispute. If the panel's finding indicates that a NAFTA signatory has engaged in a persistent pattern of failure to effectively enforce its environmental law, the parties to the complaint can agree within 60 days to a "mutually satisfactory" action plan to remedy the nonenforcement. If the parties cannot agree on a plan within 60 to 120 days, the panel may be reconvened to impose monetary fines against the party deemed at fault.

At this point in the dispute process, the treatment of NAFTA countries diverges, and this is likely to raise issues of fairness. The United States and Mexico are subject to trade sanctions in extreme cases where a cited party fails to pay the fines assessed against it or fails to enforce its environmental law. The complaining party has the right to suspend NAFTA benefits based on the amount of fine assessed. In the case of Canada, however, the Commission for Environmental Cooperation collects fines and is responsible for enforcing an action plan before a Canadian court of competent jurisdiction. Whether this will involve provincial as well as federal courts is not clear. The Canadian procedure does require a minor change in

Canadian law to obligate the courts to carry out writs of mandamus in any cases that the commission may bring before them.

A Final Note on the Side Agreement on Environment

NAFTA's side agreement on the environment does not require any of the three signatories to enact new environmental laws; it merely requires them to enforce those already on the books. It holds out the threat of trade sanctions for countries that refuse to enforce their own laws but only as a means of last resort. The road to trade sanctions is tortuously long, and the sanctions themselves are limited. Fines that could be imposed are also limited to $20 million—a relatively small amount compared to the monetary value of disputed products in trade agreements.

The rather "tame" sanctions, therefore, have left some leaders of U.S. environmental groups rather lukewarm to the parallel accord itself. Many, such as Michael McCloskey, chairman of the Sierra Club, also are worried about the environmental funding issues left unaddressed in the parallel accord. Specifically, environmentalists believe they face an ongoing battle to ensure Mexican-U.S. border cleanup operations. The fate of the integrated border environmental plan—the current vehicle for federal funding of border programs—was left dangling after the parallel accord was negotiated.

On the other hand, the imposition of any environmental trade sanctions represented a significant concession on the part of the Mexicans, who greatly fear the sanctions will be used for protectionist purposes. Other parts of the parallel accord will force Mexico to move its judicial practices closer to U.S. practices on environmental cases, which could be a step toward deeper harmonization initiatives between the two countries.

Conclusion

The European Community has developed the most detailed program for linking environmental issues to trade within today's world trading system. To some extent, NAFTA can look to the EC experience for guidance, although the ability of NAFTA countries to emulate the European experience is limited by the nature of the North American trade agreement itself.

The inability of GATT to address environmental issues works to the detriment of NAFTA. In the absence of GATT guidance on environmental issues, NAFTA negotiators forged their own environmental policy. Whether this new North American environmental policy will be considered consistent with GATT is an open question.

The environmental parallel accord for NAFTA is the beginning, not the end, of negotiations on natural resource issues in North America. The ability to assimilate polluting industries varies from country to country and region to region. Since 1991, the Mexican government has made significant progress in monitoring the emissions of industries operating within its boundaries and enforcing domestic environmental policy. But for some time to come, the Mexican government will be struggling to meet the demands for monitoring and regulatory control over current industrial activities and to absorb the increased level of industrial activity that will result from freer trade.

The Mexicans will continue to be at odds with the United States on environmental dispute resolution. The U.S. method of dealing with environmental disputes is through negotiations within the litigation process. However, the litigation of environmental responsibility is far more costly than obtaining cooperative international agreements, and it is not the Mexican method of dealing with social disputes. A country that relies heavily on litigation for enforcement increases the costs of compliance by imposing significant transaction costs on industry, the community, courts, and government.[60] Mexico is likely to balk at these costs.

NAFTA negotiations took place at a time when world attention had just begun to shift to environmental issues. Conservationists, environmentalists, and some public policy specialists had hoped to seize the opportunity that NAFTA provided to forge a new environmental policy within the context of a trade agreement that could be used by other developing and developed trade blocs. To some extent, NAFTA is likely to stimulate progress in this area, particularly because it represents negotiations between a developed nation and developing nation that share a particularly long and active border region. But many substantial environmental issues, such as industrial migration, will have to be taken up in a wider trade context. For NAFTA signatories, then, the possibility of a new GATT round with a substantial environmental component takes on special significance.

Notes

1. Fast-track is a legislative procedure under which the U.S. government can streamline the negotiating and approval process for trade agreements. The procedure involves consultations between Congress and the U.S. executive during the negotiation of an agreement. After negotiation, the final accord is submitted to Congress for a straight up-or-down vote without formal amendments.

2. See, for example, Dick Kamp, Michael Gregory, Mary Kelly, and Jan Gilbreath Rich, "Mexico-U.S. Free-Trade Negotiations and the Environment: Exploring the Issues," discussion paper, Texas Center for Policy Studies/Border Ecology Project, January 1991; Steven Shrybman, Canadian Environmental Law Association, testimony before the House of Commons, Standing Committee on External Affairs and International Trade, no. 69, Ottawa, November 5, 1990; National Wildlife Federation, *Environmental Concerns Related to a United States–Mexico–Canada Free Trade Accord* (Washington, DC: National Wildlife Federation,

1990), pp. 6–7; and Justin R. Ward, "Environmental Protection in the North American Free Trade Agreement," statement of the Natural Resources Defense Council, presented in connection with hearings before the Office of the United States Trade Representative, Washington, DC, September 3, 1991.

3. For a cogent outline of the economic and trade effects of environmental legislation, see Gote Hansson, *Harmonisation and International Trade* (London: Routledge, 1990).

4. First, the taxation model eliminates the need for specialized and expensive enforcement agencies beyond those normally associated with revenue collection. Second, a taxation model ensures that the polluter pays for polluting, regardless of enforcement activities. Third, the model gives a continuing incentive to lower pollution levels and a financial incentive to invest in cleaner technology. Fourth, once the taxation levels have been set, a culture of cooperation between the environmental and industrial communities would ensue as they jointly search for environmental solutions.

5. From "Note on the United Nations Conference on Environment and Development Held in Rio de Janeiro, Brazil from 3 to 14 June 1992," *General Agreement on Tariffs and Trade* (Geneva: L/6892/Add.3, July 2, 1992).

6. From William J. Baumol, *Environmental Protection: International Spillovers and Trade,* Wicksell Lecture Series (Stockholm: Alqvist and Wicksell, 1971), p. 21.

7. Ibid., p. 22.

8. From Jonathan Lemco, ed., *Tensions at the Border: Energy and Environmental Concerns in Canada and the United States* (New York: Praeger, 1992): p. XVII.

9. Alan M. Schwartz, "Great Lakes: Great Rhetoric," in Lemco, ed., *Tensions at the Border*, pp. 61–78.

10. Ibid., p. 76.

11. Lindsey Gruson, "Canadian Trash Flows South, Landing in Dumps in the U.S.," *New York Times,* November 27, 1991.

12. National Planning Association, *Trade Talks with Mexico* (Washington, DC: 1991), p. 42.

13. Commission of the European Communities, Task Force Report, *EC 1992 and the Environment* (Brussels: 1991).

14. Ibid., p. II.

15. George Hoberg, "Sleeping with an Elephant: The American Influence on Canadian Environmental Regulation," *Journal of Public Policy* 2, no. 1 (January–March 1991):107–132.

16. Ibid., p. 117.

17. Qualified majority voting is a weighted voting system in the European Council of Ministers, which, in effect, guarantees that a piece of legislation must be supported by a mix of large and small states. Voting strengths range from the largest states (Germany, United Kingdom, France, Italy), which have ten votes each, to the smallest (Luxembourg), which has two votes. A qualified majority vote requires fifty-four votes out of a total of seventy-six.

18. Commission of the European Communities, *Microeconomic Estimates of the Potential Gains to Be Achieved Through Completion of the Internal Market* (Luxembourg: 1988).

19. Adolfo Martera, *Marché unique européen: Ses regles, son fonctionnement* (Paris: Jupiter, 1988), p. 270.

20. See Judgement of the European Court of Justice, "Dassonville" (1974); "Cassis de Dijon" (1978), Case 120/78, Rewe-Zentralfinanz v. Bundesmonopolverwaltung für Branntwein, European Court of Justice Reports (ECR) 649, 1979.

21. Loukas Tsoukalis, *The New European Economy: The Politics and Economics of Integration* (Oxford: Oxford University Press, 1991).

22. K. Chapman, "Environmental Policy and Industrial Location," *Area* 12 (1980):209–216; H.A. Stafford, "Environmental Protection and Industrial Location," *Annals,* Association of American Geographers, no. 64 (1985):193–205.

23. T.N. Gladwin, "Patterns of Environmental Conflict over Industrial Facilities in the United States, 1970–1978," *Natural Resources Journal*, no. 20 (1980): 243--274.

24. H.J. Leonard, *Pollution and the Struggle for the World Product* (New York: Cambridge University Press, 1988).

25. Ibid.

26. Commission of the European Communities, *Task Force 1992—Environmental Implications* (Luxembourg: Commission of the European Communities, 1990), p. vi.

27. Estimate is based on 1990 U.S. and Mexican census data.

28. Dallas Burtraw and Paul R. Portney, "Environmental Policy in the United States," in Dieter Helm, ed., *Economic Policy Toward the Environment* (Oxford: Blackwell Publishers, 1992).

29. Stephen P. Mumme, "Clearing the Air: Environmental Reform in Mexico," *Environment* 33, no. 10 (December 1991).

30. U.S. General Accounting Office, *U.S.-Mexico Trade: Information on Environmental Regulations and Enforcement* (Washington, DC: U.S. Government Printing Office, 1991).

31. "General Motors Announces Plans to Move Factory out of Mexico City," *U.S.-Mexico Free Trade Reporter* 1, no. 20, (April 6, 1992):2–3.

32. Luis Donaldo Colosio, SEDESOL secretary, "Environment and Development in Mexico," a speech to the U.S.-Mexico Border Environmental Assembly and Colloquy, Santa Fe, NM, June 25, 1992.

33. From a July 1993 interview between Jan Gilbreath and Luis Donaldo Colosio, SEDESOL secretary, and from statistical information provided by the office of the Mexican Environmental Attorney General in June 1993.

34. The announcement of the performance bond program comes from an October 1991 interview between Jan Gilbreath and SEDUE Undersecretary Sergio Reyes Lujan, Mexico City.

35. Office of General Counsel, Office of Enforcement, U.S. Environmental Protection Agency, *Mexican Environmental Laws, Regulations and Standards, Preliminary Findings* (Washington, DC: U.S. Government Printing Office, 1991).

36. From a question-and-answer session with Sergio Reyes Lujan, head of the new National Institute for Environment at SEDESOL, at the U.S.-Mexico Border Environmental Assembly and Colloquy, Santa Fe, NM, June 25, 1992.

37. Tim Golden, "A History of Pollution in Mexico Casts Clouds over Trade Accord," *New York Times*, August 16, 1993, p. 1.

38. See, among other accounts, Nancy Nussar (Cox News Service), "Mexico's Credibility Sinks with Denial of Acid Spill," *Austin American-Statesman*, August 6, 1993.

39. Golden, "A History of Pollution in Mexico."

40. Richard A. Gephardt, "Address on the Status of the North American Free Trade Agreement Before the Institute for International Economics," Washington, DC, July 27, 1992.

41. See Jan Gilbreath Rich, "Planning the Border's Future: The Mexican-U.S. Integrated Border Environmental Plan," Occasional Paper 1, U.S.-Mexican Policy Studies Program, LBJ School of Public Affairs, University of Texas at Austin, 1992.

42. George Baker, "Mexican Labor Is Not Cheap," *Rio Bravo: A Journal of Research and Opinion* 1, no.1 (October 1991):7–26.

43. Statement made by Ernesto Warnholtz, head of a Mexican export association, to the *Wall Street Journal* in an article that appeared July 12, 1990.

44. From an interview between Carla Hills and reporter Steven Greenhouse; see "Hills Cites Import Curbs in Trade Pact," *New York Times*, July 8, 1992.

45. Ibid.

46. U.S. General Accounting Office, *Comparison of U.S. and Mexican Pesticide Standards and Enforcement: Report to the Chairman, Committee on Agriculture, U.S. House of Representatives* (Washington, DC: U.S. Government Printing Office, 1992).

47. Office of the U.S. Trade Representative, *Review of U.S.-Mexico Environmental Issues* (Washington, DC: U.S. Government Printing Office, 1992), p. 230.

48. The groups included the National Wildlife Federation, Natural Resources Defense Council, Environmental Defense Fund, Sierra Club, and other groups. See "Baucus Urges Stronger Panels; Groups Want Process Standards Addressed," *U.S-Mexico Free Trade Reporter* 2, no. 22 (May 3, 1993):6, and "Regional Development Bank Proposal Receives Closer Scrutiny in Congress," *U.S.-Mexico Free Trade Reporter* 2, no. 22 (May 3, 1993):7.

49. Office of the U.S. Trade Representative, *Review of U.S.-Mexico Environmental Issues,* p. 226.

50. From "A Clean Mexico: The Protection of the Environment—A Survey of Technologies Used and Investment Made by U.S. Companies Operating in Mexico," Department of Economic Services, American Chamber of Commerce of Mexico, A.C., Mexico City, March 1992. Survey respondents represented varying firm sizes and came from several sectors and geographic locations. So-called dirty industries ranged from less than 1 percent to almost 20 percent of each industry sector. The percentages of respondents representing various sectors follow: chemical, petrochemical, and pharmaceutical products, 19.2 percent; electrical and electronic products, 17.6 percent; electromechanical and machinery equipment, 11.2 percent; food and drink products, 8.8 percent; auto industry, 4 percent; bathroom products, 1.6 percent; paper products, 1.6 percent. Maquiladoras represented 10.4 percent of the respondents. A total of 75 percent of the respondents were from the Mexico City metropolitan area, and the survey was conducted in January and February 1992.

51. Ibid.

52. Patrick Low, "Trade Measures and Environmental Quality: Implications for Mexico's Exports" (Paper presented to a symposium on international trade and environment sponsored by the International Trade Division, International Economics Department, World Bank, Washington, DC, November 21–22, 1992).

53. Ibid., p. 8.

54. Jagdish Bhagwati, a Columbia University economist overseeing a report on trade and the environment for the General Agreement on Tariffs and Trade, told the *New York Times* that he was skeptical of the report's conclusion that foreign firms move into Mexico to take advantage of low labor costs but not lax environmental regulation. "I find it difficult to believe people aren't going to pay attention if the pollution abatement costs are at least 20 percent less, much less 50 percent," he said. See Keith Bradsher, "Lower Pollution Tied to Prosperity," *New York Times*, October 28, 1991.

55. Franklin Frazier, director of education and employment issues, Human Resources Division, U.S. General Accounting Office, statement on occupational safety and health and child labor policies of the United States and Mexico before

the Subcommittees on Employment Opportunities and Labor-Management Relations, U.S. House of Representatives, April 30, 1991. This source is drawn on for other statements in this paragraph.

56. From a July 1991 telephone interview between SEDUE Undersecretary Sergio Reyes Lujan and Jan Gilbreath.

57. From wire service reports and staff reports cited in "Supreme Court Deals Legal Blow to Environmentalists," *Austin American-Statesman*, June 13, 1992.

58. This trend was documented during a trip that President Salinas made to ecologically sensitive regions of Mexico in June 1993.

59. From a July 1993 telephone interview between SEDESOL Secretary Luis Donaldo Colosio and Jan Gilbreath.

60. This suggestion draws on "The North American Free Trade Area: Legal Issues," in Rafael Fernández de Castro, Mónica Vérea Campos, and Sidney Weintraub, eds., *Sectoral Labor Effects of North American Free Trade* (Austin: U.S.-Mexican Policy Studies Program, University of Texas at Austin, 1993), pp. 337–346.

Part 2

The Politics of NAFTA

4

North American Economic Integration and Canadian Sovereignty

Alan M. Rugman

From a Canadian perspective, the negotiations over the North American Free Trade Agreement were of marginal importance. The key Canadian objective was defensive: to avoid any dissipation of the U.S.-Canada Free Trade Agreement, which became effective on January 1, 1989. As is well known, there is relatively little trade or investment between Canada and Mexico (trade in 1991 was about Cdn$2 billion) compared to the predominant economic relationship between Canada and the United States (with trade of about Cdn$200 billion in 1991). Mexico is the 1 percent solution for Canada; the United States is the 75 percent solution. These economic principles lead to the three propositions explained in this chapter.

First, I will focus on U.S.-Canadian economic integration within a triad framework of global competitiveness and the implications of this arrangement. Second, I will address the issue of Canadian sovereignty, which is, for all intents and purposes, a discussion of the U.S.-Canadian relationship. In particular, concerns over Canadian cultural sovereignty are almost entirely a reflection of concerns about U.S. domination. Third, I will discuss the opportunity that NAFTA presents to mitigate the bilateral focus for Canadians and replace it with a trilateral institutional framework, based on the principles of the EC.

In the next section of this chapter data are presented on the extent of economic integration between Canada and the United States, all within a triad context. Mexico is included as a reference point, and the implications for NAFTA are drawn out. The key role of multinational enterprises (MNEs) as agents for globalization (economic integration) across the triad is discussed in two subsequent sections; in the latter section, the focus is on the concepts of globalization and sovereignty. Next, these are linked in a matrix framework, followed by discussions of the decentralization of sovereignty in Canada and in the United States. This framework is then used to discuss the FTA, NAFTA, and a potential EC-type institutional linkage. Finally, cultural nationalism in Canada is addressed.

Triad Power and Canadian-U.S. Economic Integration

To understand the nature of global competition and the role of Canada's economic integration with one of the triad powers (the United States), it is necessary to review the relative positioning of Canada's multinationals compared to those of the triad. The world's largest MNEs are drawn mainly from the triad of the United States, Japan, and the European Community. Table 4.1 shows that in 1990, 405 of the world's 500 largest MNEs came from the triad, that is, over 80 percent of the total. These large MNEs also account for most of the world's trade and direct investment. Indeed, another way of measuring the importance of MNEs is to look at the data on the world's stock of foreign direct investment (FDI), as reported in Table 4.2. (It is necessary to examine the stock of FDI, rather than the annual flow of FDI, because the investment is in physical plant and equipment and lasts for a long time.)

The Triad and Foreign Direct Investment

Changes in the stocks of outbound FDI in the triad over the 1980s are reported in Table 4.2. Although the triad's percentage of all the world's FDI stayed relatively consistent at just over 80 percent of the total, there were remarkable changes within the triad. The most dramatic change was not the growth of Japanese FDI (which increased from 4 to 12 percent between 1980 and 1989) but the replacement of the United States by the EC as the world's largest single source of FDI. By 1989, the EC accounted for 41 percent of the world's total; the United States was down to 28 percent (from 40 percent in 1980). The stock of EC FDI increased by nearly $350 billion over the decade of the 1980s, whereas that of the United States rose by $160 billion, and Japan's grew by over $130 billion. Table 4.2 also demonstrates that there is relatively little FDI from other countries, including Third World countries. Indeed, much of the 19 percent of the nontriad stock of FDI in 1989 was from Canada (at 5 percent) and other advanced, nontriad nations.

The Triad and Global Trade Patterns

The pattern of dominance of the world's FDI by the triad is repeated with data on world trade. Figure 4.1 reports data for 1990 on the annual flows of trade by the triad. Note that the United States could be extended to include Canada (and Mexico) as a "North American" bloc relevant for discussion of the North American Free Trade Agreement. Again, the value of trade accounted for by the triad is about 80 percent.

The largest number in Figure 4.1 is in the EC box; that is, trade within the twelve member countries of the EC is the largest in the world. Next largest is the trade between the United States and Canada, at nearly US$180 billion. Indeed, this is the world's largest single trading relationship. There is more trade between the United States and Canada than between the United States and Japan. Further, the United States runs a large

Table 4.1 The World's 500 Largest MNEs

Country or Bloc	Number of MNEs in 1990[a]
United States	**164**
EC	**130**
Japan	**111**
Sweden	17
Canada	**12**
South Korea	11
Switzerland	11
Australia	9
Finland	8
India	6
Other	21
Total	500

Source: Adapted from "The Fortune Global 500," *Fortune* (July 29, 1991):237–280.
Note: [a] "Number" refers to the number of MNEs listed in "The Fortune Global 500"; MNEs in the Triad = 405.

Table 4.2 Outward Stocks of Triad FDI

Country or Region	1980 (U.S.$billions)	Percent of World	1989 (U.S.$billions)	Percent of World
United States	220	42	380	28
EC	203	39	549	41
Japan	20	4	154	12
Triad Total	443	85	1083	81
Canada	22	4	64	5
All Others	59	11	195	14
World Total	524	100	1342	100

Source: Data for 1980 are from UNCTC, *World Investment Report 1991: The Triad in Foreign Direct Investment* (New York: United Nations, 1991), p. 32; data for 1989 are provided by the Policy and Research Division, UNCTC, September 1991; data for Canada's FDI (1980) are based on the data from UNCTC, *Transnational Corporations in World Development: Trends and Prospects* (New York: United Nations, 1988).
Note: Data for the EC's FDI include intra-EC FDI, and 1989 figures are based on the United Kingdom, Germany, France, the Netherlands, and Italy.

deficit in its trade with Japan, whereas its trade with Canada is pretty much in balance.

Figure 4.2 is identical to Figure 4.1 except that it depicts global stocks of FDI. It reveals a large amount of EC FDI going to North America, more than the North American FDI in the EC. There is also a lot of Japanese FDI going into North America but not nearly so much into the EC. There is a large amount of intrabloc FDI; these FDI data are part of the total EC

Figure 4.1 Global Flows of Trade in the Triad, 1990, Exports Only (U.S.$billions)

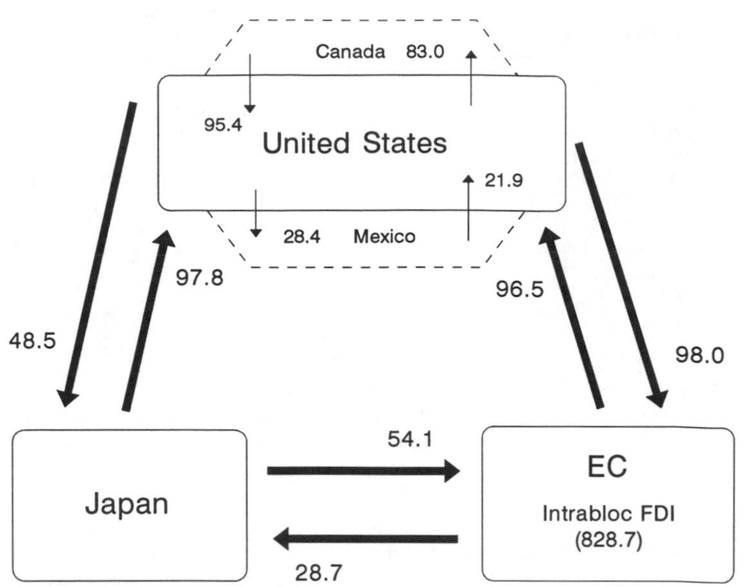

Source: Adapted from International Monetary Fund, *Direction of Trade Statistics: 1991 Yearbook* (Washington, DC: IMF, 1991).

Notes: Figures are taken from data reported by the exporting countries. EC Intrabloc Trade is based on export figures among the EC (12) as reported in Part A in the *Direction of Trade Statistics: 1991 Yearbook.*

data of Table 4.2, but here, the internal data are broken out from the external data.

Note that the EC data on both trade and FDI should be treated with caution. Each nation publishes data on its trade and FDI, but the trade data of Figure 4.1 and the FDI data of Figure 4.2 exclude intra-EC trade in order to show a proper triad picture. Unfortunately, the data in Table 4.2 cannot be constructed to exclude intra-EC data, due to statistical problems.

Canada's relationship with the triad and its dependence on the United States in particular can be further understood if its trade and investment with these markets are considered. Table 4.3 contains data on the direction of Canada's trade for 1981 and 1990. For example, over this ten-year period, Canada's exports to the United States increased from 64 percent to 73 percent of the total; exports to the EC declined to only 8 percent, and exports to Japan remained at 5 percent. Exports to Mexico were half of a percentage point in 1990, but imports were double this. A similar picture of Canada's overwhelming dependence on the United States appears in Table 4.4, except that by 1990, the stock of EC foreign direct investment in Canada was nearly 24 percent of the total.

Figure 4.2 Global Stocks of FDI in the Triad, 1990 (U.S.$billions)

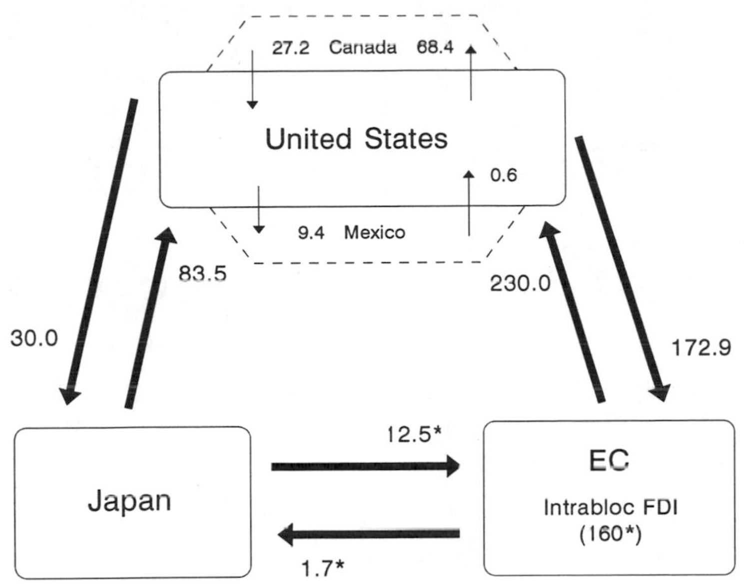

Source: Figures for FDI between North America (United States, Canada, and Mexico), the EC, and Japan are from U.S. Department of Commerce, *Survey of Current Business* (Washington, DC: Department of Commerce, August 1991); figures for FDI between the EC and Japan (*) are for 1988 from UNCTC, *World Investment Report 1991: The Triad in Foreign Direct Investment* (New York: United Nations, 1991), Figure 2 and Table 10.

Globalization of MNEs and Sovereignty

The major push behind NAFTA is globalization—the production and distribution of products and/or services of a homogeneous type and quality on a worldwide basis. The producers and distributors enjoy economies of scale through large-volume production of standardized products and services. Most of these goods and services are provided by MNEs operating across national borders.

To an extent, the MNEs of the triad homogenize tastes and help spread consumerism.[1] Throughout the wealthier nations of Europe and North America and in Japan, there is a growing acceptance of standardized consumer electronics goods, automobiles, computers, electric appliances, and so on. To a large degree, the MNEs have to respond to consumer needs and tastes, and they are successful because there is a demand for their products and services. In a remarkably old-fashioned book, Michael Porter argues that a home nation's "diamond" is the source of competitive advantages and that domestic firms that do well in that diamond can then go forth and succeed as global industries.[2] This is a zero-sum game.

Table 4.3 Direction of Canada's Trade, by Flows

	Exports to				Imports from			
Country or Region	1981 (U.S.$billions)	Percent of Total	1990 (U.S.$billions)	Percent of Total	1981 (U.S.$billions)	Percent of Total	1990 (U.S.$billions)	Percent of Total
United States	46.4	64.0	95.4	73.0	45.2	66.5	83.0	69.3
EC	7.2	10.0	10.0	8.0	5.3	7.8	13.3	11.1
Japan	3.6	5.0	7.0	5.0	3.4	5.0	8.2	6.9
Triad Total	57.2	79.0	112.4	86.0	53.9	79.3	104.5	87.3
Mexico	0.6	0.8	0.5	0.4	0.8	1.2	1.5	1.2
All Others	14.9	20.2	18.1	13.6	13.3	19.5	13.7	11.5
World Total	72.7	100.0	131.0	100.0	68.0	100.0	119.7	100.0

Source: Data for 1981 are adapted from IMF, *Direction of Trade Statistics 1985 Yearbook* (Washington, DC: IMF, 1985), pp. 126–128; data for 1990 are adapted from IMF, *Direction of Trade Statistics 1991 Yearbook* (Washington, DC: IMF, 1991), pp. 123–125.

Table 4.4 Direction of Canada's FDI, by Stocks

	Outward				Inward			
Country or Region	1981 (Cdn.$billions)	Percent of Total	1990 (Cdn.$billions)	Percent of Total	1981 (Cdn.$billions)	Percent of Total	1990 (Cdn.$billions)	Percent of Total
United States	18.6	66.4	53.1	61.2	52.1	78.2	80.4	64.2
EC	4.1	14.6	16.8	19.4	10.7	16.1	30.0	23.9
Japan	0.1	0.4	0.8	0.9	1.0	1.5	4.3	3.4
Triad Total	22.8	81.4	70.7	81.5	63.8	95.8	114.7	91.5
Mexico	0.2	0.7	0.2	0.3	0.001	—	0.001	—
All Others	5.0	17.9	15.8	18.2	2.8	4.2	10.6	8.5
World Total	28.0	100.0	86.7	100.0	66.6	100.0	125.3	100.0

Source: Data for 1981 are adapted from Statistics Canada, *Canada's International Investment Position,* Catalogue 67–202 (Ottawa: Statistics Canada, 1986); data for 1990 are adapted from Statistics Canada, *Canada's International Investment Position,* Catalogue 67–202 (Ottawa: Statistics Canada, 1991).
Note: — indicates negative FDI.

Multinational enterprises are in business; they are not social agencies. Yet over the next decade, there will be more criticism of the performance and social responsibility of MNEs, including their linkage to the environment. The goal of efficient economic performance through a simplistic globalization strategy will be compromised by the need for the MNEs to be more responsive to social needs and national interests. But sovereignty will not fade away as globalization increases. Instead, MNEs will have to deal with the twin goals of globalization and national responsiveness.[3] National responsiveness involves the need for corporations operating across national borders to invest in understanding the different tastes of consumers in segmented regional markets and the ability to respond to different national standards and regulations imposed by autonomous governments and agencies. Even Robert Reich now recognizes that MNEs are not just "national champions" and that they also respond to host-country values as well as home-country ones.[4]

The information technology revolution has helped globalization. The mass production of cheap personal computers, fax machines, and cellular telephones makes information flow faster and deeper across borders and within companies. And the greater flexibility and mobility facilitated by information technology enhances the ability of managers and companies to produce and distribute products and services on a global basis.

As explained earlier, most of the action by MNEs is concentrated in the triad markets of North America, the European Community, and Japan. In the next decade, the nature of the triad markets will change as they become more protectionist. There are already strong indications of an increase in U.S. protectionist devices, such as the super 301 trade law, the widespread use of countervailing duty (CVD) laws, and concern about Japanese MNEs operating in the United States.[5] There is also some evidence in the EC of an increase in antidumping (AD) actions and the possibility of a "Fortress Europe" developing as the single internal market emerges. However, the global economic interdependence already achieved through the activities of the large MNEs will not be halted. Indeed, a group of new MNEs, from the Asian economies of South Korea, Taiwan, and other newly industrialized economies (NIEs) will emerge, largely within the Japanese sphere of influence.

Mexico wants to be part of this trend, instead of remaining a poorer nation lacking access to one of the triad markets. Without NAFTA, there would have been increasing social and economic discontent in Mexico over the next decade because television, newspapers, and other media will continue to spread information about more affluent life-styles to a region that needs NAFTA to improve its economic infrastructure, corporate know-how, and political system in order to compete in global markets.

Information technology is a two-edged sword. Although it helps MNEs in their economic tasks, it also speeds social discontent and raises unrealistic expectations in poorer nations. Corporate efficiency is enhanced, yet the costs of doing business are also increased. The internal corporate tasks of strategic planning, financial control, research, production, human resource management, and marketing are all helped by the efficient design and use of information technology systems. But the external environment for doing business is simultaneously complicated. This means that MNEs must learn to tackle both tasks.

Responding to the twin challenges of globalization and national responsiveness requires new thinking by managers and policy advisers. The days of simple globalization are limited. Instead, MNEs must make major investments in being nationally responsive—in understanding what makes people tick and why people differ across borders. Cultural understanding is becoming as important as research and development (R&D). And even as the globalization of production and distribution feeds one desire, it also creates a hunger for more individual care and attention, a two-headed monster that needs the response of a two-pronged corporate strategy.

Put more formally, the corporation now faces a basic challenge of transaction cost economics in dealing with the public on a global basis. Because there are literally millions of consumers yet only a few hundred large MNEs, there is a problem of asymmetry in information costs—a type of buyer uncertainty. There is no way this problem can be solved by consumers because it is not in any one individual's interest to make the investment of time and money required to achieve a solution that will satisfy everyone else.[6] But the relatively few large MNEs do have this incentive. They need to stay in business, so they must be able to both achieve economic efficiency through globalization and also keep sovereignty at bay or at least accommodated to the extent that their business does not suffer. In short, the MNEs themselves must develop management strategies to be nationally responsive as well as globally efficient. It is to the method of achieving this balance that I now turn.

The Globalization and Sovereignty Matrix

Conceptually, the twin issues of globalization and sovereignty can be analyzed through the use of Figure 4.3. This is adapted from Christopher Bartlett,[7] who uses a globalization–national responsiveness matrix to analyze the strategies of nine large MNEs. This work was extended and tested on nine MNEs in the three triad blocs by Bartlett and Sumantra Ghoshal.[8] I adapt this framework to consider the nature of corporate strategies in a world in which an increasing amount of sovereignty is being exhibited.

The vertical axis captures the concept of the need for economic integration, frequently referred to as globalization. Movement up the axis results in a greater degree of economic integration. Globalization generates

Figure 4.3 Globalization and Sovereignty

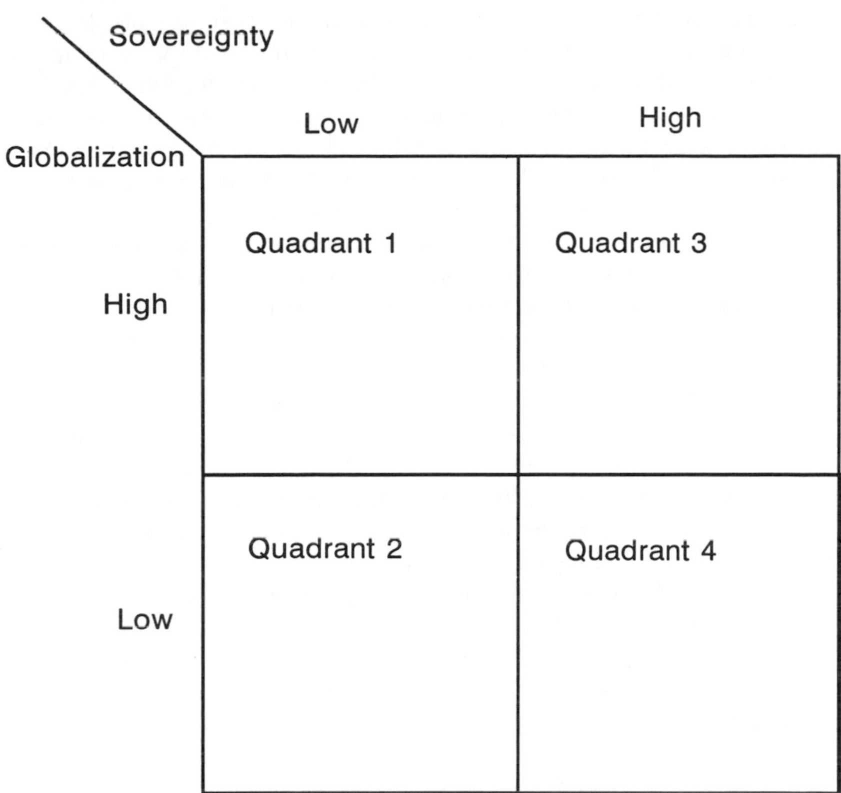

economies of scale as a firm moves into worldwide markets selling a single product or service. These are captured as a result of centralizing certain activities in the value-added chain in locations with the strongest perceived country-specific advantages. They also occur by reaping the benefits of increased coordination and control of geographically dispersed activities.

The horizontal axis measures the need for corporations to respond to sovereignty. Companies need to be nationally responsive to consumer tastes and government regulations in the countries in which they operate. The concern for sovereignty means that corporate activities must be adapted to local conditions, in terms of both content and process. This may imply a geographic dispersion of activities or a decentralization of coordination and control for individual firms. Corporations and financial institutions need either a low or a high degree of awareness of sovereignty.

On the basis of the two axes of Figure 4.3, four cases can be distinguished. Quadrants 1 and 4 are simple cases, in which the impact of an exogenous "environmental" change (such as the U.S.-Canada Free Trade

Agreement or Europe 1992) unambiguously affects the firm's movement toward a higher required responsiveness to one variable and simultaneously decreases the required responsiveness to the other variable. In Quadrant 1, the need for globalization increases, and the need for awareness of sovereignty is low. This focus on scale economies will lead to competitive strategies based on Porter's first generic strategy of price competition.[9] Usually, mergers and acquisitions will result. The opposite situation is characteristic of Quadrant 4, where sovereignty matters but globalization is low. There, niche strategies must be pursued; companies will adapt products to satisfy the high demands of sovereignty and ignore scale economies because globalization does not matter very much.

Quadrants 2 and 3 reflect more complex situations. Quadrant 2 refers to those cases where both the need for integration and awareness of sovereignty are low. This implies that both the potential to obtain economies of scale and the benefits of being sensitive to sovereignty decline. Typical strategies for Quadrant 2 would be firms and industries characterized by increased international standardization of products and services. This could reduce the need for centralized quality control and centralized strategic decisionmaking, while simultaneously eliminating requirements to adapt activities to individual countries.

Finally, in Quadrant 3, the needs for both integration and sovereignty increase, implying that different activities in the vertical chain are faced with opposite tendencies—for example, a higher need for integration in production may be coupled with higher requirements for regional adaptations in marketing. This is the most challenging quadrant and one where many successful, globally efficient MNEs must perform. Using this framework, I can analyze the impact of various government policy shocks and trends on different industries, firms, and other private-sector institutions.

In this matrix, the globalization-only view of Kenichi Ohmae[10] is shown in Quadrant 1. Here, the overarching commercial and economic interests of the MNE are paramount, and aspects of sovereignty are ignored. In contrast, in Quadrant 4, globalization pressures on the MNEs are less important than sovereignty. In Quadrant 4, governments dominate the MNE. Quadrant 2 is now of minimal interest (in it, neither globalization nor sovereignty issues dominate), but in Quadrant 3, the current problems of globalization and sovereignty coexist. Figure 4.3 can also be used to reinterpret the literature of international political economy. Quadrant 1 is a case of markets, in contrast to Quadrant 4, which is one of states. In between, Quadrant 3 is where both coexist, as pointed out by Susan Strange and Lorraine Eden.[11]

From the viewpoint of private-sector corporations, the most important business decision to be made is a judgment about where the trade-off between globalization (economic efficiency) and sovereignty (noneconomic issues) will fall. By now, it should be clear why *both* these issues are of concern to business. Today, a successful company can no longer afford to ignore sovereignty and just concentrate on globalization; Quadrant 3 matters. Each business therefore bears the costs of making the decision about the trade-off itself. Evidence that sovereignty is of growing importance and that a private-sector company must develop a strategy to respond to it can be seen in the following example.

Decentralization of Power to Canada's Provinces

The increasing power of the provinces in Canada is leading to a growing decentralization of economic decisionmaking. This is moving Canada toward Quadrant 4 of Figure 4.3. In terms of the costs of doing business, Quebec is already, in effect, a separate nation. It uses the French language for business and education, and the provincial government calls the tune in the administration of social and health services and in the regulation of the workplace. Meanwhile, there is evidence of a growing separatist feeling in Western Canada, especially in Alberta. The Atlantic provinces also form a distinctive grouping with common concerns about support for regional development.

Both the Atlantic premiers and the four Western premiers have annual meetings to discuss a common economic strategy for their regions. This is supported by a small but growing interprovincial bureaucratic infrastructure, generating data and information from a subnational point of view.

Ontario, like Quebec, has perfected the technique of a parallel bureaucracy (in its case, parallel to Ottawa). The former premier of Ontario was fond of remarking that if the province were a separate country, it would be the eleventh largest in the world. Indeed, it tries to act as if it were a separate nation, frequently stepping into areas of federal jurisdiction, including trade and fiscal policies. For example, the Province of Ontario fought the U.S.-Canada Free Trade Agreement tooth and nail both during and after the negotiations, throughout the 1986–1988 period. Only recently has Ontario learned to live with free trade.

Almost all provinces also failed to cooperate in 1991 on the introduction of Canada's goods and services tax (GST), one of the most important tax changes in Canada's history. The GST replaces the manufacturers' sales tax, which penalized Canada's exporters and subsidized importers (the latter, of course, are not subject to Canada's manufacturing tax when products are made outside of Canada). The provinces continue to have large public-sector deficits; these will likely increase in the future because the provinces must be responsive to local lobbies and social interest groups. This will compound the problems of the excessive federal deficit and lead to vicious fighting between federal and provincial ministers as their industrial, educational, social, and health programs are cut.

The failure of the Meech Lake accord in 1990 and the subsequent impasse over constitutional renewal was another example of the central government's power being eroded by the provinces. To accommodate Quebec's requests to sign Canada's constitution, the Ottawa government was prepared, with the Meech Lake accord, to let any one of the provinces have a veto over further changes to the constitution. Provinces already have the power to opt out of responsibility for some aspects of the Charter of Rights and Freedoms, in particular those dealing with language issues. This can occur when a province invokes the "notwithstanding" clause of the 1982 constitution, as Premier Robert Bourassa did in rejecting a Supreme Court of Canada decision in 1988 requiring bilingual signs in Quebec. The future prospect of senate reform will also lead to more representation from the regions and less power for the central government, especially in economic decisionmaking.

The power of the provinces is disturbing for private-sector companies and MNEs. Decentralization of power to the provinces means an increase in the costs of doing business.[12] Corporations must learn to staff offices and acquire information about eleven governments instead of one, and they also have to respond to eleven types of regulations and bureaucratic environments. This leads to confusion about standards, inefficient production, and ultimately, greater corporate expenses. In effect, the private sector is forced to deal with sovereignty at a very disaggregated level.

Canada has always been a federation, with considerable economic power delegated to the provinces. There is ongoing tension between federal and provincial powers over the economy. What is evident in Canada today is that the time is coming when the costs of political decentralization may become so great that many of the offsetting economic benefits of the federation will be lost. The end result could be something close to anarchy—not a good place to do business. In terms of corporate strategy, more and more executive time and energy must be invested in understanding the decentralized nature of political and economic power in Canada.

Decentralization of Economic Power in the United States

The United States is also experiencing considerable decentralization in economic decisionmaking. It is a country in which subnational units will continue to increase in importance. This issue should not be confused with pluralism. A variety of political opinions and parties is a strength of democracy; it can put the United States into Quadrant 3 of Figure 4.3. The problem comes when the institutional structure of the nation breaks down and business cannot operate in an efficient manner, especially relative to global competitors. This shifts the United States to Quadrant 4 of Figure 4.3.

The U.S. Constitution was designed to allow Congress to be a broker for regional and special interests. On occasion, Congress works with the executive branch, and a coordinated economic and even social policy can be both formulated and implemented. The examples of social reform and government economic activity in the Kennedy and Johnson years can be contrasted with a return to more market-based principles and a somewhat reduced role for government in the Reagan years.

However, in many areas affecting the private sector today, the overwhelming characteristic of doing business in the United States is the responsiveness of governments to special interest groups and lobbies. The more decentralized the level of government is, the more responsive the regulatory activity is to the lobbyist. Businesses themselves can sometimes be lobbyists, but there are many other groups, such as environmentalists and social activists, who seem to be growing in power. Examples of conflicts in business lobbying occur in the areas of the administration of U.S. trade remedy laws and in the current U.S. debate about the possible regulation of inward foreign direct investment.

It has been demonstrated by Alan Rugman and Andrew Anderson[13] and by others that the current administration of U.S. countervailing duty and antidumping laws is highly responsive to domestic producer interests and biased against foreign firms. Rugman and Alain Verbeke demonstrate that U.S. corporations use CVD and AD as competitive strategies to erect entry barriers against rival firms.[14] Thus, even when the U.S. government was pursuing negotiations for free trade with Canada, individual U.S. corporations still used the CVD and AD laws to build entry barriers against Canadian exporters. This was a clear example of the U.S. national interest being offset by selective producer interests. More of the same is in store in the future, although Canadian concerns about the administration of CVD and AD laws have been somewhat answered by the establishment of binational panels under the terms of the free trade agreement.

The most notorious example of U.S. producer interests offsetting official U.S. trade policy was the 1986 softwood lumber CVD, which prompted the Canadian federal government to respond by imposing an export tax of 15 percent on a major Canadian industry. The 1992 lumber CVD case is an even greater abuse of U.S. trade law procedures. Other examples over the 1986–1988 FTA negotiations period involved fresh Atlantic groundfish, potash from Saskatchewan, live swine and pork, and other goods. Over the 1980–1986 period, there were more than fifty cases of CVD and AD brought by U.S. companies against Canadian exporters, and this barrage of actions did not let up during the negotiations. None of these routine company-led applications of U.S. CVD and AD law were particularly helpful to either the U.S. or the Canadian government. In Canada, especially, the FTA was nearly sabotaged by such parochial corporate interests.

Although certain congressional leaders now wish to restrict inward FDI, most of the individual U.S. states actively encourage it. Some U.S. citizens seem to be concerned with the growing amount of Japanese FDI, which is, in practice, concentrated in the West: Over one-quarter of all Japanese FDI in the United States is in Hawaii; another quarter is in California. Many in Congress pushed for protectionist trade bills over the 1981–1988 period, leading to the passage of the 1988 trade bill, with its restrictive and protectionist super 301 provisions. Members of Congress have urged more screening of Japanese FDI, and there is a strong "Japan-bashing" stance in U.S. trade policy. Yet officials from virtually all states are actively seeking out Japanese FDI for their home districts; they want the jobs and tax base. Tennessee, for example, has attracted Nissan and Bridgestone tires; state officials there, like their compatriots elsewhere, are falling over themselves endorsing these Japanese-owned firms as good corporate citizens. This potential clash between Washington "beltway" thinking (which is anti-Japanese) and state-level activity (which is pro-Japanese) parallels Canada's experience with the regulation of FDI.

In the next ten years, the United States seems destined to repeat many of the mistakes made in Canada over the last thirty years. Canadians are experts at restricting FDI; it has not been a happy experience. In 1974, the Trudeau government introduced the Foreign Investment Review Agency (FIRA), designed to screen FDI on the basis of economic criteria to assess if there was a "net benefit" to Canada. Yet over the 1974–1985 period, FIRA responded to Ottawa's political winds, at times rejecting as many as 30 percent of the applications it received and at other times (especially 1982–1985) approving virtually everything. The administrators at FIRA and the responsible ministers abused the economics-based tests of FIRA and made political decisions just as the U.S. International Trade Commission and Commerce Department do today in U.S. trade law cases.

In 1985, FIRA was abolished, and a new agency, Investment Canada, was created with the mandate to attract FDI rather than scare it away. Throughout the lifetime of FIRA, most provinces, especially those in Atlantic Canada but also those in the West, still wanted FDI for jobs and taxes. The clash between the provinces that favor FDI and the Central Canadian economic nationalists who want to scare it off has now led to the federal government giving up many of its powers to regulate FDI by buying into the agenda of the provinces, especially their overwhelming priority about jobs. Perhaps this is some evidence of the triumph of decentralized economic power.

But a paradox emerges. In Canada, the economic nationalists, who have used central government power, are in retreat, but it appears that in the United States, economic nationalism is just beginning to take off. If Japan-bashing continues, then the U.S. proponents of restrictions on FDI should learn from Canada's unhappy experience with FIRA. In any case, the private-sector corporate strategists will need to respond to a large dose of economic nationalism and the downside of sovereignty.

A North American Economic Community

Free trade agreements are a necessary but not sufficient condition for North American economic integration. Both the U.S.-Canada FTA and NAFTA are designed to remove tariffs, apply national treatment to investment, and address some of the pervasive nontariff barriers to trade. They also provide temporary entry for designated businesspeople and attempt to remove some of the barriers to trade in services. However, both the FTA and NAFTA fall short of the type of economic and political integration achieved by the EC.

For North America, it is probably not desirable to seek the degree of political integration that exists in the EC—a common parliament, a powerful central commission, a social charter, common currency, and so on. However, it would be desirable to seek proper economic union.

Neither the FTA nor NAFTA go far enough to be designated a common market of North America. Over 70 percent of Canadians and U.S. citizens work in the service sector, yet in the U.S.-Canada FTA, major service sectors were exempted from national treatment (i.e., health, social services, education, cultural industries, and transportation). More people work in these five exempted sectors than in business services, which did receive national treatment. In any case, national treatment is a lukewarm form of economic integration because it only allows host-country rules to be applied when doing business—that is, a U.S. firm can do business in Canada but only according to Canadian laws and regulations, not U.S. ones. In contrast, in the EC, reciprocity now applies—a firm can do business according to its home-country rules. NAFTA is designed to be similar to the FTA in the sense of having provisions for national treatment and many exempted sectors.

The reason behind this particular institutional framework of the FTA and NAFTA is, of course, the Canadian and Mexican fear of U.S. domination of economic and political systems. The choice of national treatment over reciprocity (both of which are consistent with GATT) minimizes the extent of U.S. influence because it slows down the forces of harmonization. If reciprocity were applied, it would speed up harmonization, usually to U.S. standards and practices. Given the very open nature of the Canadian and Mexican economies, it would be more difficult to justify exemptions for service sectors if an EC-type model were adopted. In particular, the transport sector faces the forces of globalization, and its exemption from the national treatment provisions of the FTA has not insulated it from these forces.

The other problem with the FTA and NAFTA is that unfair national trade laws remain in place. The United States, especially, is the victim of sectoral lobbies that abuse its antidumping and countervailing duty laws to raise the prices of imported products, thereby penalizing intermediate processors and consumers. Mention of the welfare costs of such administered protection is usually drowned out by the chorus of industries demanding government help in erecting barriers to entry against rival producers.

The most appalling example of the abuse of U.S. trade law procedure is the use of CVD actions against the Canadian softwood lumber industry in 1983, 1986, and 1992. The U.S. protectionists lost the 1983 case but won in 1986 when the U.S. Commerce Department established a 15 percent duty. The Canadian government then imposed a 15 percent export tax. Subsequently, the government of British Columbia (BC) imposed a 15 percent increase in its stumpage rates so the export tax was terminated in 1991. (BC accounts for 80 percent of Canada's lumber exports to the United States.) Yet the U.S. industry pressured the U.S. government to launch a new CVD case in 1991, and the Commerce Department eventually imposed a final duty of 6.2 percent in May 1992. Commerce found that the alleged stumpage subsidy was now de minimus but applied a duty to offset the ban on exports of raw logs imposed by BC.

This lumber case, together with the Honda Canada ruling (that an engine made in Marysville, Ohio, is not a U.S. engine) and the fifty previous CVD and AD cases against Canada, led to the widespread perception in Canada that U.S. producers can use U.S. trade laws as a weapon to harass Canadian exporters.[15] The Mexicans feel the same way. In the FTA, the Chapter 19 dispute settlement panels have worked well to offset some of the most egregious legal errors in the application of U.S. trade law. In particular, the pork case led to the reversal of a blatantly protectionist decision by the U.S. International Trade Commission (ITC); an earlier case on red raspberries had reversed a technical error by the Commerce Department.[16] Yet these Chapter 19 panels cannot root out the abusive use of trade laws by industry protectionists and poorly trained officials who are too responsive to political pressures.[17] Instead, the whole system of CVD and AD should be done away with, as it has been in the EC.

The main benefit of an EC-type arrangement for North America would be the abolition of trade law actions against the member states. Instead, a new North American trade commission would only take trade law actions against Asian and European rivals. Neither the FTA nor NAFTA was able to shift CVD and AD actions to a new tripartite North American trade commission (NATC), which is logically desirable in a world of trade power and global competition. It remains the key piece on the unfinished agenda of the economic integration of North America.

The authority for a new North American trade commission needs to come from a new North American economic community (NAEC). This could be modeled on the EC itself. In particular, NAEC needs to have a new trilateral parliament or congress; a new centralized bureaucracy and set of commissioners with responsibility for trade policy, competition policy, and so on; and a new neutral site for its administrative offices. I would envisage the following components:

1. A North American economic community consisting of the United States, Canada, and Mexico as full and equal member states.
2. A North American parliament (NAP), consisting of 100 elected parliamentarians, with 50 from the United States, 25 from Canada, and 25 from Mexico. The NAC would make laws and regulations affecting the economic life of North Americans (e.g., in trade, investment, and competition policy), but it would not impose supranational laws affecting the political, social, or cultural lives of North Americans.
3. A North American commission (NAC), based on the model of the EC bureaucracy in Brussels, in which appointed commissioners would have responsibility for administering economic policies for North America, especially in the areas of trade, investment, and competition policy. One of the economic agencies would be a North American trade commission responsible for the administration of all trade law. This would require the abolition of all national trade law agencies, such as the ITC.
4. The site for the NAP and NAC should be in a neutral area, such as Puerto Rico or some other area remote from the three national capitals and their associated political, legal, and related infrastructures.

Cultural Nationalism in Canada

It is puzzling to many U.S. citizens that economics-based deals, such as the U.S.-Canada FTA and NAFTA, are opposed so passionately by many Canadians. After all, the FTA and NAFTA provide Canadians with access to the world's largest and richest market; they are good for business. Yet a majority of Canadians opposed the FTA. In the 1988 Canadian election on this issue, the Mulroney government won only because the two opposition parties split the anti-FTA vote; nearly 60 percent of Canadians did not vote for the government or the FTA. In an April 1992 opinion poll by Angus Reid-Southam, only 32 percent of Canadians supported the FTA, with 66 percent opposed. (In contrast, this poll found that in the United States, 78 percent supported the FTA and only 9 percent opposed it.) The reason is simple: Canadians are afraid of U.S. economic power and potential political, cultural, and social dominance.

To an extent, the national treatment provisions of the FTA and NAFTA should reduce Canadian fears of U.S. domination. National treatment leaves Canadian federal and provincial governments with the legal right to impose their own laws and regulations, reflecting the interests of Canadian voters. National treatment does not invite harmonization; rather, it spotlights the economic pressures of globalization and forces an internal Canadian debate whenever there are economic pressures to harmonize. Thus, national treatment is a safeguard for Canadian sovereignty. Nonetheless, most of the opponents of the FTA remain unaware of this institutional protection and continue to blame the agreement for a perceived loss of sovereignty that has nothing to do with the FTA itself.

In a similar manner, Canadian opponents of the FTA have not acknowledged that the exemptions from the agreement preserve key aspects of Canadian sovereignty. For example, the exemption for health services protects the Canadian medicare system. There are economic pressures on the provinces due to the escalating costs of delivering a universal health care system, but these pressures were not caused by the FTA. The introduction of realistic user fees could help reduce the excess demand for health care under a subsidized medicare program, but this potential solution has nothing to do with the FTA itself. Similarly, the economic problems facing Canada's social, transport, education, and cultural services are all real and urgent, but none of them are due to the institutional provisions of the FTA.

The reason why many Canadians are still confused by this is that the nationalist lobby opposing the FTA continues to dissemble to the Canadian public, stating repeatedly that the agreement threatens health, social, and cultural programs. In the infamous cartoon booklet he wrote during the election, left-wing columnist Rick Salutin depicted the FTA as an instrument that would force the harmonization of Canada's health and social services to U.S. values. Indeed, opponents of the FTA alleged that Canada's sovereignty would be eroded by the agreement and objected when better-informed trade observers stated that the FTA exempted these sectors.[18] Yet three years after the FTA was put in force, Canada's sovereignty is not diminished; the FTA has made no difference to the ability of Canada's politicians to create internal chaos in areas affecting the constitution, tax policy, health, culture, and so on.

Having lost the argument that the FTA would diminish Canadian sovereignty, opponents of the agreement switched to attacking it on economic grounds. In a series of economically illiterate and blatantly distorted books, economic nationalists like Maude Barlow and Mel Hurtig have argued that every job loss in Canada since 1989 is due to the FTA.[19] The "research" team at the Canadian Labour Congress, headed by Don Campbell, kept a list of job losses due to the FTA, but an examination of this list, reproduced in Barlow,[20] reveals that it is inaccurate. It includes jobs lost in sectors that were exempted from the FTA, such as breweries, transport, and cultural industries. The only sector with substantial job losses is food processing, but these losses are due to the exemption of agricultural marketing boards from the FTA, which kept up the input costs of dairy and feather products and drove food processors to the United States where there are scale economies and cheaper inputs.

The economic nationalists in Canada, having lost the 1988 election on the FTA, then continued to oppose it on grounds that can only be portrayed as naked anti-Americanism. They stated that the FTA is part of a neoconservative, right-wing business agenda designed to cripple Canadian sovereignty and deliver Canada into the arms of the United States. They stated that even if the job losses may not have been due to the FTA itself, they were caused by the Tory government's devotion to free trade, deregulation, market forces, and the GST. Readers who find it difficult to believe the internal contradictions and economic errors in this reasoning should consult the books by Salutin; Barlow; Hurtig; Linda McQuaig; and Barlow and Bruce Campbell.[21] Their titles dominated the best-seller lists in Canada, and the Canadian media, especially the CBC and *Toronto Star,* continue to showcase such left-wing thinkers. This led to a poisoned intellectual climate in Canada, where journalists and media commentators turned to well-known economic nationalists for the easy story, dumping on the Mulroney government and blaming the FTA and the United States for Canada's own problems.

Conclusion

In Canada, the phrase *cultural nationalism* is an excuse for being anti-American. There is a large and voluble Canadian industry advocating this line. It receives a disproportionate amount of media attention, and it serves to polarize opinions into simplistic categories of pro- or anti-FTA. The business groups that support the FTA are caricatured as a pro-U.S. lobby, with no moral commitment to Canada. This insulting dismissal of perfectly valid economic concerns has alienated most business leaders and independent commentators. Indeed, it is a waste of time debating narrow-minded economic nationalists who still have not read the FTA, nor acknowledged the exemptions from it for cultural, social, health, education, and transportation industries. There is little or no learning curve for old-fashioned nationalists; the facts of globalization and triad power are dismissed as a probusiness agenda. Many Canadian nationalists are like environmentalists: They would rather have no business at all. This is the Canadian burden—to perform in an economically successful manner on a world stage where the actors are following nineteenth-century scripts.

Notes

1. Kenichi Ohmae, *The Borderless World: Power and Strategy in the International Economy* (New York: Harper Business, 1990).

2. Michael E. Porter, *The Competitive Advantage of Nations* (New York: Free Press, Macmillan, 1990).

3. Christopher A. Bartlett and Sumantra Ghoshal, *Managing Across Borders: The Transnational Solution* (Boston: Harvard Business School Press, 1989).

4. Robert Reich, *The Work of Nations* (New York: Free Press, Macmillan, 1991).

5. Alan M. Rugman and Alain Verbeke, *Global Corporate Strategy and Trade Policy* (London and New York: Routledge, 1990).

6. Alan M. Rugman, *Inside the Multinationals: The Economics of Internal Markets* (London: Croom Helm, and New York: Columbia University Press, 1981).

7. Christopher A. Bartlett, "Building and Managing the Transnational: The New Organizational Challenge," in M.E. Porter, ed., *Competition in Global Industries* (Boston: Harvard Business School Press, 1986), pp. 367–401.

8. Bartlett and Ghoshal, *Managing Across Borders*, 1989.

9. Michael E. Porter, *Competitive Strategy: Techniques for Analyzing Industries and Competitors* (New York: Free Press, Macmillan, Binch, 1980).

10. Ohmae, *The Borderless World*, 1990.

11. Susan Strange, "Big Business and the State," *Millennium* 20, no. 2 (Summer 1991):245–250, and Lorraine Eden, "Bringing the Firm Back In: Multinationals in the International Political Economy," *Millennium* 20, no. 2 (Summer 1991): 197–224.

12. Alan M. Rugman and Joseph R. D'Cruz, "Quebec Separation and Canadian Competitiveness," *American Review of Canadian Studies* 21, no. 2/3 (Summer/Autumn 1991):253–259.

13. Alan M. Rugman and Andrew Anderson, *Administered Protection in America* (London and New York: Routledge, 1987).

14. Alan M. Rugman and Alain Verbeke, "Strategic Management and Trade Policy," *Journal of International Studies,* no. 3 (1989):139–152, and Rugman and Verbeke, *Global Corporate Strategy and Trade Policy.*

15. Rugman and Anderson, *Administered Protection in America.*

16. Tom Boddez and Alan M. Rugman, "Effective Dispute Settlement: A Case Study of the Initial Panel Decisions Under Chapter Nineteen of Canada-U.S. Free Trade Agreement," in Earl H. Fry and Lee H. Radebaugh, eds., *Investment in the North American Free Trade Area: Opportunities and Challenges* (Provo, UT: Brigham Young University, 1991), pp. 93–126.

17. Rugman and Verbeke, *Global Corporate Strategy and Trade Policy.*

18. Rick Salutin, *Waiting for Democracy: A Citizen's Journal* (Toronto: Viking, 1989).

19. Maude Barlow, *Parcel of Rogues: How Free Trade Is Failing Canada* (Toronto: Key Porter Books, 1990), and Mel Hurtig, *The Betrayal of Canada* (Toronto: Stoddart, 1991).

20. Barlow, *Parcel of Rogues.*

21. Salutin, *Waiting for Democracy;* Barlow, *Parcel of Rogues;* Hurtig, *The Betrayal of Canada;* Linda McQuaig, *The Quick and the Dead: Brian Mulroney—Big Business and the Seduction of Canada* (Toronto: Viking, 1991); and Maude Barlow and Bruce Campbell, *Take Back the Nation* (Toronto: Key Porter Books, 1991).

5

The U.S. Domestic Politics of the U.S.-Mexico Free Trade Agreement

Howard J. Wiarda

Mexico will poison us.
—Ralph Waldo Emerson

When the great American writer and moralist Ralph Waldo Emerson penned these words more than one hundred and fifty years ago, he was referring to the U.S.-Mexican War of 1846–1847 in which the United States took nearly one-third of Mexico's national territory, the present-day U.S. Southwest, and annexed it. Emerson feared the consequences of the aggressive U.S. strategy of Manifest Destiny and, particularly, the moral implications *for the United States* of a war of conquest. He believed such an aggressive war would come back to haunt the United States; hence, his comment that U.S. seizure of Mexican territory would serve as poison in the U.S. body politic.[1]

It appears from the debate over the U.S.-Mexico free trade agreement that Mexico still has the capacity to poison the United States. In the present circumstances the term *poison* is both a figurative expression, as it was in Emerson's day, and a literal one, if we accept one of the arguments advanced by critics of the agreement that Mexican pollution poses a major threat to U.S. border areas. The proposed agreement has been a divisive issue, a politically sensitive one, and one that has the capacity to turn U.S. domestic politics into a nasty, bitter broil. It has unleashed nationalist, xenophobic, demagogic, and even racist currents. Even before the serious political bargaining over the treaty's terms had begun, the issue was deeply controversial.

Every empirical study that we have suggests a free trade agreement with Mexico will bring significant benefits in terms of job creation, lower prices on many goods, and stimulus to the economies of both the United States and Mexico.[2] And yet the opposition to the pact, which is so mutually advantageous, has been intense. This chapter explores why that is so, and it discusses the nature of the opposition, which arguments are valid, and which arguments are spurious. It tries to sort out the serious arguments from those that are red herrings, driven by hysteria and irrationalism. The debate over the U.S.-Mexico free trade agreement makes it clear that many issues and currents are loose in the land besides a relatively straightforward trade agreement. In the process of sorting out the arguments over U.S.-Mexican free trade, we may also discern signs of a new style of interest group politics in the United States and of far larger moral, political, economic, and even cultural issues that have recently driven the country. Nothing is simple anymore.

Hypotheses and Conjectures

The debate surrounding NAFTA has been a divisive issue in the United States. Trade policies overall and the proposed U.S.-Mexico agreement in particular are touching some strong defensive and nationalistic nerves. The agreement came at a time when U.S. industries faced stiff competition from abroad, the economy was in recession, U.S. workers were perceived as paying the price of a declining U.S. edge in world markets, unemployment was rising, and the U.S. public was deeply worried about the future. In addition, NAFTA has unleashed some deeper and meaner sentiments, including racial and cultural prejudices and the bashing of a weak neighbor that serves, in part, as a surrogate for a stronger Japan. The present analysis discusses those issues, the players on both sides of NAFTA, the partisan implications of trade politics, and the impact of the Hispanic voting population on the issue, as well as the politics of competing regional interests—for example, those of the sunbelt versus those of the rustbelt.

Economists are in virtually unanimous agreement that NAFTA will be mutually advantageous.[3] Free trade helps create jobs in the long run (although there may be some short-term dislocations), it has a multiplier effect on economic growth (usually put at 1:2—for every dollar that goes into trade, two dollars are generated in economic growth), and it keeps the quality of goods high and prices low. It helps promote stability in Mexico, helps the United States solve the problem of unchecked immigration, and may even give the United States a handle on the troublesome drug issue. One would think that a proposal whose benefits are almost universally recognized would have generated little opposition. Yet NAFTA has been strongly attacked by the leaders of organized labor (principally the American Federation of Labor–Congress of Industrial Organizations [AFL-CIO]), by environmental groups, and by such privileged sectors as the textile industry and Florida growers who already enjoy special government favors and subsidies that protect them from foreign competition. These groups often distorted the facts about NAFTA, exaggerated the potential harm accruing, spawned myths that NAFTA would harm both the United States and Mexico, and even invented arguments that are downright spurious. If NAFTA had been defeated, it would have harmed U.S. global competitiveness, destroyed even more U.S. jobs, raised prices for numerous goods and services, lowered the quality of U.S. products, restricted choices for U.S. consumers, and run the unacceptable risk of economically and politically destabilizing Mexico. And yet the opposition was so vocal that NAFTA's passage by Congress was in serious doubt. Furthermore, the controversy surrounding NAFTA is unlikely to disappear even though it was passed in the House of Representatives on November 17, 1993.

What is going on here? Clearly, the NAFTA debate has become something more than just a trade debate. But what precisely is it? What is at stake? Why is the issue so hot? For what other issues and agendas does NAFTA serve as a smoke screen? Those are the questions that I try to answer here.

The last major global trade pact before NAFTA was concluded in 1979 in the General Agreement on Tariffs and Trade.[4] In contrast to the present disputes, that agreement was arrived at relatively placidly and with near unanimity. Earlier trade agreements were usually reached by a few technicians and specialists meeting behind closed doors. Sometimes, a few heads had to be knocked together, but the discussions were seldom made public, nor was the public involved in the debate. Though the issues were often crucial, they were seldom politicized or made the stuff of mass politics.

Today, all that has changed. The arguments over NAFTA illustrate how much trade policy has changed in the last two decades and how international and domestic politics have become intertwined. Tariffs used to be the main concern, but this was a subject that was remote from most people's consciousness and without high political stakes or even visibility. A handful of experts and interest groups got together, hammered out their differences if necessary, and worked out an agreement. But now, the U.S. and Mexican trade negotiators must also deal with "hot" or "new agenda" political topics such as pollution, the environment, drugs, human rights, and democratization. In addition, the negotiators must deal with subjects such as farm and industrial subsidies, patents and trademarks, industrial standards, child labor, minimum wages, unionization and labor rights, government purchasing, and investment issues—all areas that are close to the bone of national economic policymaking. Furthermore, these issues are coming to the fore in the midst of a severe U.S. recession, in a post–Cold War era when all foreign policy issues have been increasingly politicized, and in a charged electoral arena where jobs and economic growth are the key and virtually only issue. As these new and more complex issues entered into trade discussions, both the intensity of the debate and the decibel level have risen.[5]

In earlier times, trade discussions with Mexico over an issue like the bracero (or Mexican labor programs) were relatively simple and clear-cut.[6] Growers were in favor of lowered restrictions on the use of the cheaper Mexican labor, and organized labor was opposed. Republicans tended to be in favor, and Democrats were opposed—unless they lived in states where grower interests were strong. This is a comparatively straightforward division, unencumbered by the hosts of accompanying, often peripheral interests—and their respective lobbies—that exist today. Now, the issues are broader and more complex, and they reach deeper down into society; hence, the political and economic stakes are higher. Undercutting a Floridian's vegetable market, a Georgian's peanut subsidy, a New Englander's dairy subsidy, a rustbelt industry, or some "buy American" preferences in Pentagon purchasing involves political risks and the vociferous denunciation of groups that are no longer content to be silent. The dispute over NAFTA has become like the Supreme Court nominations of Robert Bork and Clarence Thomas or the debates over spotted owls and snail darters. The issue has become intensely politicized, a variety of new groups and interests are involved, and masses of voters and lobbyists are mobilized. The public agenda frequently serves as a smoke screen for various private agendas, and the issue has become so partisan and so politicized that it wreaks great harm on the fragile national community. Prejudice against Mexico or Mexicans, expressed in disguised form, may also be a sub-rosa factor in the debate.

This narrative discussion can be summarized in a series of hypotheses—really, at this stage, more like conjectures—that point to the differences between earlier and present trade disputes.

1. Many more interest groups—environmental, human rights, population, ethnic, and others—are involved in the issue.
2. In a time of economic recession, the stakes are higher for many people, and the public gets involved.
3. Recession issues are compounded by electoral politics. Both the White House and the Congress have sought to get political mileage out of the issue.
4. Prejudice against Mexico for a variety of reasons—racial, cultural, religious, or because of Mexico's often anti-American foreign policy in the past—may also be involved. But because racial or ethnic bias can no longer be expressed publicly, such prejudice is now expressed in other forms—such as opposition to NAFTA. Opposition to NAFTA may also be used as a way to "get at" Mexico for other reasons, perhaps involving natural gas policy, drugs, pollution, or any one of the host of issues that connect the United States and Mexico.
5. Some of the issues raised—the purported use of child labor in Mexico, for example—seem to be red herrings; certain issues that are brought up are really smoke screens for other, larger issues.

6. Along the national political and cultural divide, NAFTA has sometimes been used as a way to attack President Bush and President Clinton, to polarize the debate, and to divide the country by provoking conflict and acrimony. The goal may be larger than just trade. In this new era of guerrilla theater and guerrilla politics, issues are purposely used to destroy a presidency or an administration rather than to resolve specific problems.
7. Things are not always what they seem. In the case of NAFTA, the real reasons for U.S. support of the proposal may be geopolitical (stabilizing a neighbor with whom the United States shares a 2,000-mile border) rather than economic. Similar deceptions and smoke screens are used by the opposition.
8. The dissembling, the guerrilla tactics, and the overkill of interest group positions (as in the debates on Central America in the 1980s) produce paralysis and ineffectiveness in the U.S. government.
9. Out of this kaleidoscope of clashing interests, rival political and cultural conceptions, and complex maneuvering, the public interest may be lost or only partially served. Meanwhile, the public policy process tends toward fragmentation and dysfunction.

The Groups and Their Positions

If, as Theodore Lowi says, interest group liberalism is *the* ideology of U.S. pluralist democracy,[7] the debate over NAFTA bears out that contention. Literally hundreds of interest groups have now taken stands on the issue. The Congress and the White House serve as channels, referees, filters, and, ultimately, interpreters of this interest group competition, meanwhile exercising their own considerable independent influence. According to the theory, good public policy comes out of this winnowing process and the balancing of competing interests. But the process may also produce biased views, a lopsided interest group situation in which most groups (however thin or weak in numbers) are lined up on one side of the issue, and, in the end, national sclerosis and deadlock.[8] It is sometimes hard to tell if genuine pluralism or effective public policy is produced by these struggles.

Groups in Favor of NAFTA

Most of the major U.S. business groups, especially the peak associations, lined up behind NAFTA. These include the National Association of Manufacturers (NAM, whose member companies account for 85 percent of U.S. manufacturing output and jobs), the U.S. Chamber of Commerce, the Business Roundtable (a New York City–based group that represents more than 200 major U.S. corporations), the Council of the Americas (which represents U.S. business concerns in Latin America), and the U.S. Council of the Mexico-U.S. Business Committee (a branch of the Council of the Americas). Most small business groups and associations also believe that the free trade agreement will result in a net gain in jobs and income for both countries. In addition to the large, umbrella organizations, more specialized associations such as the Automotive Parts and Accessories Association support the agreement, even though they recognize that their members—depending on location or specialized product—might be negatively affected.[9] The pro-NAFTA forces also put together a larger, all-encompassing organization to lobby more effectively for ratification.

Not all business groups supported NAFTA without reservations, however. The NAM, for example, said its final decision would be based on the actual negotiated agreement and that it would not support any agreement that did not "clearly serve the interests of U.S. manufacturers."[10] NAM also said that "under no circumstances" should the negotiations with Mexico undermine the achievements of the U.S.-Canada Free Trade Agreement signed in 1988. Ultimately, the NAM did support the passage of NAFTA. The Chamber of Commerce similarly supported the proposal but also introduced some reservations. It recognized that orchestrating business and congressional approval for a free trade agreement with Mexico would be harder than it was for the Canada agreement (where U.S. business has a far greater stake) and that it would be more difficult to mobilize a coalition. William Archey, the international vice-president of the U.S. Chamber of Commerce, warned that "the cost to companies of being out front will be greater."[11]

The vast majority of mainstream U.S. academics are also in favor of the agreement. This includes both economists as well as Latin American specialists. Unlike other groups surveyed, academics have no particular axes to grind on this issue; their views are largely value-free. The academics argued that a U.S.-Mexico free trade agreement was a win-win situation that would benefit both countries and that *not a single* serious quantitative study had been produced that would contradict that assessment. They recognized that some U.S. workers would likely be hurt in the short run by increased imports from Mexico, but the numbers would not be great; those who are hurt, they suggested, should be compensated and retrained. In the longer term, all the economic boats (Canadian, U.S., Mexican) would rise as a result of a free trade agreement. Academic scholars shared the view that increased trade should not come at the cost of environmental degradation (which is one of the main claims made by the pact's foes) but that an environmental understanding should be worked out on a parallel track by environmental experts, not in the agreement itself. Significantly, a letter signed by prominent economists and other academics and sent to all members of Congress in April 1991 (and reprinted in the *Wall Street Journal)* carried the names of persons associated with both

Democratic administrations (Richard Feinberg, Robert Pastor, Sally Shelton-Colby) and Republican administrations (Paul Boeker, Rudiger Dornbusch).[12]

A new and potentially explosive force on this issue is the Hispanic community in the United States. At some time in the 1990s, Hispanics will become the largest minority in the United States; they are registering to vote and getting involved in politics on an increasing scale; they are organized for national political action as never before; and on this issue, they have particularly strong views. What makes NAFTA such an explosive issue is that most Hispanic groups have traditionally been associated with the U.S. Democratic Party, but because of the Democratic National Committee's (DNC) earlier opposition to a fast-track agreement, many Hispanics became alienated from the party. As Elaine Coronado of the umbrella Hispanic Alliance for Free Trade noted, "A lot of Hispanics are now questioning their loyalty to the Democratic Party." Similarly, Cesar Collantes of the League of United Latin Americans lobbying groups said the Democratic National Committee "should reconsider their close alliance with the AFL-CIO [which has led the opposition to NAFTA] on this issue." Democrats have found themselves under rising attack from the increasingly influential Hispanic lobby, some of whom are accusing the party and the AFL-CIO of running a racist ad campaign against the proposed pact.[13] The Democrats have had to make a painful choice between their Hispanic and their labor constituencies—a choice most Democrats would prefer to avoid.

Not all Hispanics are in favor of NAFTA, incidentally. Many Hispanics in the United States fear the competition for their own jobs that would come from Mexican industry or from increased Mexican immigration. For some Hispanics who are already in the United States, now that they are aboard the boat, they would like to pull up the gangplank and keep others out. But officially at least, the major Hispanic lobbying organizations have been strongly in favor of the pact.

Groups in Opposition to NAFTA

In Washington, it is probably easier to organize a coalition against something than it is in favor of something. This fact is illustrated by the seeming ease with which individuals of radically different views have papered over their differences to solidify their opposition to NAFTA. Patrick Buchanan, Ralph Nader, Ross Perot, and Jerry Brown, for instance, have little else in common except their opposition to NAFTA. In addition, some groups, such as organized labor, have long had a veto power over legislation. Passing legislation has been complicated in recent years by the tremendous proliferation of interest groups (now over 50,000 in Washington alone) and by the phenomenon of "networking," which brings diverse groups together under a single banner for the sake of mobilizing greater strength on individual issues. Often, these groups consist of little more than letterheads and mail drops, but they may seem impressive for their titles and form parts of larger, more influential coalitions.

Organized Labor

Organized labor, principally the AFL-CIO, has been the key group opposed to NAFTA. As far as labor is concerned, the critical issue is jobs. The AFL-CIO argues that NAFTA will result in hundreds of U.S. companies relocating in Mexico to take advantage of cheap labor, which will produce a loss of jobs in the United States. In taking this position, U.S. labor is responding to the fears of its membership, as distinct from the larger national interest; moreover, its focus is on short-term job losses rather than the long-term job gains that NAFTA holds out as its promise. However, the jobs that may be created are unlikely to be unionized (and certainly not by the AFL-CIO), whereas many of the jobs that may be lost are union jobs. Labor's interests are thus the interests of the union itself and of its present membership, not necessarily the interests of other working people, job seekers, or the public at large.

Because of their significance, it is important to understand the positions of organized labor and to present them objectively, rather than casting them only in a negative light or "straw-manning" them. The AFL-CIO, for example, argues that it wants good relations with Mexico, that it favors stronger ties with all of Latin America, and that it advocates a reduction of Latin America's debt so the area can begin to recover and progress economically. But big labor opposed even a limited free trade agreement on the following grounds.[14]

1. NAFTA between the United States and Mexico would change the "continental" economy in ways that would provide great advantages to capital investors at the expense of workers.
2. NAFTA would hurt U.S. workers by paving the way for "hundreds of thousands" of U.S. jobs to be exported to Mexico.
3. It would also, the AFL-CIO alleges, harm Mexican workers by forcing them to work at "substandard" wages. Ignored in this claim, of course, is the fact that without the jobs provided by U.S. firms, Mexican workers would be even worse off and have far fewer job prospects at even lower salaries.
4. NAFTA provides for "increased labor mobility," but the AFL-CIO says that is a euphemism for hiring temporary and nonunionized workers and keeping them at low wage rates.
5. The AFL-CIO believes that NAFTA would turn all of Mexico into a giant maquiladora that would contribute little to industrialization, technological growth, or international competitiveness.

6. Labor argues that NAFTA has been established hastily to serve as a counterpoint and check on the now more integrated European Community, and that this policy is "mean, short-sighted, and simplistic."
7. In contrast with the EC, the AFL-CIO says, U.S. and especially Mexican workers have only a limited social safety net on which to fall back and no social charter comparable to that of the EC providing for minimum wages, social assistance, collective bargaining, vocational training, and health and safety protection—put in place, in part, to discourage "runaway" plants. Again unlike the North American accord, the EC also has a regional development fund to narrow the gap between rich and poor areas.
8. The AFL-CIO says that NAFTA is more a political than an economic initiative, designed to shore up a corrupt, potentially unstable regime, and that the proposal puts the "jobs of U.S. workers, our members, and your [Congress's] constituents in jeopardy."
9. NAFTA would result in "North American workers" (presumably both U.S. and Mexican) being "laid off, exploited, and poisoned" —one supposes from pollution. "The working women and men of the United States and Mexico cannot bear such a burden," says the union, "and they should not be required to take it on."

To argue its case, the AFL-CIO has trotted out some hoary issues, not all of which are directly relevant to the case at issue. Some of these, in fact, may be red herrings. For example, in trying to build support for its case, the U.S. labor movement has emphasized the problem of child labor in Mexico—which is, indeed, a problem but one that has little or nothing to do with the advantages of a free trade agreement.[15] The AFL-CIO has also emphasized that the Mexican labor movement is corporatist and largely state-controlled—again, this is true, but it has always been that way, and this is of doubtful relevance to the issue at hand. Organized labor has also joined with environmentalists in a somewhat strained marriage of convenience to argue that NAFTA will result in environmental damage and pollution of the air and rivers in the border areas—as if Detroit's or Gary's industries did not pollute. In the past, however, the AFL-CIO has often been against environmental controls in U.S. industries, arguing that it would cost jobs. These arguments seem forced, but they are useful to labor in mobilizing political support.[16]

Organized labor is, in some ways, in a difficult political position on the NAFTA issue. Its membership has been declining drastically in the past two decades, so its political clout is not what it once was. At the same time, organized labor's public image is not a very good one. Moreover, a too-strong position in opposition to NAFTA will drive a wedge between big labor and Hispanic voters and could tear the fabric of the Democratic Party.

Meanwhile, even with its declining membership, big labor still has veto power over many issues, maybe not in the country at large but certainly in Washington, DC. Politicians are unwilling to stake out positions unfavorable to organized labor for the same reason they are afraid of other single-issue lobbies. The AFL-CIO provides major voting blocs and financial support in election campaigns, and its leadership may "target" a recalcitrant member of Congress with sufficient numbers of hostile voters to cause defeat. In addition, big labor has been able to channel the current national anti-Japanese sentiment in ways that also help its cause vis-à-vis Mexico. It plays upon today's concern for jobs, jobs, jobs in ways that lead to strong protectionist sentiment against *all* foreign products. And in picking on Mexico, the AFL-CIO knows that it has an easier target than if it were to focus on Japan. Mexico has thus become a surrogate for anti-Japanese and antiforeign sentiment. To counter the AFL-CIO's opposition, the Clinton administration agreed to negotiate separate labor and anti-dumping agreements with Mexico to protect U.S. jobs. President Clinton was forced to take on the unions in an aggressive, high-profile manner in the final weeks of his battle to win congressional approval of NAFTA. This rift between a Democratic president and his traditional party constituencies may have some impact on Clinton's ability to mobilize union support on future issues.

Growers

In earlier years, U.S. growers preferred lax U.S. immigration laws that would allow inexpensive Mexican farm workers to enter the United States. But now that it is cheaper agricultural products and not just the workers that are coming in, many U.S. farmers are very worried. South Florida farmers and many in the Southwest and California initially joined with labor leaders and environmentalists in opposing NAFTA. The California tuna industry, fearing Mexican competition, also opposed the pact. The growers argued that the agreement would give Mexican farmers an unfair advantage. U.S. farmers must pay someone $6 per hour to drive a tractor, but in Mexico, it costs about a tenth of that; consequently, Mexican fruits and vegetables are much cheaper than U.S.-grown products. In addition, U.S. growers are far more heavily regulated than their Mexican counterparts, which further adds to their costs. In Florida's Dade County (Miami) alone, the Farm Bureau estimates that NAFTA could cost 17,000 jobs.[17]

As one farmer said, "I don't see how we can compete with people who don't have to follow our laws and pesticide regulations. . . . Maybe in the overall picture it may be good for the nation, but what happens if the farmers are out of business?" Health concerns were also cited by the Florida growers: Mexican farmers use pesticides like DDT and chlordane, which have been banned in the United States. Hence, the Florida Fruit and Vegetable Association appealed to Congress for a "level playing field" and "fair trade." The Florida and California growers argued that they could lose 30 percent of their volume once protectionist tariffs are lifted, and they have had the support of their state congressional delegation.[18]

When they were unable to block Congress from approving President Bush's request for fast-track negotiating authority for NAFTA, U.S. growers sought to curb agricultural imports through packaging regulations. Grower and packaging groups, along with the International Brotherhood of Teamsters, filed suit to force the U.S. Customs Service to enforce laws already in effect requiring that imported goods be conspicuously marked to show their country of origin. The Court of International Trade agreed, but the decision was appealed by Washington-based lawyers representing Mexican farm interests.[19] Ultimately, the support of the citrus and horticultural lobbies was won with eleventh-hour modifications to NAFTA that provided their industry with special safeguards.

Not all U.S. growers agree with these positions. For example, corn, wheat, and grain producers do not feel as threatened by Mexican products. In addition, some of the biggest U.S. growers, such as the Minneapolis-based Pillsbury Company, are well positioned to take advantage of NAFTA: Pillsbury's Green Giant division already owns agricultural land as well as a food processing plant in Mexico that is almost exclusively dedicated to serving the U.S. market.[20]

Environmental Groups

With the ending of the Cold War, a "new agenda" of U.S. foreign policy issues has come to the fore. These include democracy, drugs, human rights, and immigration, as well as pollution and environmental concerns. As the Cold War has receded, these new agenda items have achieved greater salience.[21]

A partial listing of the environmental and consumers groups that came out against the U.S.-Mexico free trade agreement includes:

- Environmental Action
- Friends of the Earth, U.S.
- Greenpeace
- Natural Resources Defense Council
- Sierra Club
- Center for Science in the Public Interest
- Community Nutrition Institute
- Consumer Federation of America
- National Consumer League
- Public Citizen
- Public Voice

- Arizona Toxins Information Project
- Child Labor Coalition
- Community Nutrition Institute
- Southern Arizona Environmental Management Society

A number of these organizations have national constituencies; others are known in Washington as "paper organizations." The latter may be leftovers from the New Left of the 1960s who have learned that organizational politics and not revolutionary rhetoric is the way to influence the political process. Nevertheless, by pooling their resources, networking, and projecting a united front, the "greens" have been able to make their voices heard. The criticisms stemming from the environmental groups include the following:[22]

- NAFTA largely ignores increased population, traffic, and waste problems along the border area.
- The assessment of potential environmental problems is superficial and incomplete.
- NAFTA omits analysis of environmental laws and institutions.
- NAFTA lacks concrete implementation strategies to protect the environment.
- NAFTA does not marshal sufficient funds specifically to protect the border environment.
- The U.S. Environmental Protection Agency has not had a strong enough hand in the formulation of the plan.
- Mexican environmental protection laws and institutions are too weak to offer adequate safeguards.
- Under the agreement, U.S. safety and environmental standards could be classified as "trade barriers" and thus preempted.

For the most part, these are reasonable concerns. Both the Bush administration and the Mexican government responded positively to them and attempted to build into NAFTA stronger safety and environmental regulations.[23] The Clinton administration also has negotiated a separate environment agreement. That is, after all, how U.S. interest group politics work. But those environmental concerns that are reasonable and can be accommodated within NAFTA must be distinguished from those that are so extreme that they cannot possibly be implemented. In the same vein, those environmental groups that are serious (and that present reasonable demands) must be distinguished from groups who hoped to use environmental issues to scuttle the entire agreement and sabotage the Bush and Clinton administrations or whose private agendas may differ from their publicly stated ones.

Not content with the added environmental agreement, some environmental groups continued to try to undermine the entire trade pact. They brought suit against NAFTA and seemed to have triumphed temporarily when a federal judge ordered the Clinton administration to prepare an environmental impact statement on NAFTA, a judgment that was later overturned. Nevertheless, other large and more responsible environmental groups, such as the National Wildlife Federation, disassociated themselves from this suit and took the position of being in favor of NAFTA as long as their environmental concerns were satisfactorily addressed in the parallel agreement.

Ross Perot

In the 1992 election campaign, Ross Perot zoomed like a rocket over the U.S. political landscape. He appeared suddenly and rose rapidly in the polls. Perot's electoral fortunes waxed and waned; at one point, he pulled out of the campaign and suffered a severe credibility loss in the process, only to reenter later. Perot was very adept at diagnosing and articulating the nation's ills; his problems stemmed from the solutions he offered, which often struck observers as far-fetched. Perot wound up with zero electoral votes but 19 percent of the popular vote.

Among Perot's main issues were jobs and the economy. He was strongly opposed to NAFTA. Among the phrases he made famous was the "sucking sound," which he said was the sound of U.S. jobs fleeing to Mexico if NAFTA were to be approved. More serious economists, while conceding some short-term job loss, responded that the real sucking sound was the sound of U.S. exports going to Mexico: Exports *create* U.S. jobs. The fact is that Mexico has recently surpassed Japan as the second-largest trading partner in the world for the United States, behind only Canada. NAFTA would increase such exports and thus add to a brighter, long-term U.S. jobs picture. Various efforts were made by pro-NAFTA groups to diminish the popular appeal of Perot's anti-NAFTA message, but none was as effective as the debate between Perot and Vice-President Al Gore on the "Larry King Live" show on Cable Network News (CNN). Gore's quiet persistence provoked a display of Perot-style irascibility, which led to Perot's prompt decline in the polls.

The Radical Left and Right

As the debate heated up, a variety of radical right, "progressive," and Marxist groups also joined the campaign against the agreement. Patrick Buchanan entered the anti-NAFTA contingent by raising the specter of mass immigration and calling for an "America-first" strategy. The Citizens' Trade Campaign was the umbrella organization under which groups on the radical left rallied. Many of the same groups and individuals who were part of the anti–Vietnam War protests of the 1960s, active in the radical effervescence of the 1970s, and opposed to U.S. action in Central America in the 1980s joined the new movement. These included religious groups, black power groups, gay and lesbian organizations, radical environmentalists, and Jesse Jackson's Rainbow Coalition. Some consumer groups, under Ralph Nader's leadership, also joined the fray. Employing familiar Marxist ideology, the leaders of the campaign argued that under NAFTA, capitalism would prosper at the expense of the workers. Broadening their campaign to include GATT and free trade, these groups pointed out that under GATT agreements, international business had a mechanism to bypass U.S. environmental laws. Thus, the radicals appealed to workers and environmentalists, and Buchanan appealed to the darker forces of xenophobia.

The strength of the fringe groups, taken by themselves, was minuscule. But their message had enough plausibility to appeal both to campus radicals and to other well-meaning groups. The United Methodist Church, Unitarian Church charities, and even the Humane Society and the American Society for the Prevention of Cruelty to Animals (not previously known for their expertise on trade issues) joined the cause. The radicals got local governments in some university cities to pass resolutions condemning NAFTA. Even some state governments began to express concern, worried that their ability to regulate goods shipped into the state would be undermined under NAFTA. Hence, although these groups lacked electoral support, they were able to garner broader sympathy by touching all the right emotive buttons: jobs, the environment, the poor, and so on. Furthermore, at some levels in the Clinton administration, they now had a receptive ear. These ground swells at the grassroots—Jesse Jackson, Ross Perot, Patrick Buchanan, the blame-everything-on-NAFTA sentiment, the radicals with their seductive, usually bumper-sticker-level messages—of course made it increasingly difficult for members of Congress to support the trade agreement.

In the Balance

Think Tanks

Because of the salience of the issue, many of the scholars operating within the think tank community have issued opinions on NAFTA, most of them generally positive. The Center for Strategic and International Studies (CSIS) Mexico Project, directed by M. Delal Baer, has a long list of publications, meetings, and testimony to its credit.[24] Others among Washington's think tank community have likewise expressed positive interpretations of NAFTA—Jeffrey Schott and Gary Hufbauer of the Institute for International Economics (IIE), also known for their work on the U.S.-Canada Free

Trade Agreement; scholars associated with the Brookings Institution (particularly its Mexico analyst, Nora Lustig); and the Heritage Foundation's Wesley Smith, whose positive views on NAFTA in the 1990s contrast sharply with the foundation's criticism of Mexico in the 1980s (a position also generally representative of CSIS).[25]

Opposition has come from more marginal institutions. The Institute for Policy Studies (IPS), which has been a signatory to several anti-NAFTA statements, is a left-wing think tank that has been opposed to every U.S. defense and weapons system of the past thirty years. The Council on Hemispheric Affairs (COHA), also a signatory on several anti-NAFTA statements, is a one-man think tank with a handful of dedicated interns. The Economic Policy Institute has strongly criticized NAFTA in what is almost a one-man crusade largely echoing the arguments of the AFL-CIO.[26]

Among the think tanks, therefore, the balance of scholarly and mainstream sentiment is clearly in favor of a U.S.-Mexico free trade agreement.

Congress

NAFTA was a proposal of the Republican Bush administration, and that means that congressional Republicans have been supportive, although there was some erosion of that support. The Clinton administration also supported the pact, although sometimes lukewarmly. The real rub has been with congressional Democrats and the unprecedented number of first term representatives, all of whom are very independent from House suasions and skeptical of the trade agreement.

Within the Congress and particularly within the Democratic majority, the issue is a tricky one. On the one hand, most of the congressional Democrats are, in the abstract, in favor of free trade. They understand its advantages and are generally committed to a free or perhaps a "fair trade" (limited management) trade agenda. At the same time, these same congressional Democrats want good relations with Mexico, understand the dangers of a destabilized Mexico, and would be willing to assist Mexico to help achieve stability and economic growth. Other things being equal, most members of Congress would prefer to vote for free trade over protectionism.

But of course, within the Congress, other things are not equal. Many members are torn between their free trade proclivities and the protectionist demands of their constituents. They do not want factories to close in their districts. There are regional differences, and the drug issue and environmental concerns enter in. The depressed state of the U.S. economy also made a difference. There are efforts to gain political mileage out of the issue, and there are interest group counterpressures—on environmental and other tangential matters. There are also concerns about congressional prerogatives.

1. Many members of Congress accept the argument of the AFL-CIO that a U.S.-Mexico free trade agreement will cost U.S. jobs. This fear is particularly strong in the so-called rustbelt states of New England and the Midwest where older industries (textiles, shoes, automobiles) are in decline and may flee to Mexico or other countries to take advantage of cheap labor. Many U.S. industries have already taken such a southerly route. The members of Congress recognize the long-term prospect that NAFTA will create jobs, but for most, it is the short-term concern—reelection—that is most important.[27] Hence, the Democratic congressional delegations in the New England and Midwest states voted strongly against the earlier fast-track Bush initiative.[28] Members of Congress from other areas, including Democrats, did not feel such heavy pressures over jobs and could vote in favor. At the same time, Republican members from states like Florida, where grower interests are strong, also tended to have strong reservations about the proposal.

2. The issue has been made more difficult by the depressed state of the U.S. economy. Members of Congress who would have voted for NAFTA in prosperous times cannot do so in a situation of depression. When jobs are scarce and people are hurting, it is difficult to vote for a measure that might result in greater short-term job loss. It was precisely because of these pressures in an election year that further action on NAFTA was postponed from 1992 until 1993.

3. As many members of Congress know, organized labor is in decline nationwide, but that may not be true in particular districts. In older industrial states like Michigan, Ohio, New York, Pennsylvania, Massachusetts, Illinois, and many others, going against organized labor would be the kiss of death politically. In other states where big labor is not so strong, representatives would still prefer to have labor as a friend rather than an enemy. In addition, many Democratic members of Congress are heavily dependent on the AFL-CIO for campaign contributions. Because money is the "mother's milk of politics," as the old saw puts it, representatives cannot afford to vote against the wishes of their main contributors. Hence, although organized labor seems to be in decline nationally, it is still a potent force at local, state, and regional levels and may still have veto power nationally.

4. Although the Democrats obviously want to retain the support of organized labor, they do not want to do so at the cost of losing the Hispanic vote. Naturally, they would prefer to keep both. At the national level during the Bush presidency, the Democratic National Committee chose to side with its big-labor constituency, concluding that labor supporters vote in greater numbers than do Hispanics and provide far more money to the party. This opened up the DNC to the charge that it was anti-Hispanic, anti-Mexican, and even racist, a charge that the Democrats would clearly like to avoid. So below the DNC, it will depend on the electoral district: Where Hispanics vote in large numbers, members of Congress will vote

accordingly; where Hispanics are small in numbers, these members will be more likely to vote with organized labor. The Clinton administration demanded that Democratic representatives support the president on this issue.

5. In the wake of the Cold War, drugs have now become, according to some public opinion polls, *the* number one foreign policy issue in the United States.[29] About 50 percent of the cocaine coming into the United States passes through the Mexican border, and the members of Congress like Charles Rangel (D, NY) fear that NAFTA will open up the border to even greater drug traffic.[30]

6. Similarly, a majority of representatives favor NAFTA but also want to be on the "right side" on environmental issues. They do not want to lose what have long been considered Democratic constituencies: labor, farmers, and environmentalists. Though favorable toward NAFTA, they also wanted to build in strong environmental, safety, consumer protection, and pollution control provisions—hence, the separate or side agreements on labor and the environment.

7. The issue of congressional prerogatives revolves around the way NAFTA was originally proposed by the Bush administration. The administration asked for fast-track authority. That means that it would negotiate the agreement and present it to Congress as an up-or-down issue, and no amendments or revisions to take care of special constituency interests could then be tacked on. But in an era when many representatives wish to micromanage every last detail of policy, cutting them out of the process and restructuring their ability to amend and modify the proposal was not acceptable. This was a procedural issue but was important to Congress. Some members, such as Senator Carl Levin of Michigan, used the procedural concern as a smoke screen for opposition to NAFTA on other grounds.[31]

8. The temptation was also strong among congressional Democrats in 1991–1992 to sabotage the entire NAFTA and use it as a campaign issue to castigate Bush. Democrats hoped that if the case was made that NAFTA would damage U.S. jobs, they would be in a position to reap the political benefits. A deepening recession, rising unemployment rates, and the loss of U.S. jobs and prosperity overseas provided weapons with which to slam the president. The current wave of Japan-bashing also fits into this: Japan is too big, powerful, and important for anyone to do very much about it besides making rhetorical and symbolic gestures (smashing Toyotas with sledgehammers). But Mexico, now *there* is a tempting target—close by, less powerful, and with less capacity to hit back—or so it seems, unless the United States stupidly succeeds in destabilizing it. In terms of job loss and potential political damage, therefore, NAFTA could not have come at a worse time. Of course, the advent of the Clinton administration in 1993 and its support for the agreement changed the political dynamics.[32]

During the 1992 election campaign, as representatives went back to their districts to run for reelection, a new and disquieting phenomenon occurred that was very damaging for NAFTA. The agreement began to be blamed in the popular mind for everything that was wrong with the U.S. economy. In Michigan, for example, if the automobile industry was in trouble, it was NAFTA's fault; in North Carolina, the problems of the furniture industry were blamed on NAFTA; in the Northeast, the troubles of the shoe and textile industries were blamed on NAFTA. It mattered little that these industries were in trouble anyway and not because of NAFTA. Instead, *all* the problems of the economy were being laid at NAFTA's feet before NAFTA even existed. This sentiment was not based on an accurate assessment of the roots of U.S. economic troubles, but the foul public mood did make it harder for members of Congress to support the free trade agreement.

A growing problem was the opposition of the Congressional Black Caucus to NAFTA. Spurred on by Jesse Jackson's Rainbow Coalition, which came out against the agreement, and bolstered by a rising number of new black representatives and the growing seniority of some of its members, the caucus argued that the agreement would cost U.S. jobs. Specifically, it was worried about jobs for African-Americans, which it believed would be lost to the rising tide of Hispanics. The caucus also raised the drug and environmental issues. Although these concerns were no doubt sincere, the caucus was also trying to withhold its support of NAFTA as a bargaining ploy with the Clinton administration over appointments, the shape of the Clinton economic reform package, and other policy concerns. NAFTA had thus become a political football, a part of the political bargaining over other issues that had nothing to do with the agreement and for which NAFTA might be sacrificed. The Black Caucus ended up divided on the issue, with first-term Congresswoman Eddie Bernice Johnson and other supporting the agreement. The voices of prominent black Americans, such as former U.S. Ambassador to the United Nations Andrew Young and former Congresswoman Barbara Jordan, reinforced members of the Black Caucus who voted in favor of NAFTA.

Most congressional Democrats adopted a wait-and-see attitude. The Democratic leadership—House Ways and Means Chairman Daniel Rostenkowski House Speaker Thomas Foley, House Majority Leader Richard Gephardt, then Senate Finance Committee Chairman Lloyd Bentsen—supported President Bush's request for fast-track authority. But they also experienced strong concern over the possibilities for job loss and saw the potential for a gathering storm. Particularly in the House, the leadership was pressed by other lawmakers to break with the president and make this a 1992 campaign issue. When Gephardt (who sought the presidential nomination in 1988 on a protectionist platform and voiced strong reservations about NAFTA) decided to take a low profile on the issue and not become a presidential candidate for 1992, the tension was eased somewhat. But as unemployment spread and the recession deepened in 1990–1991, the temptation to "go demagogic" on the Mexico agreement increased. In 1992, an election year, Bush could not have gotten his fast-track authority as he did in 1991, which is why further negotiations with Mexico over the issue were put off until 1993.[33] The Clinton administration negotiated new side agreements in that year, but many members of Congress were still noncommittal. Indeed, Majority Leader Gephardt pronounced the side agreements unacceptable in August 1993, and Majority Whip David Bonier declared his opposition to NAFTA. This forced the Clinton administration to rely heavily on Republican Minority leader-in-waiting Newt Gingrich, who provided the votes for a surprisingly comfortable pro-NAFTA majority in the House of Representatives.

Analysis and Response

A great variety of arguments in opposition to NAFTA have surfaced in these pages. By no means did they all have to do with the merits of the case. This was an emotional, nationalistic, highly political, and even xenophobic issue, in which rational argument was often sacrificed to deeper emotions. Among opponents, the approach was a shotgun one: Fire lots of pellets in the hope that some of them hit targets. But some of the arguments offered, to switch metaphors, truly were red herrings or smoke screens designed to disguise other issues or agendas—tangential issues and false issues that had little to do with the real debate. It therefore becomes important to sort out the real from the bogus issues, the red herrings from the real dangers.

Press accounts, literature on the subject, interviews, and scholarly analysis reveal the following list of reasons for opposing the U.S.-Mexican pact:

1. Fear of U.S. job loss—but this fear often has a regional basis
2. Fear of competition, experienced by some growers and tuna fisheries
3. Fear of pollution of border streams and air
4. Fear of environmental damage
5. Complaints about lax consumer standards in Mexican plants
6. Complaints about inadequate health and safety provisions
7. Complaints about use of child labor in Mexican factories
8. Fear of increased drug trafficking
9. Dislike of Mexico for various reasons
10. Use of Mexico as a surrogate for bashing Japan
11. Defensive and nationalistic sentiments

12. Racism
13. The timing in the midst of a recession
14. The desire for electoral advantage
15. Mexico seen as authoritarian, corporatist, nondemocratic
16. Democratic Party reliance on AFL-CIO support, financial and otherwise
17. Desire not to antagonize big labor and environmental groups
18. Attempts to embarrass Bush and Clinton and undermine their administrations
19. Isolationist and America-first sentiments
20. Human rights concerns
21. The desire for stronger protectionism
22. Condescension toward Mexico; prejudice and a sense of superiority

Thus, I found twenty-two reasons advanced in the various arguments opposing a North American Free Trade Agreement. For analytical purposes, I have divided the twenty-two into four categories: (1) solid, substantial reasons that need to be addressed, (2) worrisome issues about which something can be done, (3) red-herring or straw-man issues, and (4) political issues that respond to different agendas.

Of the twenty-two reasons, two seem to me to be particularly solid and substantial. These are numbers 1 and 2 on the list: The potential loss of U.S. jobs and the damage done to some U.S. sectors, such as the Florida citrus and vegetable growers and the California tuna fisheries. To take the latter issue first, these tend to be localized or regional issues. They help explain why representatives from these states, of both political parties, tended to vote against the fast-track authority in 1991. But because they are regional issues, they do not resonate as strongly as national issues. Indeed, if they did resonate nationally, the argument could be presented that Mexican fruit, vegetables, and tuna would help keep U.S. consumer prices down. The NAFTA vote could not be won without addressing the concerns of the growers, and in the end, the special deal for citrus and vegetable growers unlocked crucial votes in the Florida and California delegations.

Far more worrisome is the issue of job loss. Most economists believe that though NAFTA will result in short-term job displacement, it will ultimately create more jobs. But the first question is, What kinds of jobs? Not unionized jobs, surely. Again, most economists believe that, in the long run, some U.S. industries (such as textiles) are largely doomed to disappear anyway within approximately twenty years; it is far better, therefore, to get the change over with quickly rather than letting it drag on for two decades. That is a powerful argument, but meanwhile, what of the people who lose their jobs? Probably, their numbers will be larger than the Bush or Clinton administrations admitted;[34] probably, too, the job retraining that will be put in place will be less than adequate. Efforts will be made to minimize this wrenching transition, but there is likely no alternative but to admit this realistically, meanwhile putting in place measures to cushion the blows (retraining, long-term unemployment benefits, relocation, early retirement). The Clinton administration sought to address these concerns in its side agreements on labor and dumping.

Seven of the twenty-two reasons for opposing NAFTA fall into my second category, "worrisome issues about which something can be done." These are numbers 3, 4, 5, 6, 7, 15, and 20: fear of polluting border streams and air, fear of environmental damage, complaints about lax consumer standards, complaints over inadequate health and safety provisions, complaints about the use of child labor in Mexican factories, complaints over Mexico's authoritarian and often nondemocratic political system, and human rights concerns. It should be noted that, in contrast to the previous category that focused on the possible harm of a U.S.-Mexico FTA to the United States, every one of the issues mentioned here is an internal Mexican problem. They are the institutional problems and by-products of an underdeveloped economy and political system trying to live up to U.S. standards. They are the kinds of issues that come up when a Third World country like Mexico shares a long border with a First World country like the United States, where different laws or different capacities to implement the laws apply.

These are also the kinds of issues about which something can be done. In fact, the Bush and Clinton administrations strenuously pressured Mexico, which very much wanted and needs NAFTA, into speeding up implementation of these programs and safeguards as a way of easing passage of the legislation through the U.S. Congress. For example, Mexico has now created a commission to study environmental and pollution issues along the border. It also has new legislation aimed at bringing Mexico into compliance with U.S. environmental standards, and it was pressured to actually implement the new legislation. It has committed over $400 million to resolving pollution and environmental issues. The Clinton administration insisted on a separate agreement with Mexico on environmental concerns, although opponents insisted to the bitter end that the agreement failed to provide for swift trade sanctions against environmental offenders. Mexico similarly has new laws dealing with health and safety issues, and some of these will be implemented. Mexico has also moved to beef up its consumer protection and quality control standards to international expectations. And it has tried to tighten up its child labor laws, particularly in border industries and where internationally based firms are the employers. With regard to Mexican politics, the country has been moving for some time—even before NAFTA became an issue—toward a more open, more broadly based, more representative political structure, although it will probably not be democratic in precisely the U.S. mold.[35] The same is true for human rights: Under both domestic and international scrutiny, Mexico's observance of human right standards has, in general, improved in recent years, although some violations continue to occur.

On every one of the issues deemed worrisome but improvable, Mexico is already making progress. It is probably too much to expect that a modernizing but still Third World country can, within a matter of a few years, bring its reforms and enforcement in all these areas up to U.S. standards. Furthermore, if Mexico tries to implement all these changes simultaneously and too rapidly, it runs a considerable risk of destabilizing what is already an uncertain and shaky regime.[36] That was also a dilemma for the Clinton administration. It needed to push Mexico hard and quickly on all these fronts to satisfy opposition interests and get its free trade agreement through Congress. At the same time, if it pushed too hard, it ran the risk of destabilizing Mexico. And because of the possible reverberations in U.S. foreign and domestic policies (massive immigration and huge strains on schools, social services, and law enforcement), Mexico is *the last country in the world* that the United States would want to see destabilized.

The third category is composed of red-herring or straw-man issues. I have listed six of the reasons for opposing a U.S.-Mexico free trade agreement in this category. These are numbers 8, 9, 11, 12, 21, and 22: the fear of increased drug trafficking, dislike of Mexico for various reasons, defensive and nationalistic sentiment, racism, the wish for stronger protectionism, and condescension toward Mexico—prejudice and the sense of North American superiority. With regard to drugs, although truck and container traffic across the border will increase, there is no evidence nor any reason to believe that the flow of drugs into the United States from Mexico will expand under a free trade agreement. For the most part, drugs are a domestic U.S. problem, which is largely unaffected by U.S.-Mexico trade relations; further, one could make the case that NAFTA will make it easier for authorities to police the border, for Mexico to resist the lure of drug money, and for U.S. and Mexican counternarcotics efforts to be better coordinated. This, then, is purely a red herring. So is dislike of Mexico, whether it comes from the right because of Mexican opposition to U.S. policy toward Central America in the 1980s or from the left because of Mexico's continuing intolerance toward the principal leftist standard-bearer, Cuauhtémoc Cárdenas.

The United States in 1992–1993 appeared to be in a defensive, nationalistic, America-first mood. But there seems to be no rational reason why those sentiments need to be directed at Mexico—or *especially* at Mexico. Racism is also a simmering problem in the United States, including, at times, racist sentiments particularly directed at Hispanics. But there is an irrational basis to such racism and, again, no reason why it should be directed specifically toward Mexico. Similarly, inclinations toward protectionism and, along with it, condescension toward Hispanics and their institutions are irrational fears, self-defeating fears, and fears that are directed at Mexico seemingly because the proposed free trade agreement makes that country an inviting target. All these are red-herring issues that have little substantive basis.

The fourth category is political issues. Seven of these may be found on the list (numbers 10, 13, 14, 16, 17, 18, and 19): use of Mexico as a surrogate for bashing Japan, the unfortunate timing of NAFTA in the midst of a recession, the desire for electoral or political advantage, the Democratic Party's heavy reliance on the AFL-CIO for political and financial support, the desire by that same party not to embarrass big labor or environmental groups, the related political desire in 1992 to embarrass Bush's White House and derail his reelection possibilities, newer efforts to embarrass Clinton or extract political favors from him, and isolationist and America-first sentiments.

These are all contentious issues for several reasons: (1) They have little to do with the merits of NAFTA; (2) these reasons are seldom expressed publicly but are usually sub rosa concerns derived from private comments and analyses, which makes it very difficult to respond to them, much less offer a refutation; and (3) because they involve congressional and White House political and reelection considerations, they may be the most important of all the reasons listed here.

To fully understand this last point, one must have a clear sense of Washington policymaking as it has evolved over the last two decades. It is a context of fierce ambition, of reelection considerations that outweigh all others (including considerations of the public interest), of intense and often nasty conflict between Congress and the White House, and of heavy politicization of all issues, whether domestic or foreign.[37] This last set of reasons for opposing NAFTA therefore represents a wild card, a joker in the deck, because they are not amenable to "rational" consideration of the issue. They respond to political and personal advancement agendas on the part of politicians, not to the agenda of the public interest. Hence, the issue bends in the political winds and depends on multiple circumstances and currents whose outcomes are often unpredictable. Perhaps the greatest illustration of the opportunistic nature of the Washington political game has been the unlikely anti-NAFTA alliance of Jesse Jackson, Patrick Buchanan, Ralph Nader, Ross Perot, and Jerry Brown.

Conclusion

The proposed U.S.-Mexico free trade agreement provides a wonderful case study of how things work or do not work in Washington, DC. Objectively, almost all economists and scholars without axes to grind agree that NAFTA is a positive development—good for the United States and good for Mexico. Recognizing the possible short-term dislocations, these scholars nevertheless argue that in long-range terms, more jobs will be created than lost, economic growth will be stimulated in both countries, per capita income will rise, new social programs can be advanced, inflation and higher costs can be avoided, and political stability (especially for Mexico) can be assured. The prospects are so favorable and the unanimity of opinion among experts so certain that it is difficult to be against NAFTA on the merits of the case. Even members of Congress privately recognize the strength of these arguments. All things being equal, NAFTA should have been approved with little difficulty.

But in Washington, as I mentioned earlier, all things are not equal. Issues are seldom dealt with on their merits alone. Rather, a variety of other agendas come into play. In this case, the other agendas include the effort of some groups to embarrass or "get" the Clinton administration, the Democratic Party's need for the support (financial or otherwise) of big labor, and the effort by members of Congress to gain electoral or political advantage from the issue. NAFTA came under attack on the basis of arguments that had little or nothing to do with the merits of the case; conversely, it may have been passed on the same basis.

My analysis has shown that the one substantive issue that grows out of the proposed U.S.-Mexico free trade agreement is the potential that U.S. workers may lose jobs. That issue should be taken very seriously. Environmental concerns also have come to weigh heavily. Many of the other issues are smoke screen issues; still others are amenable to new policy initiatives on the part of Mexico or the United States to satisfy the concerns raised. These are, in Washington parlance, "do-able" matters; something can be done about them.

The jobs issue is the most pressing concern, one that cannot be easily glossed over. Nor is it readily susceptible to fixing. It will not do for proponents of NAFTA to try to inaccurately minimize the number of jobs that will be lost under this program (in long-range terms, they would almost certainly be lost anyway, but that is small comfort to those persons whose jobs are, in fact, lost sooner rather than later). Nor will it work to simply argue that NAFTA will eventually create more jobs than are lost. Rather, we must be prepared to spend scarce money in the form of job retraining, relocations, and long-term unemployment benefits. To be sure, the issue of jobs, particularly during a recession, was the vital one. But it is not an issue without solution. Pollution and environmental issues were similarly addressed in the side agreements negotiated by the Clinton administration.

The real "sleeper" issues in all this involve political variables: reelection possibilities, embarrassing the president, using NAFTA, and political bargaining over other issues that have little to do with NAFTA. These are so infinitely changeable, often depending on the sense in Congress of how strong or how vulnerable a president is depending on the way the political winds blow, that almost any outcome is possible. Still riding the crest of his early popularity, President Bush was able to get fast-track authority through a Democratically controlled Congress in 1991. But as his poll ratings fell precipitously later that year and in 1992, the Democrats, sniffing vulnerability if not the chance of victory, forced the White House to postpone further consideration of the proposed agreement until 1993, after the elections.

Clinton favored NAFTA, and for the first time in fourteen years, the United States had a Congress and White House of the same party. But the political climate in early 1993 was such that NAFTA was in severe trouble; most observers thought that if the vote were taken then, the agreement would fail. The merits of the agreement were clear, but for NAFTA to be approved, the same political and logrolling arrangements that threatened the package also, in adept leadership hands, were necessary to save it.

Notes

1. The Emerson quote was previously used by Ramon Mestre in a provocative op-ed piece on the U.S.-Mexico free trade agreement; see *Washington Post*, May 10, 1991.

2. See especially the balanced assessments of Sidney Weintraub, *A Marriage of Convenience: Relations Between Mexico and the United States* (New York: Oxford University Press, Twentieth Century Fund Report, 1990), and Sidney Weintraub, *Free Trade Between the United States and Mexico?* (Washington, DC: Brookings Institution, 1984).

3. See the letter signed by twenty-four economists and Latin America area specialists in the *Wall Street Journal*, April 24, 1991.

4. For the background, see Saryn O'Halloran, "Congress, the President, and U.S. Trade Policy: Process and Policy Outcomes" (Paper delivered at the Annual Meeting of the American Political Science Association, San Francisco, September 1, 1990); *National Journal* 22, no. 24 (June 16, 1990):1486–1487; *Economist*, June 16, 1990; and *Congressional Quarterly*, March 16, 1991.

5. An excellent assessment is in the *New York Times*, May 28, 1991.

6. Vernon M. Briggs, *Immigration Policy and the American Labor Force* (Baltimore: Johns Hopkins University Press, 1985), and Sidney Weintraub and Stanley R. Ross, *"Temporary" Alien Workers in the United States: Designing Policy from Fact and Opinion* (Boulder, CO: Westview Press, 1982).

7. Theodore Lowi, "The Public Philosophy: Interest Group Liberalism," *American Political Science Review* 61 (March 1967):5–24; also Lowi, *The End of Liberalism* (New York: Norton, 1969).

8. William Connolly, *The Bias of Liberalism* (New York: Atherton, 1971), and James McGregor Burns, *The Deadlock of Democracy* (Englewood Cliffs, NJ: Prentice-Hall, 1967).

9. The Business Roundtable, *Building a Comprehensive U.S.-Mexico Economic Relationship* (New York: Business Roundtable, n.d.); National Associations of Manufacturers, *NAM News*, February 11, 1991; U.S. Council of the Mexico-U.S. Business Committee, statement of Ambassador Thomas O. Enders before the Subcommittee on Trade of the Committee on Ways and Means, U.S. House of Representatives, February 28, 1991; *Wall Street Journal*, May 13, 1991.

10. NAM, Board of Directors news release of February 9, 1991.

11. *National Journal* 22, no. 24 (June 16, 1990):1486–1487.

12. *Wall Street Journal,* April 24, 1991.

13. *Washington Times,* May 15, 1991.

14. Testimony of Robert M. McGlotten, director, Department of Legislation, AFL-CIO, before the Subcommittee on Labor Management Relations, U.S. House of Representatives, on the "North American Free Trade Agreement," April 30, 1991; statement of Thomas R. Donahue, secretary-treasurer, AFL-CIO, before the Committee on Finance, U.S. Senate, on the "Proposed U.S.-Mexico Free Trade Negotiations," February 6, 1991; AFL-CIO Executive Council, "U.S.-Mexico Free Trade Agreement, May 24, 1990," in *Statements Adopted by the AFL-CIO Executive Council* (Washington, DC.: AFL-CIO, May 23–24, 1990); statement of Mark A. Anderson, international economist, AFL-CIO, before the Subcommittee on Trade, Committee on Ways and Means, U.S. House of Representatives, on "U.S.-Mexico Economic Relations," June 28, 1990. For a discussion of some of the tougher choices facing the Democratic Party's coalition as organized labor's clout wanes, see *Washington Post,* July 16, 1991, A5.

15. See "Underage Laborers Fill Mexican Factories, Stir U.S. Trade Debate," *Wall Street Journal,* April 9, 1991.

16. All these issues came together in the U.S. House of Representatives Committee on Small Business Hearing of the U.S.-Mexico Free Trade Agreement, April 24, 1991, in which the AFL-CIO, environmentalists, and prolabor lobbyists all testified.

17. *Miami Herald,* May 14, 1991, A1.

18. *Miami Herald,* April 10, 1991, A4.

19. *Journal of Commerce,* June 20, 1991, A1.

20. Ibid.

21. Howard J. Wiarda, *On the Agenda: Current Issues and Conflicts in U.S. Foreign Policy* (Glenview, IL: Scott Foresman/Little, Brown, 1990).

22. See the statement in *Public Citizen,* March 4, 1991; the comments of the Natural Resources Defense Council, submitted to the Environmental Protection Agency, September 30, 1991; the Capitol Hill Forum put on by Agricultural, Environmental, and Labor Groups on January 15, 1991, as well as the lists of organizations supporting these positions. See also the balanced statement of Timothy Atkeson, Environmental Protection Agency, before the Subcommittee on Rules of the House, Committee on Rules, U.S. House of Representatives, October 16, 1991.

23. For the Bush administration response, see the letter and accompanying materials issued by the White House Press Office and dated May 1, 1991, sent by the White House to every member of Congress; Mexico's response is contained in "Mexico's Environmental Initiative for the Northern Border: A $460 Million Commitment," a paper issued by the Mexican Embassy, October 23, 1991.

24. Wesley Smith, *Refuting Six Myths About the U.S.-Mexico Free Trade Accord* (Washington, DC: Heritage Foundation, 1991).

25. *Wall Street Journal,* April 24, 1991; see also the writings of M. Delal Baer and Sidney Weintraub on NAFTA.

26. See Faux's testimony before the U.S. House of Representatives Committee on Small Business Hearing, April 24, 1991.

27. David Mayhew, *Congress: The Electoral Connection* (New Haven: Yale University Press, 1974).

28. See the roll call on the extension of fast-track authority for the North American Free Trade Agreement, in the U.S. House of Representatives, May 23, 1991, and in the U.S. Senate, May 24, 1991.

29. John E. Reilly, "America's State of Mind," *Foreign Policy* (Spring 1987): 39–56.

30. *Washington Times,* June 15, 1990.

31. See Senator Carl Levin's letter of June 12, 1991, addressed to Scholars for Free Trade with Mexico.

32. *Christian Science Monitor,* April 15, 1991, *Washington Post,* April 23, 1991, H1.

33. David S. Cloud, "Democrats Weigh the Politics of Battling Bush on Mexico," *Congressional Quarterly* (March 16, 1991):660–663.

34. See the administration's letter to Congress of May 1, 1991.

35. For further discussion, see Howard J. Wiarda, *The Democratic Revolution in Latin America* (New York: Holmes and Meier, 1990).

36. See my essay, "Mexico: The Unraveling of a Corporatist Regime," in Daniel Pipes and Adam Garfinkle, eds., *Friendly Tyrants: An American Dilemma* (New York: St. Martin's Press, 1991), pp. 307–327.

37. Glen Gordon, *The Legislative Process and Divided Government* (Amherst; Bureau of Government Research, University of Massachusetts, 1966); for application to foreign policy, see Howard J. Wiarda, *Foreign Policy Without Illusion: How Foreign Policy Works and Fails to Work in the United States* (New York: HarperCollins, 1990).

6

The Changing Face of Mexican Nationalism

Soledad Loaeza

In June 1990, Presidents George Bush and Carlos Salinas de Gortari announced their support of official negotiations to establish a free trade agreement between the United States and Mexico. To several Mexican opinion groups, the announcement represented a break with past policies. However, it was no surprise. Since the beginning of the 1980s, the Mexican government had undertaken a series of radical changes in the economy intended to establish a new model of development. These changes meant opening the economy and replacing the import-substitution model that had led Mexican growth since World War II with an export-led model. In this context, a free trade agreement seemed like a natural derivation of the new lines of policy.

When the announcement was made, many observers and politicians in both countries predicted a strong nationalist reaction against the two presidents' proposal. This possibility seemed particularly likely in the case of Mexico, where multilateral agreements traditionally had been preferred to bilateral agreements with its powerful northern neighbor. Past experience showed that any Mexican government suggesting close cooperation with the United States automatically aroused suspicions about its ability to defend national interests. This situation was even more delicate in 1990 because nationalism was a central issue for the left-wing opposition led by Cuauhtémoc Cárdenas. The appeal of Cárdenas, many believed, was based on his commitment to economic nationalism and on his association with the legendary expropriation of oil companies decreed in 1938 by his father, President Lázaro Cárdenas.

Since the presidential campaign of 1988, Cárdenas had persistently denounced Carlos Salinas and the policies of modernization he proposed as an assault on national sovereignty. This line of argument holds that an agreement for the liberalization of trade and investment with the United States was an attack on national industry. According to this thesis, such an agreement would mean the end of economic self-determination and the final subordination of the Mexican government to U.S. interests.

Moreover, closer cooperation with the United States could have divisive effects on a political situation in which the wounds of the presidential election of July 1988 were still fresh. The allegations of fraud made by the opposition had cast serious doubt on the validity of the triumph claimed by the candidate of the Party of the Institutional Revolution (PRI). By 1990, the political situation had been stabilized, and President Salinas had managed to overcome most of the accusations of illegitimacy. However, in the process of organizing for democratic elections, the opposition parties were confronted with many crucial points of contention concerning political reform—the power of the presidency, the privileges of the official party, and all the obstacles, legal and otherwise. The subject of a new approach to the United States could easily be used to exacerbate political differences. Some would applaud the economic benefits of opening the apparently prosperous North American market, others would protest the political costs of the rapprochement, and still others would fear that closer ties with the United States would lead to the downgrading of Mexican culture. Therefore, many believed that this new policy toward the United States had a very high potential for nationalist mobilization.

Prediction and Reality

More than two years after the trade negotiations between Mexico and the United States started, predictions of a wave of anti-Americanism in Mexico as a reaction against a trusting approach to the United States had not come to pass. There was no deeply held consensus in Mexico in relation to the free trade agreement, but the subject had not aroused significant opposition. And although some disagreements were expressed, these were concentrated on trade issues and appeared mainly among business organizations, industrialists, and merchants. Even the cardenista opposition reversed its original outright rejection of the agreement and sought to develop more nuanced views based on the now well-recognized need to improve Mexico's position in international markets.[1]

The relative calm that prevails in Mexico concerning the policy of closer ties with the United States is somewhat surprising. The same can be said of the acceptance of the bilateral trade agreement between the two countries, given the troubled history of the relations between them and given the tensions of the 1990s, when the bilateral agenda seemed charged with explosive issues ranging from drugs to Mexico's foreign policy in Central America. The prevailing lack of opposition to the FTA in Mexico is even more puzzling to U.S. observers because nationalist reactions in Mexico had been almost an automatic reflex to any proposal of cooperation advanced by Washington.

There are several explanations to the mystery of why there has not been an anti-American reaction in Mexico to the new policy vis-à-vis the United States. Mexico's left-wing opposition explains this relative passivity by arguing that the FTA negotiations were imposed upon Mexican society by what they consider to be the undemocratic government of Carlos Salinas.[2] Others believe that the apparent acceptance of an increased U.S. presence in Mexico is proof of the weakening of a national identity that has already been penetrated by U.S. culture. However, the official version maintains that the Mexican people were consulted and that the agreement had public approval and ample support.[3] Opponents to this assertion answer that Mexico's population was brainwashed.

The weak response of the nationalist opposition, combined with the fact that opposition parties are still concentrating on electoral problems and have not succeeded in making the FTA negotiations a rallying point for their cause, indicates that the FTA is not a matter of general discontent. The debate surrounding the agreement centered on its economic aspects, and as the negotiations progressed, they became increasingly technical. They seemed to be centered on debates between specialists on concrete themes, such as the textile and automobile industries, conflict resolution mechanisms, or rules of origin. In contrast, discussions about the foreseeable political effects of the agreement have all but disappeared from the media or even from the list of political issues presently confronting the Salinas government. If there is something like a general attitude in Mexican public opinion regarding the FTA, this could be described as one of attentiveness or unprejudiced interest, although not entirely lacking in distrust.

It may be that the absence of a negative reaction against the FTA is the result of two years of government publicity exalting the advantages of trade liberalization, the free market, and a friendly relationship with the United States. However, it may also be that other influences have weighed upon public opinion, modifying former attitudes regarding other countries. In the last two decades, Mexican society has been exposed to an unprecedented flow of information and images from the outside world, thanks to an impressive development of the media and also to the increase in exchanges—personal and other—with the United States. The result has been a less parochial society and a change in perceptions regarding the international context, which many Mexicans have begun to see more as an opportunity than a threat.

This chapter will try to explain Mexicans' unexpected response to closer cooperation with the United States by exploring the following hypothesis: Since the beginning of the 1970s, Mexico's relationship with the international community has become more open and responsive. Related changes have affected the traditionally inward-looking Mexican nationalism, although it is still too early to define the new attitudes and values associated with the Mexican "imagined political community"—to use Benedict Anderson's definition of *nation.*[4] Until the end of the twentieth century, it seems clear that the international environment will continue to be an important dynamic force in transforming this community. Today, most of Mexican society seems able to integrate a foreign component as part of a specific identity. The acceptance of a new relationship with the United States must be understood in this context.

To analyze this hypothesis, the next section of this chapter will describe central aspects of nationalism in Mexico as a cultural and political phenomenon. The following section will present two elements that since the 1970s have contributed to the opening of Mexico to the outside world: the prosperity of the 1970s and the foreign policy of the successive governments that have since recognized the need to develop a new relationship with the international system. The last section will discuss some cultural differences between Mexico and the United States that may be central for perpetuating their respective identities.

Historical Dimensions of Mexican Nationalism

Mexican nationalism is a cultural process as much as a political ideology, and it cannot be understood unless both sets of elements—cultural and political—are considered. Nationalism is the expression of a specific identity built on the language, customs, images, values, and symbols that have been recognized as specific to a given group of people. In addition to these cultural elements, political components are also present in these identities. Usually, this combination is the result of a particular historical experience and the importance of each set of elements—cultural or political—in the definition of a given identity, which will depend on the characteristics of the society: In a multicultural society, the creation of a political community is an alternative to the more stable structure of a culturally homogeneous society. In the case of Mexico, the nationalist formula has sought to conciliate historical continuity and political ideology in order to attain two different but related goals: to introduce homogeneity in a society characterized by diversity and to counter the disintegrating influences of the outside world.

Since the second half of the nineteenth century, the Mexican state has assumed the responsibility of preserving the integrity of the nation, threatened from the inside by social differences and from the outside by powerful and ambitious countries. The political community represented by the state has given coherence to a society that could have been torn apart by its internal contradictions. Nationalism has been the instrument used by the state to stabilize a heterogeneous society, which has been accomplished by recognizing what is common to the members of this community and also by drawing frontiers that differentiate them from others. This means that in the long process of nation-building, the shaping of Mexican identity, the consciousness of the outside world, the cultural traditions of the Indian past, the colonial experience, and the struggles for modernization have been equally important.

In the case of heterogeneous societies, political ideology can substitute for historical continuity as the basis of nationality, as happened in the United States where "being an American . . . is an ideological commitment. It is not a matter of birth."[5]

In these terms, a comparison can be drawn between Mexico and the United States, but it does not take one very far. Both nationalist formulas may share the intolerance and exclusionary impulses of any other nationalism (which, in both these cases, is aggravated by the political component), but the differences in content are very profound. The "American creed" can be subsumed in words that express solely political values: antistatism, individualism, populism, and egalitarianism.[6] The Mexican identity, on the other hand, includes cultural traditions as well as political values.

However prevalent these varied cultural traditions may be in today's Mexican nationalism, it would be a mistake to see them as a set of static emotional and cultural constraints that have remained constant since the nineteenth century. Such a view flows from a basic misunderstanding of the very nature of nationalism. Nationalism is the result of a dynamic process—it is a historical construct that absorbs social changes and experiences. Since 1910, not to mention the previous century, Mexican society has undergone a far-reaching process of modernization that was accelerated by economic change after the 1940s. These phenomena have had a significant impact on national identity, that is, on the meaning and content of what is understood as being specifically Mexican. In other words, modernization has not crushed this identity; it has transformed it.

Today, the notion of "being Mexican" does not necessarily evoke the picture of a peasant in a rural setting waiting passively for the rain to fall. That image corresponds to a Mexico that has long since disappeared. At the turn of the century, 80 percent of the population was registered as Indian, but today, only 20 percent falls into that category. Agriculture was then the center of the Mexican economy, but in 1992, it represented less than 10 percent of the GDP (as against 24 percent for manufacturing and 27 percent for commerce, restaurants, and hotels). Only 33 percent of Mexicans could read and write in 1920; by 1980, that percentage had risen to 80 percent. And more than 65 percent of the Mexican population now lives in cities. Although it is true that almost 40 percent of the population lives below the poverty level and has not benefited from economic modernization, this does not mean that these Mexicans have remained marginal to a modern culture in which change is a value in itself.

The diversity of traditions that have come together in the making of a Mexican identity explains some of its contradictions. The national culture includes numerous expressions—artistic and other—of ancient ethnic communities, together with the Western values and institutions that were brought from Spain and have been assimilated into a complex whole. In addition to the complexity derived from a multicultural origin, the Mexican identity integrates conservative values associated with Catholicism. It maintains hierarchical social relations, respects the family or the local community, and combines all this with the appeal of progress and change. It also considers the individual and private property as legitimate pillars of the social and political systems. All this occurs within the framework of a common "immemorial past."[7] Moreover, the urban environment and the increased contacts with the United States resulting from what seems to be an endless current of Mexican migrants to that country[8] favor a spontaneous change of attitudes and values that escapes all institutional control.

The Revolution of 1910 defined the features of the Mexican identity of the twentieth century by retrieving the indigenous cultures, but the importance of this experience in the creation of Mexican nationalism derives from the renewed political content that the Revolution gave to this identity. In it, the nation as represented by the state was identified as a value superior to any particular interest, and economic self-determination became the essence of change and national sovereignty; in the nineteenth century, by contrast, attitudes and values had been considered the basis of progress and the cradle of the national identity. The revolutionary state promoted an almost inseparable association between the Mexican cultural community and the postrevolutionary regime.

The original motivation of Mexican nationalism was autonomy and self-determination. Thus, nationalism was the result of the assertion of a unique identity as opposed to the colonial power, Spain, initially and then to other countries, especially to the United States. Therefore, Mexican nationalism also originated as a defensive response to the international environment, which provided a general framework for the definition of Mexico's characteristics. As mentioned before, in defining a Mexican identity, common cultural features count as much as those features that differentiate Mexicans from others. That is, the sense of community is also built on the consciousness of the existence of other communities. The different experiences Mexicans have had with other countries have contributed in a very important manner to the shaping of Mexican identity.

Mexican nationalism had, from the beginning, a defensive quality that only in times of crisis turned into xenophobia, as during wartime—the War of Independence, the civil wars of the mid-nineteenth century, and the 1910 Revolution. However, these explosions are isolated examples.[9] The occasions in which nationalism appears as an expression of superiority or as an instrument of aggression are very rare; in fact, the preservation of independence and self-determination seems sufficient to the defensive Mexican nationalism.

The international experience of revolutionary Mexico also contributed to the shaping of mistrustful attitudes with respect to the outside world.

The Mexican civil war was seen by some foreign countries (such as Germany, Great Britain, and the United States) as an opportunity to intervene in internal affairs with different purposes: to protect interests already established in Mexico; to benefit from political fragmentation and the disappearance of the national government by consolidating and expanding their presence; or—particularly in the case of the United States—to participate in shaping the political and economic reorganization of the country. Whatever the motives, the Mexican Revolution was a time of intervention.[10] For instance, in 1914, U.S. troops occupied the port of Veracruz in an attempt by President Woodrow Wilson to force democratic elections on the military dictator, Victoriano Huerta. One of the consequences of this experience was a closer identification of the revolutionary government with the defense of self-determination and the national interest.

During those difficult years, the international environment had been as hostile to Mexico as it has historically been to any revolutionary country. It was only in 1934 that Mexico was admitted to the League of Nations, and it was not until World War II and the ideological and strategic arrangement it brought that Mexico was considered a reliable and full member of the international community.

Nevertheless, this new international status did not modify Mexico's basic attitude of suspicion toward the outside world, and it was the basis for an attempted ideological and economic self-sufficiency. This attitude was reinforced by the import-substitution model of economic development, which pursued the creation and development of a national bourgeoisie and inward-looking growth. Economic self-determination became synonymous with sovereignty and national independence. Protectionism and state control over natural resources were integrated into a political identity that was understood as being specifically Mexican.

The opening of the economy and the introduction of an export-led model of growth in the 1980s represented something more than a new economic policy; they were part of a political initiative that involved a profound revision of the Mexican perception of the outside world and, therefore, of the established notions of nationalism, sovereignty, and self-determination. As will be discussed in the following sections, this revision started at the beginning of the 1970s.

In the process of building a new relationship with the United States, the political aspects of Mexican nationalism were expected to show more rigidities than the cultural aspects. The political system had been identified with the defense of national sovereignty for such a long time that political changes could be seen as a threat to the nation. Defense of the nation was one of the arguments made by the official party to justify its virtual monopoly of power, and party leaders presented the opposition as an instrument of foreign intervention. Thus, political continuity posed obstacles to a change of policy toward the United States.

The depth of the economic crisis of the 1980s was so great and the tensions it created in the political system were so acute that Mexicans were prepared to accept radical solutions, even a complete overturn of the relationship with the outside world based on the recognition that self-sufficiency was an illusion. Moreover, the course of political events in Mexico in those years revealed that the cultural changes that had transformed Mexican society had also paved the way for political change. Thus, among the various components of Mexican nationalism, cultural heterogeneity has finally imposed itself on the political homogeneity of that same nationalism.

Mexico and the World Since the 1970s

The relationship of Mexican society to the outside world has experienced remarkable changes since the beginning of the 1970s. These changes are the result of the coincidence of two different factors: the acceleration of social modernization due to the economic expansion of the 1970s and the foreign policies of the last four governments, which sought to increase Mexico's participation in international affairs.

The administrations of Presidents Luis Echeverría (1970–1976) and José López Portillo (1976–1982) are remembered primarily for excessive waste, corruption, political demagoguery, and elite irresponsibility. Nevertheless, during most of these same years (1970–1982), the Mexican economy showed annual growth rates that oscillated between 6 percent and 9 percent. During the Echeverría years, economic expansion was possible thanks to international credit; oil revenues were the basis of the economic boom of the López Portillo period. Political reform is also one of the hallmarks of these years. Echeverría pursued policies of reconciliation toward the middle classes that had been alienated by the 1968 crisis, and López Portillo believed that economic prosperity made the opening of the political system affordable.

The combination of economic expansion and political reform favored important changes in Mexican political culture. A participatory culture did not develop fully, but economic growth in a general context of tolerance created unique opportunities for economic and political participation, transforming the attitudes and conduct of Mexicans with regard to power.[11] Passive submission to the dictates of authority was replaced by an awareness that society could set limits on this authority. Many groups, mostly within the middle classes, developed a new feeling of competence with regard to public affairs and the ability to influence the decisions of those in power. In the process, public opinion gradually became a component of the power structure.

The mass media also underwent a significant transformation, bringing the outside world closer to Mexico. In the worst years of the recession, from 1980 to 1987, the number of radio listeners in Mexico grew from sixty to eighty million, and the number of television viewers went from thirty to fifty-five million. National and international radio and television news bombarded the population (as it still does) with an intensity that would have been unimaginable fifteen years before. Today, the electronic media play a crucial role in the general socialization process of Mexicans and also in the shaping of their political opinions and attitudes.

The impact of prosperity on Mexican political culture was evident in the case of the middle class, which benefited most from the economic growth of the 1970s. The patterns of consumption of middle-class individuals were modified, and many began to model their life-styles on their counterparts in the United States, to the point that the same groups that historically had been committed to building a national identity seemed to have been turned into instruments of U.S. cultural influence. Prosperity increased their participation and also their sense of self-confidence, and, as a result, it also changed their political attitudes.

The extent of these changes was highlighted by the tensions of the critical period that followed the end of the José López Portillo administration. Miguel de la Madrid's government recognized the limits of economic nationalism and protectionism, and during his term in office, from 1982 to 1988, Mexican society seemed to have explicitly recognized the limits of political self-sufficiency. One of the distinctive characteristics of political change in these years was that its points of reference were not exclusively Mexican. The political events in other countries served as examples for many Mexicans. The Spanish democratic transition after the fall of Franco, the end of military regimes in other Latin American countries, and the collapse of Socialist regimes in Eastern Europe seemed to offer solutions that could also be applied to the Mexican situation.

Thus, the international context became part of the Mexican internal process of change. The development and expansion of information media gave Mexico access to the international ideology market; it broadened the country's political horizon in terms of options for change. Mexico lived through the crisis of the 1980s as if it were in a crystal box: It looked to the outside in search of solutions to its economic and political problems, just as it was looked upon from the outside. This means that in the last twenty years, in times of prosperity and in times of hardship, Mexican society built a new relationship with the world, a relationship that both enriched its perspectives and limited its options.

The new attitudes of Mexican society regarding the outside world were also a reflection of governmental decisions. Traditionally, Mexican foreign policy had been used mainly as an instrument for the defense of self-determination and as a means to differentiate Mexico politically from the rest of the world, especially the United States. Therefore, an independent foreign policy—which amounted to a kind of isolationism—was considered a central component of the national identity.

The government of President Echeverría changed the predominantly political character of Mexican foreign policy. It attempted to use foreign policy as an instrument to solve some of the economic problems that were manifest by the beginning of the 1970s. For instance, the Echevarría government used foreign policy to promote better terms of trade for Mexican commerce. Although there are many differences between the Echeverría administration and its successors, this shift in the conception of Mexican foreign policy became permanent. And it has been increasingly accentuated to the point of subordinating diplomacy as an instrument of defending political autonomy and redefining diplomacy as a tool of elevating economic priorities that stress similarities, complementary trends, and parallelisms with other countries. The FTA negotiations illustrate this development because in the 1990s, all issues in the bilateral agenda of U.S.-Mexican relations were subject to the course of those negotiations.

At first sight, the comparison between Echeverría's and López Portillo's foreign policies and those of De la Madrid and Salinas shows more discrepancies than similarities. During the 1970s, Mexico became the champion of sovereignty as an absolute value. President Echeverría pursued a policy of international leadership based on moral denunciations of the growing breach separating rich and poor countries, and President López Portillo aspired to the same policy but with the support of oil revenues.[12] As a consequence of the policies of international leadership and multilateralism, Mexico had to learn to negotiate its own positions with the governments it wanted to rally to its cause. This meant that Mexico had to recognize some limits to self-determination. In doing this, the country relinquished the relative autonomy it had traditionally derived from a foreign policy that shunned group action. Then, the true meaning of what has been called an "active" foreign policy was the end of the Mexican unilateralism that, until the 1970s, had been considered the only effective means for protecting self-determination.

In the 1980s, however, Presidents De la Madrid and Salinas struggled to restore the margin for maneuver that Mexico had lost in the previous decade by discarding any pretense to active international leadership and by resorting to bilateralism. This chapter has not judged the appropriateness of this strategy in terms of the recovery of the Mexican economy or the relationship with the United States. Suffice it to say that the international vulnerability of Mexico in those years amounted to what many saw as an effective loss of sovereignty. The point to be made in regard to the change of Mexican attitudes toward the outside world is that, in spite of their evident differences, the last four Mexican administrations all saw in the international environment an opportunity to find new solutions to the country's problems. This was true even in the 1980s, when economic crisis and external debt created a situation in Mexico that amounted to a loss of national sovereignty. In those years, the international system was not seen as an opportunity but as a heavy burden; nevertheless, however hostile the environment was, autarky or an inward-looking strategy were never seriously considered. It was generally accepted that part of the trouble came from the outside world, but it was also understood that an important part of the solutions to that trouble would have to come from that very same environment.

Mexico and the United States

The decision of the Mexican government to negotiate a free trade agreement with the United States marks a profound shift in the history of the relationship between the two countries because it recognizes the inevitability of geography.[13] Except under extraordinary circumstances, both countries had tried to ignore each other for many years, either by exaggerating their cultural differences, as if the distance such differences created between them was an insurmountable obstacle, or by dealing indirectly through third countries or in the framework of multilateral organizations. Now, however, the increasing complexity of the border and the natural consequences of territorial contiguity have imposed themselves on the two neighbors.

This mutual indifference was only a pretense because interdependence between Mexico and the United States has steadily increased since the second half of the nineteenth century. The interest of the United States in Mexico stems primarily from military and strategic reasons, although in the last twenty years, economic ties between the two countries have been expanded by an intense process of interpenetration. Since the 1970s, the strategic importance of Mexico to the United States was enhanced for several reasons: Mexico's oil resources, the dimensions of the country's foreign debt that endangered the stability of the U.S. banking system, an impressive increase in bilateral trade, the inflow of Mexican migration to the United States, and, last but not least, drug traffic.

These and other issues created a full and intertwining network of relations that were shared during the Mexican economic crisis of the 1980s. It was then, when many of their common interests reached a critical point, that Mexico and the United States were forced to sit at the negotiating table and establish direct contact.[14]

Until the 1980s, Mexico had never had a clear, long-term, and comprehensive policy toward the United States. Successive Mexican governments seemed to prefer practical and short-term solutions to the bilateral problems, instead of making explicit the constraints, contradictions, costs, and benefits of the relationship with the United States. It was as if Mexicans turned their backs on their northern neighbor, leaving the intense, nongovernmental exchanges to follow a natural course. Mexico would defend the principles of national sovereignty and self-determination in international organizations in general terms—although it was no secret to whom the messages were addressed—and in relation to third countries, if possible. This strategy seemed to make the point and reduce the risks of a direct confrontation with a too-powerful and, at times, disagreeable neighbor.

In this perspective, the importance of the FTA lies in the fact that it appears to be the direct result of the first long-term Mexican policy toward the United States. This policy establishes objectives, priorities, and means to attain those objectives within a general framework of cooperation between the two countries—a framework that today seems more advantageous than coexistence or even simple harmony.

In Mexico, there are many who fear the new scheme because they know cooperation among unequal partners may turn into subordination. Others believe that closer cooperation with the United States will deepen and accelerate the Americanization of Mexican culture and the loss of national identity. The risk of subordination seems greater than the risk of Americanization. Although the process of modernization in Mexico has certainly reduced the cultural differences between the two societies, some of the basic values on which each society is built are visibly distinct. Individualism, for example, is at the very heart of Americanism, whereas in Mexico, the notion of community is stronger and has greater social legitimacy than that of the individual. The community in Mexico has survived in spite of the state's authoritarianism, liberal policies, and the imbalances of the capitalist development, so much so that groups and social organizations are key to the modernization project of President Carlos Salinas. Instead of fighting them, Salinas seems to have recognized their strength and resilience and also their usefulness for his own purposes.[15]

Consequently, in Mexico, the superiority of the general interest over particular interests has a moral appeal that seems completely absent from U.S. culture. The importance of these values in understanding the cultural distinctiveness of Mexico and the United States stems from their derivations in terms of the basis of society and of the state's authority as a representative of the general interest, which in Mexico, has been recognized once again as without substitute.

The evolution of the international environment in the last quarter of the twentieth century has made the United States the main political and cultural challenger to the Mexican nation. A strategy of closer cooperation between the two countries is inaugurating an original alternative to the problems posed by geography, the consequences of which are still difficult to predict.

Notes

1. See Cuauhtémoc Cárdenas, "TLC: Una propuesta alternativa," *Nexos*, no. 162 (June 1991):51–56.

2. See Adolfo Aguilar Zínser, "El tratado de libre comercio, dimensión política," in Bárbara Driscoll de Alvarado and Mónica C. Gabrill, eds., *El tratado de libre comercio: Entre el viejo y el nuevo orden* (Mexico, DF: Universidad Nacional Autonomo de Mexico, Centro de Investigaciones Sobre Estados Unidos de América, 1992), pp. 159–172.

3. That was the result of a round of hearings organized by the Mexican Senate in May 1990 to discuss the advantages of negotiating a free trade agreement with the United States (*Foro Nacional de Consulta Sobre las Relaciones Comerciales de México con el Exterior*). As expected, the Senate recommended the negotiations.

4. Benedict Anderson, *Imagined Communities: Reflections on the Origin and Spread of Nationalism* (London: Verso, 1983).

5. Seymour Martin Lipset, *Continental Divide: The Values and Institutions of the United States and Canada* (New York and London: Routledge, 1990), p. 19.

6. Ibid., p. 27.

7. Anderson, *Imagined Communities*, p. 19.

8. In 1990 alone, the Immigration and Naturalization Service of the United States arrested 1,092,258 undocumented Mexicans: see *Immigration and Naturalization Service Statistical Yearbook, 1990* (Washington, DC: Government Printing Office, 1991), p. 167.

9. In a historical account of xenophobic explosions during the Mexican Revolution, Alan Knight insists that anti-Spanish feelings were stronger than anti-American feelings. According to him, Americans or American interests were not an important target for Mexican revolutionaries. See Alan Knight, *The Mexican Revolution,* vol. 2 (Cambridge and London: Cambridge University Press, 1986).

10. See Friedrich Katz, *The Secret War in Mexico: Europe, the United States and the Mexican Revolution* (Chicago and London: University of Chicago Press, 1981).

11. For an extended treatment of recent changes in the Mexican political culture, see Soledad Loaeza, "The Emergence and Legitimization of the Modern Right, 1970–1988," in Wayne A. Cornelius, Judith Gentleman, and Peter H. Smith, eds., *Mexico's Alternative Political Futures* (San Diego: Center for U.S.-Mexican Studies, University of California, San Diego, 1989), pp. 351–360.

12. See Mario Ojeda, *México: El surgimiento de una política exterior activa* (México: Secretaría de Educación Pública, Foro 2000, 1986).

13. For an analysis of closer cooperation between the two countries as a positive response to geography, see Sidney Weintraub, *A Marriage of Convenience: Relations Between Mexico and the United States* (New York and Oxford: Oxford University Press, 1990).

14. See, for instance, the "rescue operation" designed by U.S. financial authorities in August 1982 to save Mexico from bankruptcy, described in Joseph Kraft, *The Mexico Rescue* (New York: Group of Thirty, 1984).

15. See PRI, "Discurso pronunciado por el Presidente Constitucional de los Estados Unidos Mexicanos, Carlos Salinas de Gortari," Ceremonia del LXIII aniversario del partido revolucionario institucional, March 4, 1992.

7

The Pressures for Political Reform in Mexico

M. Delal Baer and Sidney Weintraub

Few non-Communist economies were more closed than Mexico's at the onset of the 1980s. Few developing economies are more open today. This change in development philosophy began slowly in 1982 and then accelerated after Mexico joined the General Agreement on Tariffs and Trade in 1986. The main features of this opening have been amply described.[1] They include drastic reduction of import barriers, privatization of many state-owned enterprises, deregulation of key economic sectors, sharp reductions in the public-sector deficit, and a vigorous anti-inflation effort involving wage and price controls. The state has ceased to be the *rector,* or moving force, of the economy.

What has been less analyzed outside Mexico is how many political taboos had to be jettisoned to accomplish this transformation. Vested interests in the deeply entrenched system of protection and state ownership had to be overcome. Because of the salience of the United States in Mexico's push to export manufactured goods, a new bilateral relationship had to be forged. The previous two-track policy in dealing with the United States—political distancing, on the one hand, and economic coexistence, on the other—ceased to be viable. It became clear that Mexico had to become more active abroad, particularly in the United States, if the country were to achieve its economic objectives. Mexico found that it was necessary to engage in foreign lobbying, which meant that it had to accept foreign lobbying in Mexico in return. The combination required a basic redefinition of what previously was considered unacceptable, lest national sovereignty be compromised. The most basic shattering of precedent came with the Mexican request for North American free trade. This goal required not only toleration of closer political-economic relations with the United States but also an embrace that had been unthinkable since the Revolution eighty years earlier.

As it opened the economy, Mexico's leaders followed a nuanced policy of gradual but grudging political opening. The authorities sought to limit the electorate's free choice until the economic changes were seen to be raising incomes and employment, which would then permit the Partido Revolucionario Institucional to win elections in an open environment. This, to a large extent, was accomplished.

Once other taboos were shattered, however, the Mexican authorities found it impossible to fully contain the process of internal political change. First, there has been a boomerang effect in U.S.-Mexican relations. Once Mexican government officials put their domestic development agenda on the table in relations with the United States, the repercussions returned home with great force. A host of actors ranging from U.S. environmental groups to Mexican political activists have discovered that they can pressure Mexican authorities by airing Mexican domestic issues in the United States. Second, it is proving impossible for an authoritarian Mexico to increase the intensity of its economic and social relations with its democratic neighbor without affecting Mexico's political institutions. Finally, the economic reforms themselves have removed many of the tools by which Mexican authoritarianism sustained itself.

What follows is a discussion of the forces that shaped Mexican political and economic policies during most of this century and an analysis of the pressures that led to the shattering of these precedents. The concluding section dissects the interplay among economic, social, and political events. The central conclusion of the chapter is that once the Mexican government opened the economy and sought closer economic relations with the United States, it also lost its tight control of the internal political process. Political opening can be slowed for a time, but it cannot be halted forever.

Forces Shaping Mexico Prior to the 1980s

A number of features of Mexican policy were taken as axiomatic until the 1980s. The main one was that foreign intervention in Mexico's internal affairs was unacceptable. Mexico had suffered greatly from U.S. intervention in the nineteenth and first half of the twentieth centuries. These interferences included the Mexican War (in which half the country's territory was seized), the occupation of Veracruz, the incursion into Mexico to capture Pancho Villa, and U.S. pressure to dictate Mexico's policy toward foreign oil and other companies. Texans remember the Alamo, but this is trivial compared with the multiple humiliating memories of Mexicans.[2]

The principle of nonintervention by foreign powers in the internal affairs of other countries thus came quite naturally to Mexico. This precept carried a reciprocal obligation: that Mexico not interfere in the internal affairs of others. This was a simple enough constraint when it dealt with Mexican-U.S. relations, in which Mexico was mostly powerless to intervene in any event, but it carried some weight in Mexico's relations with weaker powers like those in Central America. This restraint also affected Mexican relations with Cuba after Fidel Castro came to power. Mexico's strict adherence to the principle of nonintervention did not permit it to join the United States and other countries of the Organization of American States in isolating Cuba.

Nonintervention was expressed in more subtle forms as well. Mexico did not engage in extensive lobbying in foreign countries, and it frowned on foreign lobbying in Mexico. For many years, the Mexican Embassy in Washington dealt with the U.S. State Department and avoided direct contact with members of Congress and even with other U.S. government agencies. This was explained as being consistent with the principle of nonintervention, but it may also have reflected Mexican ignorance of the role Congress plays in the U.S. scheme of things. Because the Mexican Congress was relatively powerless, it was assumed that the U.S. Congress was similarly a nonpotent arm of government.[3]

The distrust of U.S. motives was particularly great in the economic sphere. Mexico had experienced forceful intervention by the U.S. government on behalf of U.S. corporations operating in Mexico. The expropriation of foreign oil companies in 1938 was so popular and it remains an issue around which Mexican emotions can be aroused to this day precisely because of the historical experience of the oil companies and the U.S. government acting in concert to impose their will on Mexico. The Calvo Doctrine, which states that disputes between foreign corporations and national governments in Latin America must be settled in the courts of the country where the investment is located, proved so durable because of a fear that the United States would engage in gunboat diplomacy on behalf of U.S.-based corporations.[4]

This need to protect sovereignty against more powerful interventionist powers was a potent historical motive for restricting foreign direct investment. In the modern era, this concern for sovereignty went beyond a fear of the threat of force by the government of the home country. Sovereignty, by extension, soon was interpreted as the ability of Mexico to determine its own policies and be independent of decisions made in head offices of corporations located beyond its borders. Mexican legislation limiting the foreign equity share to a maximum of 49 percent has been the practice for decades; it was codified in the 1973 foreign investment law.

Much foreign investment in Mexico took place during the long dictatorship of Porfirio Díaz (1876–1910). The Díaz era was later seen as an era of exploitation, one in which national economic groups joined forces with foreign business interests to exploit the majority of Mexicans. The Revolution of 1910 was thus seen as a movement for social justice in which foreign economic interests were also seen as being implicated.[5]

Finally, pre-1980s thinking in Mexico was conditioned by the nature of the country's development program. Mexico was not alone in adopting a program of import-substituting industrialization (ISI), or development from within, as it was labeled. This was the reigning philosophy throughout Latin America, beginning out of necessity because of the foreign exchange shortage during the Great Depression and then hardening into a well-articulated philosophy under the tutelage of the Economic Commission for Latin America and its charismatic leader, Raúl Prebisch. In Mexico, ISI was also seen as a way to achieve economic independence from the United States. As practiced, ISI entailed establishing domestic industries and protecting them against import competition. It went further in that it also involved prescribing levels of domestic content for final products, thereby seeking to force national production of intermediate goods and services.

The conditioning economic elements in Mexico at the start of the 1980s, therefore, involved a strict and expansive interpretation of nonintervention, distrust of foreign direct investment, and a rigorous program of ISI. Each of these elements had as either a stated or unstated motive the achievement of greater economic and political independence from the United States.

This independence was never fully achieved, much to the frustration of Mexican nationalists. The United States remained the dominant market for Mexican exports and the main source of imports. About two-thirds of the foreign direct investment that was permitted came from U.S. corporations. Moreover, U.S. domestic economic policy, whether it dealt with interest rates or inflation control, had a profound effect on Mexico. This became evident in the early 1980s, when high U.S. interest rates and low inflation contributed to Mexico's foreign debt crisis.

Mexico's discomfort with its economic interdependence led it to pursue a dichotomous policy of separating economic and political relations with the United States. Politicians in Mexico often ran on antigringo platforms, and the nation regularly voted against U.S. positions in international organizations. Mexican textbooks invariably portrayed the United States in a bad light. The selection of stories for the *primeras planas* ("front pages") of leading Mexican newspapers were consciously chosen to depict the worst of U.S. society. Although Mexican authorities sought to prevent this low-grade anti-Americanism from contaminating economic relations with the United States, they were not always successful for Americans could, of course, read the Mexican press and listen to Mexican politicians.

Mexican-U.S. relations were inevitably tense under these circumstances. Indeed, it was quite natural for two informed authors, one an American and the other a Mexican, to entitle their widely cited book ***Limits** of Friendship* (emphasis added).[6] It is therefore not remarkable that developments in Mexican-U.S. relations over the past decade were labeled as impossible as recently as 1980.

The foregoing were among the features that shaped Mexico-U.S. relations prior to the 1980s. However, the internal political structure in Mexico was determined by other forces. When attempting to understand the PRI's long rule, it is important to keep in mind that the Mexican economy performed well under an authoritarian structure.[7] From the 1930s to the early 1980s, gross domestic product in Mexico grew by more than 5 percent a year and by more than 2 percent a year on a per capita basis. Although political protest erupted periodically, basic political changes did not immediately follow. The old pillars of the edifice began to crumble only when dissatisfaction with authoritarian politics was combined with economic downturn and restructuring in the 1980s.

The ISI model as practiced in Mexico succeeded in delivering growth at the macro level, but it also resulted in a highly skewed distribution of income.[8] Opportunities for education were not readily available throughout the country. It seemed, however, that as long as most Mexicans—or at least most *influential* Mexicans—were benefiting, this inequality led to little political turmoil. A growing middle class favored social stability, and the ISI model, whatever its social shortcomings, delivered this. Nationalism, as it manifested itself under the ISI model, became the banner under which Mexican entrepreneurs extracted unearned rents from the general public: The consumer was offered inferior goods at a high price.

The inequalities were explained away by the argument that only after economic growth was attained could attention be turned to the question of distributive justice. This, in fact, was the historical sequence in most currently developed countries. The favoritism shown to owners of capital was rationalized under the "infant-industry" thesis, and this, too, was the policy once followed by most of today's industrialized countries. The results in Mexico, however, were deeply ingrained inequalities that, even under the best of circumstances, will take decades to rectify. President Salinas has stated that about 40 percent of the Mexican population still lives in conditions of absolute poverty.

Mexico's highly controlled economic practices functioned hand in glove with corporatist social organizations and authoritarian political control. Beginning with President Lázaro Cárdenas's administration (1934–1940), key segments of society were incorporated into the bosom of the PRI. The party's dominance was sustained by the obligatory affiliation of state-sponsored rural and working-class organizations, such as the Confederation of Mexican Workers (CTM) and the National Confederation of Campesinos (CNC). Although some independent *campesino* ("peasant") organizations emerged, the movement as a whole was controlled by the central political authorities. Mexican labor unions were subject to similar pressures. Government-owned industries created an environment in which the distinction between economic and political decisions was blurred. Independent unions were weak, and political loyalty was made a condition of employment.

The private sector was equally dominated by an overweening state. The import license structure and a complex web of concessionary permits for business activity were the tools with which authoritarian political elites ensured a politically submissive business community. The ever-present possibility of falling out of favor with the political elite—and losing import licenses or concessionary permits—hung like the sword of Damocles over the heads of individual business people.

This framework of governance served the utilitarian purpose of maintaining social stability for many years. However, it was not democratic. Although peasants and labor were the stuff of revolutionary legend, they were not the vanguard of electoral democracy in Mexico. Instead, their votes and their loyalty were controlled by the PRI. The winners of national and statewide elections were known in advance; they would be the candidates of the PRI. Until quite recently, the PRI's electoral victories were usually genuine, the product of an absence of effective alternatives, authentic historical legitimacy, and a formidable political machine of mass corporatist organizations. Indeed, Mexico's ruling party has not recognized a single presidential loss in fourteen successions since it established itself in the late 1920s. It was not until the 1980s that non-PRI candidates demonstrated true force. A political system with this degree of durability, rooted in the very structure of the nation's economic and social life, is not transformed into a full democracy in a single season.

The Collapse of the Old Economic Order

The 1980s were a precedent-shattering decade in Mexico. The old economic model gave way to a new paradigm as the result of the calamitous years that began in 1982. It had become evident to many Mexican economists and outside observers by the early 1970s that the "easy" phase of import substitution had run its course, and Mexico was producing most of the consumer goods required for its population. The words *import substitution* can be misleading if they imply that the policy will reduce the level of required imports. In Mexico, what actually happened was that the nature of imported products changed. Mexican imports during the ISI period were primarily intermediate and capital goods, the products needed for domestic production of the goods previously imported.

As long as a policy of looking inward delivered high rates of economic growth, the relative inefficiency of production was considered a secondary issue. Industrial exports might not increase, but protection kept out competitive imports. Mexican politicians therefore saw little reason to alter the economic model. Producers who benefited from this captive market were able to extract rents, and they became a powerful vested interest for the status quo. The poor hardly mattered in the political equation. Their votes were delivered by the PRI, and, if not delivered, they could be counted as if they were.

The need for change in the ISI structure was masked during the 1970s because large oil discoveries allowed Mexico to earn vast amounts of foreign exchange. The availability of oil in the ground also facilitated borrowing by Mexicans, in both the public and private sectors, of vast sums from the world's bankers. Mexico's external debt grew to over $100 billion, more than half the size of the country's GDP. The Mexican leadership at the time, under the presidency of José López Portillo, made the calculation, consciously or otherwise, that oil prices could go in only one direction—upward. Consequently, they consumed and invested and stole as if there were no tomorrow. No attention was paid to nonoil exports, causing Mexico to suffer from what economists refer to as the "Dutch disease"—the distortion of prices of all other goods when a natural resource bonanza floods the country with foreign exchange.

Oil prices, of course, eventually did decline, and the economic house of cards collapsed with the shortage of foreign exchange. The onset of the debt crisis in the 1980s and its consequences to this day were set in motion when the Mexican authorities went to Washington in August 1982 to inform officials of the U.S. Treasury and the international financial institutions that there were no more reserves and that interest on the foreign debt could not be paid. Mexicans have since paid a heavy price for the miscalculation by the authorities during the 1970s. This is evident to the population and has undermined the credibility of the PRI.

When Miguel de la Madrid Hurtado became president (1982–1988), it was clear that the old economic model had led to disaster and that a change was needed. But there was no inevitability as to the form this change would take. Many in Mexico argued that the problems could be corrected by increasing the role of the public sector. The most visible symbol of the economic collapse was the pressing need to service the external debt. There was thus much clamor for renouncing this debt as having been foisted on Mexico by overeager foreign bankers. Those who had benefited from the old system—the protected businesspeople, the powerful unions in government-owned enterprises such as the national oil company Pemex, and the PRI politicians—wanted cosmetic change.

What they got instead was a new development paradigm, the outline of which will only be sketched in here because it has been described elsewhere.[9] Hesitantly at first but then abruptly after 1986, Mexico opened its economy. This was symbolized by its entry into the GATT in 1986, a step that had been explicitly rejected six years earlier after much lobbying by protected groups of small-scale industrialists and those intellectuals who were fearful that a more open economy would lead to closer ties with the United States. They were correct: The opening of the economy has, indeed, led to closer ties with both the United States and the outside world generally.

Mexico made commitments to liberalize its import structure when it entered the GATT, but its actions went well beyond these commitments. Once Salinas became president in 1988, there was a veritable rush to liberalization. Within three years, import permits, the key instrument for keeping out competitive imports, had been eliminated for practically all goods except agricultural and automotive products; these will gradually disappear under free trade. Import tariffs now range between zero and 20 percent, and the average, trade-weighted tariff is about 10 percent. Tariffs against U.S. goods will disappear in ten to fifteen years under free trade. The reason for the rush to openness was based partly on timing: The vested interests opposed to open markets had little influence, providing an opportunity to create an entirely new set of vested interests in a new development model. The new policy looks outward, not to a protected internal market. Thus, after 1986, Mexico joined the rest of the trading world from which it had deliberately isolated itself for more than fifty years.

The Mexican initiative for free trade with the United States and within North America generally also grew out of the desire to set in place a new structure that would be extremely difficult for future governments to reverse. If the policy of looking outward is to be successful, the U.S. market is crucial for Mexico. Omitting oil, for which there is a world market, some 80 percent of Mexico's exports go to the United States, and earnings from manufactured exports are now greater than those from oil exports. Thus, one of Mexico's motives in seeking free trade is to find some insurance against U.S. protectionism. Mexico also seeks foreign investment to set up plants that can exploit economies of scale, and assurance of access to the U.S. market will promote this. Therefore, rather than resisting foreign direct investment, Mexico now solicits it. Many of these investments will come from parent companies in the United States and other industrial countries, which will then export on an intrafirm basis. Mexico's goal is to increase industrial productivity, thereby facilitating higher real wages. The intent is to use the free trade opportunity as the basis for converting the country into a North American tiger by following policies similar to those of the Asian tigers.

The rush to open the economy also originated in the philosophic approach of the policymakers in the Salinas administration. It is clear from their writings (former academics abound in the government's economic policy positions) and also from their actions in government that they believe Mexico's economic future can be made more prosperous and more secure by looking outward, rather than continuing a policy of seeking development from within the relatively small Mexican market. It is also evident from the extensive privatization and deregulation programs that have been implemented that the technicians have more confidence in the market than in government dominance. This is a technical point of view, one that might ordinarily have been frustrated by entrenched politicians. But technocrats have dominated the economic policy process, even as political leaders have called the tune on gradual political opening.

The Collapse of the Old Political Order

It was not a coincidence that electoral pluralism and discontent with PRI dominance came to the fore simultaneously with the collapse of the ISI model and the deterioration of the economy during the 1980s. The transition to a market economy undermined the traditional structures of Mexican authoritarianism by challenging vested interests, decentralizing decision-making, eroding corporatist social organization, and awakening civil society. Economic reform inevitably required political reform, perhaps to an extent unanticipated by the economic reformers who began the process.

Initially, the decay of the old political order was hastened by mass discontent with the sacrifices required by economic restructuring. The early years of economic reform were a purgatory for politicians trying to convince the public that there was light at the end of the tunnel. It was easy for the ordinary citizen to feel that the statist past, no matter how illusory and flawed, was better than the excruciating present. And public dismay was inevitable when deficit reduction and the need to transfer resources abroad in order to meet debt obligations produced sharp drops in living standards during the 1982–1988 stabilization period. These declines in living standards affected not only the poor, most of whom have been inarticulate regarding the political structure, but also the middle class. This was the first setback faced by this influential group since the 1930s. Naturally, Mexicans blamed political authorities for the nation's dire economic straits.

Mexico's initial years of economic reform were traumatic. Federal deficit reduction efforts led white-collar unions and government employees to abandon the PRI in droves. The decline of the PRI's share of the vote in Mexico City in the 1988 presidential election was partially attributable to the desertion of disgruntled bureaucrats. Similarly, the removal of long-standing price subsidies in Mexico City, for everything from the subway to tortillas to gasoline, had its political consequences. Efforts to establish realistic product pricing and exchange rates had devastating political effects. Sharp devaluations throughout the 1980s led to a drop in purchasing power and an increase in the inflation rate. The opposition sentiment was strongest in the northern states, where commercial relations with the United States were most intense, and in Mexico City.

The privatization of state-owned industries also meant reductions in the work force and pay scales. The privatization of Teléfonos de México, for example, entailed trimming jobs. Similarly, the temporary closure and later privatization of the Cananea copper mine, an icon of Mexico's revolutionary history, meant a loss of jobs and an opportunity for populist opposition leaders to score political points. The shutdown of industries, such as the Fundidora Monterrey steel mill, dealt sudden blows to local economies. Presidents de la Madrid and Salinas both had to alienate union constituencies that had been key to the PRI's political power. Parastatal employment could no longer be used as patronage for grassroots constituents in return for political loyalty.

Economic reform required a frontal assault on the elite power centers of the regime. Mexico's political elite expected that the state-run economy would redound to their political and personal benefit, senior politicians came to expect cushy retirements as the managers of large parastatal industries, and union leaders expected lucrative contract arrangements as service providers to government businesses. Known in Mexican Spanish as *dinosaurios*, this generation of politicians perpetuated their access to wealth and power by wrapping themselves in the mythology of the Revolution and equating the eternal rule of the PRI with the defense of national sovereignty. Clearly, this powerful set of interests was deeply resistant to change.

The economic adjustment of the 1980s turned passive resentment into active voting for opposition parties. The economic crisis that unfolded in 1982 implied a failure of Mexico's traditional institutions, and the remainder of the decade was characterized by a propensity toward punishing the incumbent PRI. Voters first turned to the opposition Partido Acción Nacional (PAN), a conservative party with confessional overtones that has taken strong anticorruption and free market stances. As the PAN, long the second most powerful political force in Mexico, gained momentum and captured the protest vote in state and local races during the mid-1980s, the government responded harshly.[10]

The PAN was supplanted as a catalyst for discontent by the 1988 presidential candidacy of the PRI breakaway populist Cuauhtémoc Cárdenas. Cárdenas captured the voter's imagination by invoking memories of his father, former President Lázaro Cárdenas. He ran on a platform opposing the PRI's economic reform, describing the program as a betrayal of the Mexican Revolution's heritage. President Salinas entered office with a keen sense of the need to defend economic reform from political challengers—he was declared the presidential victor with a bare absolute majority of the vote, and hardly anyone believed the figures. What started out as an internal PRI conflict over economic policy ended with the shattering of the unchallenged, sixty-year, single-party rule of the PRI.

Cárdenas, although wearing the guise of the reform outsider, represented Mexico's combined Socialist and ex-Communist parties merged with the PRI wing that was most wedded to state participation in the economy. He was widely believed to have won the sympathy and under-the-table collaboration of the traditional dinosaurios of the PRI in 1988, including the petroleum workers' leader Joaquín Hernández Galicia and the teachers' union leader Jonguitud Barrios. A number of the small political parties that joined his coalition in 1988 had a dubious past of intimacy with the government, suggesting that a rebellious PRI electoral machine was partially responsible for the surprisingly strong Cárdenas showing. Ironically, although protest voters thought that Cárdenas was an agent of change, he actually represented a philosophy of economic counterreform that would return Mexico to the pre-1982 philosophy. This has led the PRI to castigate his followers as "the new reactionaries," implying that they are nostalgic for the old taboos. In the upside-down world of

Mexican politics, apparent reformers are reactionaries, and sitting incumbents are revolutionaries.

Incumbent economic reformers, especially those whose party has been in power for over sixty years, face special dilemmas. The same regime that was responsible for getting Mexico into economic straits in the 1970s reformed the economy in the 1980s. The same regime that nationalized the banks in 1982 completed their reprivatization in 1992. The fact that the PRI regime has been identified with both Mexico's economic problems and their solutions creates credibility problems for reformers. De la Madrid carried the burden of accumulated public resentment and blame of previous presidents. His successor, Salinas, enjoys more popularity, but significantly, he cultivated the image of a reformer willing to take on the system. The legitimacy of the system was at an all-time low when it embarked on six years of fiscal adjustment in 1986 that transformed the public-sector deficit of 16 percent of GDP into a surplus by 1992. Mexico's economic reform is not the product of a revolution from below; rather, it has been implemented from above by an embattled incumbent regime.

Mexico's 1988 presidential election represents a historical breakdown of the ancien régime, induced by a traumatic economic reform combined with anachronistic political institutions. However, the 1988 vote sent contradictory signals. On the one hand, Cárdenas represented a backward-looking reaction to economic reform. The danger of political backlash among elites is most acute during the early phases of reform, when the old has not yet died and the new has not yet been born. Economic reform entails phasing out political personalities, patronage practices, and institutions associated with the state-run economic model. But dinosaurs resist extinction. This is quite clearly what occurred in Mexico in the presidential elections of 1988. On the other hand, the 1988 vote also signaled the emergence of a newly assertive democratic culture. Economic reform eroded the institutional and corporatist controls associated with ISI, unshackling an autonomous civil society. Inexorably, economic reform generated unexpected political consequences that have eluded the control of economic planners.

Democratization and Economic Reform

Mexican authoritarianism in the 1980s and 1990s was, in part, a response to the backlash to economic reform as expressed in the electoral arena. Miguel de la Madrid absorbed the political punishment for the dislocations of reform, and President Salinas made it clear that he would not jeopardize the success of his economic reform for the vagaries of a potentially unstable democratization. Russia's struggle to manage political and economic liberalization simultaneously was prominent in President Salinas's thinking, as were the economic successes of the Asian tigers that had delayed political opening.[11] In the nations of the former Soviet bloc, apparatchiks and nationalists have effectively utilized the mechanisms of democracy to frustrate attempts at economic and political reform. President Salinas and the PRI, moreover, received a temporary political reprieve after the 1988 elections. The benefits of economic reform, in the shape of lower inflation and a return to economic growth, began to produce political benefits by the early 1990s.

Despite the desire to limit political opening, Mexico has experienced more political change since 1989 than it had in the previous sixty years. And Salinas's popularity and a successful reform have not dampened the desire for greater democratization that was unleashed during the 1980s. The PRI remains dominant, but it must now adapt to a more competitive electoral game and share some power with the opposition. The Mexican Congress, particularly the Chamber of Deputies, is gaining influence, and legislative compromises that were unnecessary in the past are now commonplace. Such compromises will become even more routine under the electoral reform passed into law by the Congress during the second half of 1993. Political change has also taken place within the PRI—the old corporatist party controls are a shadow image of those of the past, leading to profound social changes in the countryside and in the labor union movement. The PRI can no longer take its dominance for granted and must field attractive candidates and compete effectively in elections that are now largely open.

In the years after Salinas's turbulent election, the battle for political opening shifted to the state and local levels. Initially, the imperative of defending economic reform from opponents in the electoral arena led to a tightly controlled, discretionary political opening. The pace of political opening was deliberately slowed to prevent the cardenista opponents, who had sworn to obliterate the PRI and economic reform, from gaining momentum. Local contests in the states of Michoacán, México, and Guerrero in 1989 left a bitter aftertaste because of regime heavy-handedness, cardenista flirtations with violence, and unclear electoral preferences.

Although some commentators have suggested that Salinas has pursued perestroika without glasnost, political closure was not absolute.[12] The Salinas government was a master of the mixed message. It displayed flexibility and a new respect for the electoral process when opposition parties accepted economic reform and gradual political opening. Watershed electoral victories were ceded to the PAN in the 1989 gubernatorial race in the border state of Baja California but only after the PAN mobilized a vigorous organizational machine to defend its victories, polling booth by polling booth. Some declared that the seeming receptivity to PAN victories and the apparent hard-line attitude toward Cárdenas amounted to a policy of "selective democracy." Cardenistas argued that the PAN had been co-opted by the PRI and had accepted a position of power-sharing cohabitation within a fundamentally unchanged authoritarian context.

Continuing pressures for political liberalization were evident in the 1991 midterm elections, but by then, the reform measures were producing economic growth, and the cardenistas offered no viable economic alternative. The August 1991 elections chose 500 deputies (the full Chamber), three-fifths on the basis of single-member districts and the remainder by proportional representation, as well as 32 senators (half the Senate). Cárdenas had lost popularity, and his Partido de la Revolución Democrática (PRD) did quite poorly. PRI candidates won 31 of the 32 Senate contests; the lone non-PRI winner was a PAN candidate in Baja California Norte, a state where the PAN already held the governorship. In the Chamber of Deputies contests, the PRI obtained 320 of the 500 seats, or 59 more than it had won in 1988. The PRI sweep was even greater in the single-member district contests, in which its candidates won 290 of the 300 elections. The other 10 were won by PAN candidates. Overall, the PRI received 61 percent of the votes, the PAN 17 percent, and the PRD only 8 percent. The PAN won its traditional share of the vote; the PRD seemed to be collapsing.

The PRI apparently won the federal elections without excessive recourse to manipulation. In this respect, the strategy of implementing economic liberalization first and then using its success as the springboard for victories in openly contested elections seemed to be working.[13] The 1991 midterm elections took place against the backdrop of three years of growth and declining inflation. The Brady Plan had removed the debt crisis from the economic agenda, and the worst adjustments of trade liberalization and privatization had passed. Mexicans were clearly better off than they were in 1988.

The PRI's improved showing in the 1991 federal elections also can be attributed to the fact that President Salinas realized that the party's corporatist and patronage styles required updating. He encouraged grassroots organization rather than the traditional sectoral modes of political mobilization. Salinas also restored the flow of resources to the states and regions of the country while preserving the nation's macroeconomic gains by creating the Solidarity program, a $3-billion public works initiative designed to combine local sweat equity with federal resources. Although Solidarity was touted as a nonpartisan program, its projects redounded to the political benefit of the PRI. The Solidarity program, with its cell-like territorial structure, reinforced and paralleled the PRI's political reorganization. There was even speculation that the program was a political party in the making, ready to be launched in the event that the PRI proved to be unreformable.[14]

The PRI's political comeback at the federal level, combined with the cession of the 1989 Baja California gubernatorial race to the PAN, gave the impression of an overall plan to permit limited doses of political opening while proceeding rapidly with economic reform and reconstruction of the PRI. Moreover, the PRI hoped to restore not only its electoral dominance but also the credibility of the election process: It wanted not only to win but also to have its victories believed. Toward this end, extensive new legislation was passed in 1989 requiring the creation of a new federal election registry, new voter registration cards, and the construction of a new, supposedly more impartial and professionalized electoral bureaucracy. However, the strategy went awry.

Simultaneous with the 1991 federal elections, races were held for six gubernatorial positions. There were significant differences in the probity of federal, as opposed to state and municipal, elections.[15] The complaints about the federal elections were modest compared with those in a number of state and local elections, particularly in the gubernatorial races in Guanajuato and San Luis Potosí, two states with a long history of fervent opposition sentiment. There, a successful economic reform was not enough to deactivate an assertive opposition and the resurgent strength of the PAN. Yet, unlike the Baja California case, the PAN met with resistance there. This could scarcely be explained on the grounds of defending the economic reform for the PAN is philosophically in tune with that reform. Rather, the prospect of conceding more than one governorship seemed to stimulate an inertial authoritarianism, the result of ingrained practices and local machines, that has proved hard to shed. State and local elections are governed by state, as opposed to federal, laws and institutions and thus did not benefit from the greater transparency achieved at the federal level.

The adoption of mass postelectoral civil disobedience generated enough pressure to force the resignation of the PRI candidates in San Luis Potosí and Guanajuato. The resignations were designed to control damage and to avoid tainting the overall national PRI victory. The phenomenon of elections followed by civil disobedience followed by negotiations and PRI resignations soon came to be tagged the *segunda vuelta,* or "second round." The second round was the price paid by the regime for failing to establish its credibility on the issue of electoral transparency. The PRI had claimed victory on so many questionable occasions in the past that now, when it may, indeed, have won elections in a cleaner environment than ever before, it was not believed. Procedural irregularities at the state level remained serious enough to cast doubt on the announced results and the regime's good faith.

Ironically, the PRI candidate may have won in both states; Mexico's opposition parties had failed to organize effectively. Rather than take responsibility for their failings, they often sought refuge in accusations of fraud. To avoid an embarrassing defeat and to achieve a tactical advantage, some opposition forces fudged the democratic principles they said they were defending. Under these circumstances, hopes for establishing a consensus on a legal framework for elections and resolving political questions were fading rapidly.

Residual authoritarianism of the PRI's most retrograde elements, combined with radical opportunism on the part of some opposition forces, was undermining the electoral process and replacing it with a raw test of political wills on the streets and in backroom deals in Mexico City. The second round pattern, which began in 1991, marked a crucial moment in which President Salinas began to lose control of the pace and dynamics of political opening.

The pattern of gradual opening and fierce postelection conflict at the state and local levels continued after 1991. The gubernatorial race in Chihuahua in 1992 saw the popular PAN candidate, Francisco Barrio, win a victory in which the results were accepted by all parties. By contrast, the gubernatorial race in Michoacán in 1992 saw the defeat of PRD candidate Cristóbal Arias, followed by claims of PRD victory, postelectoral demonstrations, and the resignation of the PRI candidate, Eduardo Villaseñor.[16] Because the prospect of admitting the loss of Michoacán, the home state of Cárdenas, would have sealed the political fate of the PRD, it was preferable from the standpoint of PRD strategists to cast doubt on the election results.

The Michoacán resignation precipitated a serious crisis within the PRI. The party's dinosaurs, viewing a democratic transition with as much enthusiasm as they felt for the already unpopular economic reforms, were on the verge of revolt. Even PRI leaders of a more liberal mindset observed that elections were being decided in the streets rather than at the polls. It would be difficult to convince anyone to run as a PRI candidate if the victories would not be respected and if their efforts were sacrificed to appease opposition strategies. President Salinas convoked an emergency private gathering of the party leadership to assure them that Guanajuato and Michoacán would be the exception to rather than the rule of Mexican politics. "To try to convert the exception to the rule," he asserted, "would mean weakening the democratic life of the nation . . . and pushing the rule of law to the limit."[17] Opposition forces mobilized second round protests after the gubernatorial races in Tamaulipas and Puebla in late 1992, but they were unsuccessful.

The message of the Salinas-era elections is that, in spite of the PRI's remarkable political recovery and the restoration of economic growth, the anti-incumbent sentiment of the 1980s will translate into continued pressure for a democratic transition in Mexico in the 1990s. The political restoration of the PRI and of President Salinas in the federal elections of 1991 can be interpreted as public approval of his economic policies. Performance matters, and the PRI and Salinas won a new lease on political life by dint of stellar policy results. A vote for the PRI's economic leadership should not, however, be interpreted as a vote for the restoration of single-party authoritarianism. The experiences of 1991–1992 in the states of San Luis Potosí, Guanajuato, and Michoacán demonstrated that the

Mexican electorate could approve the economic reform of a PRI president yet still desire greater political liberalization.

Salinas will find himself impelled by the logic of economic reform to take actions that are likely to further accelerate the erosion of the regime's traditional sources of authoritarian political control. The disbanding of Mexican corporatism is occurring ever more rapidly, decisionmaking is growing ever more decentralized, and Mexican society will grow more sophisticated as economic reform succeeds. This is abundantly evident with the second phase of economic reform, which began with Salinas's 1991 introduction of a constitutional reform bringing market forces into Mexico's ejido system. Peasants will be permitted to rent, sell, or incorporate their landholdings with one another or in association with foreign capital. One implication of this reform is that by breaking the decades-long economic dependence of the *ejidatario* ("a peasant who belongs to an ejido") on the state, it is likely to break the PRI's stranglehold on the rural vote.

Similar forces are at work in Mexico's private sector and trade unions. The dismantling of import licensing, together with the structuring of a more uniform and less arbitrary tax code, frees entrepreneurs to participate in the political arena without fear of capricious authorities. The privatization of parastatal industries exposed them to the cold wind of economic reality and pressure to negotiate labor contracts in accordance with market forces. Decentralized wage and salary negotiations simply increased the unions' independence from government control.

Finally, Mexico's growing urban middle class is coming of age. The urban electorate defected from the PRI in large numbers in the 1980s. For these voters, corporatist structures have little to offer, and they are no longer able to mobilize electoral loyalties. Mexico's middle class has been a ticking time bomb since the student movement of the late 1960s. Yet economic modernization relies on an educated middle class, precisely the sector least amenable to the suasions of corporatist loyalty and most likely to lead the demand for political democracy. Thus, as Mexico's push toward modernization progresses, the forces of democracy are likely to be strengthened.

The Political Impact of the Free Trade Initiative

The North American Free Trade Agreement is best seen not simply as an important economic step involving the three countries but also as one that has significant implications for their cultural interaction and political relations. The relationship between the United States and Mexico has gone through a profound change during the past ten years. For Mexico, the free trade initiative represents a fundamental shift in attitude for it formally links the nation's future to its relations with the United States. Although the most important aspect of this transformation is economic, Mexican behavior has been altered in other ways. Incidents that would once have inflamed the nation with nationalistic fervor are now calmly dealt with as aberrations that can be corrected in an otherwise friendly relationship. The best example of this was the government's handling of the 1990 U.S. kidnapping of a Mexican doctor implicated in the murder of Enrique Camarena, an official of the U.S. Drug Enforcement Administration.

For its part, the U.S. government has been satisfied with Mexican overtures. When a neighbor's hand has been visible mostly as a clenched fist, it is hard to spurn that hand when it stretches out in friendship. This was clear to the conservative Bush administration. The congressional debate authorizing the procedures for the negotiation showed, however, that many Americans retained a vision of Mexico as it was and, to a decreasing extent, as it still is—not as it will become. The U.S. debate was fierce, pitting the executive branch and business and academic supporters in favor of free trade against labor unions, many environmentalists, and others who wondered whether it was appropriate to forge a close economic link with a country that still lacked democratic maturity.

The final decision on NAFTA rested with the Clinton administration and a Congress controlled by Democrats. The argument that the United States should not enter into free trade with a country that is not yet a democracy in the mold of the advanced industrialized countries is, in our view, misguided. Mexico is moving in that direction, prodded by the stimulus of an open economy and the prospect of free trade.

Mexico's economic opening, coupled with the privatization that has taken place, means that the bulk of day-to-day economic decisions (such as what to import and from where, to give but one example) will be dispersed among thousands of actors rather than centralized in the bureaucracy. This dispersion in the economic sphere has already stimulated much concern over the slow pace of political and administrative decentralization. Meanwhile, the increase in trade between the two countries has already spawned a great number of nongovernmental and social alliances across the border.[18] The Mexican environmental movement received much stimulus from pressure exerted by its U.S. counterpart during the free trade negotiations. As trade and investment deepen, the producers and traders of the two nations will have to reach agreement on thousands of product standards.

Mexico considers itself to be in the Western cultural sphere and wishes to be accepted in this manner externally. The Mexican reaction to outside concern over electoral fraud is one manifestation of this. The boomerang effect referred to earlier has augmented these contacts. The door to increased cross-border influence was opened with Mexico's recognition that it was going to have to become more active in the United States if it was to accomplish its domestic objectives. It became evident in Mexico that the fate of free trade was in the hands of many decisionmakers, ranging from union leaders to Latino chambers of commerce to members of the U.S Congress. Mexico found that it could not ignore events in the United States that were so vital to its own national interest.

Mexico has made a quantum leap in trying to influence this disparate group, although the very notion of attempting to influence another nation's domestic policy decisions violated the central Mexican taboo on interfering in the sovereign affairs of other nations. The decision to hire lobbyists in the United States was made with great concern that U.S. interests would most likely become active in Mexico in like manner.

Ironically, it was Mexican opposition party activists who encouraged the U.S. government to pressure Mexican governmental authorities to open the political system. The intense desire of Mexico's leaders to achieve free trade, combined with the political uncertainty surrounding U.S. congressional ratification, created leverage with which to extract concessions. The opposition realized the force of the boomerang effect.

This effect was first seen after the disputed 1986 Chihuahua gubernatorial race in which the PAN candidate was believed to have been denied a legitimate victory. Frustrated PAN activists went to Washington without the authorization of their national headquarters and met with several U.S. senators (including Jesse Helms) and representatives of Washington think tanks and held a press conference at the National Press Club to call attention to their grievance. They also registered a formal complaint with the Human Rights Commission of the Organization of American States.

These early opposition party efforts brought on nationalistic hyperventilation in all quarters. The left made pointed historical references to the nineteenth-century Mexican conservatives who had mobilized French influence to install Emperor Maximilian, seeking to conjure up images of a reactionary PAN alliance with conservative interventionism from the United States. The PRI nationalists fumed about national security, and the PAN national leadership disowned its own activists.

As it happened, these early PAN militants paved the way for later, extensive opposition party activities in Washington and elsewhere in the United States. Once the Mexican left realized that the boomerang effect might work for it, extensive tours throughout the United States were organized for Cuauhtémoc Cárdenas after the hotly contested 1988 presidential election. His swings through Chicago and Los Angeles were designed to mobilize the Mexican-American population. These visits precipitated similar trips by President Salinas. The Mexican foreign ministry now has a full-time senior official devoted solely to cultivating the Mexican-origin population in the United States. Mexico's competitive partisan politics had definitively taken the competition across the border.

Mexico's antigovernment democratization advocates found that the complex political process related to the negotiation and ratification of NAFTA provided them with considerable leverage. They argued that

NAFTA should be conditioned on a completed democratic transition—political transition first and free trade thereafter, exactly the reverse of the sequence chosen by the government. Cárdenas's *Foreign Policy* article was representative of these views.[19] Senator Porfirio Muñoz Ledo, a senior figure in the PRD, made a series of visits to Washington to make the same case with U.S. congressional figures, such as Senator Christopher Dodd and Representative Robert Torricelli. He trod a fine line between conditioning NAFTA on democracy first and U.S. intervention in Mexico's internal affairs. Representative Torricelli, as chair of the Western Hemisphere subcommittee of the House, held two hearings on human rights and the electoral situation in Mexico and utilized the hearings to send a clear signal to the Mexican government that "free trade is a democracies only club."[20] Other legislators later picked up on this theme.

Activists and intellectuals among Mexico's populist opposition parties have found they have little Mexican support in contesting the economic aspects of NAFTA, and they have designed their electoral strategies with a U.S. audience in mind. Organizing mass postelectoral demonstrations and attempting to make states ungovernable, then bringing these disturbances to the attention of the international press are now part of the repertoire in leveraging U.S. audiences to internal Mexican politics. Even when the PRI legitimately seems to have won elections, as in the 1992 gubernatorial contest in the state of Michoacán, there are enough irregularities to make these protests credible. The effectiveness of these strategies resides in the Mexican government's sensitivity to its international image and the prospect of U.S. congressional reaction to events.

The responsiveness of the Mexican government to international media coverage was evident during the 1991 midterm and gubernatorial elections in the states of Guanajuato and San Luis Potosí. The prospects of extensive coverage of prolonged election protests by the *New York Times* and the *Wall Street Journal* were assessed after both newspapers issued blistering editorial comments. The prospect of negative coverage was reinforced by the presence in Mexico of a number of well-known U.S. academic specialists during the elections. The resignations of the apparently victorious PRI candidates were the result of sensitivity to external pressure at a moment when the outcome of NAFTA negotiations was uncertain. What was new here was that internal pressure reported outside the country reverberated back to Mexico and led President Salinas to void the electoral results. Mexican authoritarianism, therefore, is no longer a fortress protected by an impenetrable moat.

An important component of the second round experience is attributable to the internationalization of the Mexican economy. The international repercussions of Mexico's domestic politics have become as important as the formal electoral process in determining many political outcomes. Indeed, so powerful are the international dimensions at play in the second round phenomenon that they worked to overturn the results in Michoacán in 1992 despite a report by international observers from the Carter Center of Emory University that the elections were generally conducted fairly.[21]

We have dwelt on the democratizing influence of NAFTA because it precipitated events that encouraged opposition parties in Mexico to actually seek U.S. intervention. This was taboo-breaking of a major nature. However, the democratizing aspect of what is happening in Mexico is not limited to NAFTA. The unilateral opening of the Mexican market, the entry into GATT, and the search for foreign direct investment has led to the formation of significant social and economic links between Mexico and the United States. And Mexico's aspiration to enter the First World economically has had a contagious effect on its politics. The range of cross-border governmental and nongovernmental points of contact have multiplied in the business, managerial, technical, and academic communities. Moreover, both the government and the opposition now realize that the Mexican-origin population in the United States can be a potent force for influencing U.S. opinion about Mexico, but this same community has its democratizing influence in Mexico as well.

Mexican human rights organizations are now in direct contact with counterpart nongovernmental organizations in the United States. Alliances were forged between nongovernmental actors in both countries, some designed to prevent and others to obtain approval of the fast-track negotiating authority. These alliances were carried out in the process for congressional approval of NAFTA and the side agreements on environmental and labor cooperation. Mexico is finding it impossible to accept international standards of behavior in the trade arena while disregarding international norms in the political arena. NAFTA, now that it is in existence, will have to deepen in thousands of ways as trade and investment relations increase—in setting standards, harmonizing environmental practices, upgrading workplace standards, and consulting about future policies—and this will not happen unless the political opening catches up with the economic opening.

Ultimately, the Mexican economic and investment climate will be affected by the uncertainty surrounding Mexico's transition to stable, multiparty politics. The reversibility of economic reform will continue to be associated with the possibility of a tormented electoral transition that brings an antireform figure to the presidency. Such uncertainty would seem to argue in favor of single-party stability, at least for those who welcome Mexico's economic opening and the free trade initiative. However, a transition that strengthens moderate opposition party forces would confirm the existence of a wide and deep consensus in favor of economic reform. This is the best assurance of continuity of reform. Mexicans are aware of the Chilean experience, where the transition from the Pinochet dictatorship to the democracy that now exists was predicated on a continuation of the economic reforms put in place by the Chicago boys.

This is why Mexico's political maturity is an important issue to the United States—as it obviously is to Mexicans. Relations between Mexico and the United States cannot become intimate if Mexico remains an authoritarian society. Although South Korea and Taiwan proved able to resist political opening for decades, their political traditions are quite different from those of Mexico.

The Mexican experiment of opening its economy boldly and opening its political structure more cautiously is in midstream at present. The economic policy seems to be working. Despite some slowdown in 1992 (to about 2.6 percent) and again in 1993 (to only 0.4 percent), GDP growth remains positive as inflation declines. Public opinion polls show that both economic opening and free trade with the United States are favored by a majority of the population.[22] If the national midterm elections of 1991 are a reasonably accurate reflection of popular sentiment, Mexico's economic policy is restoring confidence in the ability of the PRI government to manage the economy. The collapse of popular support for Cárdenas is another manifestation of the preference for the PRI's economic management.

The limits to political opening, by contrast, are bringing Mexico and the PRI into tension with the United States. This duality is unlikely to endure. The government stimulated the beginning of the end of the old politics when it opened the economy, and the initiative for free trade with the United States is accelerating the process of political opening, as Mexico's reaction to external criticism of political manipulation shows. Once it becomes clear that laggardly electoral behavior in Mexico will limit the deepening of the total North American relationship, the external pressure for democracy will become intense. As economic reform proceeds, Mexican authorities will no longer have the luxury of compartmentalizing politics and economics. At that point, these two strands of national life will rapidly become part of the same process.

Notes

1. For a comprehensive discussion of Mexico's transformation, see Nora Lustig, *Mexico: The Remaking of an Economy* (Washington, DC: Brookings Institution, 1992).

2. One of the authors of this chapter lives in Texas and hopes he is not lynched for saying this!

3. George Grayson, *Politics of Mexican Oil* (Pittsburgh: Pittsburgh University Press, 1989).

4. The Calvo Doctrine was promulgated in Argentina but was applied in most of Latin America, including Mexico.

5. There was a brouhaha in Mexico in 1992 when a new history textbook for elementary school children portrayed the Díaz era in a relatively benign light. This incident is worth mentioning because it demonstrates how thoroughly the conditioning forces discussed here are inculcated in Mexican children.

6. Robert A. Pastor and Jorge Castañeda, *Limits to Friendship* (New York: Alfred A. Knopf, 1988).

7. The rule of the Liberal-Democratic Party in Japan has also been long, and this, too, was supported by successful economic outcomes.

8. The data have been consistent over the last thirty or more years in showing that the lowest 40 percent of families receive less than 12 percent of the national income.

9. Sidney Weintraub has discussed this transformation in *A Marriage of Convenience: Relations Between Mexico and the United States* (New York: Oxford University Press for the Twentieth Century Fund, 1990).

10. See Enrique Krauze, *Por una democrácia sin adjectivos* (Mexico: Joaquin Mortiz Planeta, 1986); M. Delal Baer, "The 1985 Mexican Midterm Elections," *Latin American Election Study Series* no. 3 (Washington, DC: Center for Strategic and International Studies, July 31, 1985), and "The 1986 Mexican Elections: The Case of Chihuahua," *Latin American Election Study Series* (Washington, DC: Center for Strategic and International Studies, September 1, 1986).

11. Sidney Weintraub and M. Delal Baer, "The Interplay Between Economic and Political Opening: The Sequence in Mexico," *Washington Quarterly* (Spring 1992):187–201.

12. Lorenzo Meyer, "Aqui perestroika sin glasnost," *Excelsior,* December 13, 1991. Two sensitive assessments of the mixed messages of the Salinas administration on political reform can be found in Wayne A. Cornelius, "El PRI en la encrucijada," *Nexos* 149 (1990), and Lorenzo Meyer, "El limite neoliberal," *Nexos* (1991).

13. See M. Delal Baer, "The 1991 Mexican Midterm Elections," *Latin American Election Study Series* (Washington, DC: Center for Strategic and International Studies, October 1, 1991).

14. M. Delal Baer, "Mexico's Second Revolution: Pathways to Liberalization," in Riordan Roett, ed., *The Politics of Economic Liberalization in Mexico* (Boulder, CO: Lynne Rienner Publishers, 1993).

15. Ibid.

16. George W. Grayson, "The 1992 Mexican State Elections," *Latin American Election Study Series* (Washington, DC: Center for Strategic and International Studies, July 7, 1992).

17. Carlos Salinas de Gortari, *El Norte,* October 22, 1992, p. 1.

18. Cathryn Thorup, "The Politics of Free Trade and the Dynamics of Cross-Border Coalitions in United States–Mexican Relations," *Columbia Journal of World Business* 26, no. 2 (Summer 1991).

19. Cuauhtémoc Cárdenas, " Misunderstanding Mexico," *Foreign Policy* 78 (Spring 1990):113–130.

20. See Robert G. Torricelli, "Update on Recent Developments in Mexico," U.S. House of Representatives Hearing Before the Subcommittee on Western Hemisphere Affairs, 102nd Congress, first session, October 16, 1991.

21. The Carter Center of Emory University, *Report of the Team Sent by the Council of Freely-Elected Heads of Government to Witness the Observation of the Elections in Michoacán and Chihuahua* (Mexico: The Carter Center, July 13, 1992); idem, "Serias reservas sobre denuncias de grupos nacionales," *El Nacional,* July 14, 1992.

22. Polls consistently show that about two-thirds of Mexicans support NAFTA. A Gallup Mexico Poll of September 1991 (as reported in *El Nacional,* October 7, 1991, p. 11) is representative of other surveys. It showed that 64 percent of those queried favored NAFTA, and only 16 percent were opposed; further, 62 percent favored the economic opening, and only 26 percent were opposed. Subsequent polls continue to show a majority in favor of NAFTA.

Part 3

Conclusion

8

New Patterns of Conflict and Cooperation

M. Delal Baer

The North American Free Trade Agreement has been replete with unanticipated consequences and unconventional approaches to trade policy. The effects are still rippling through the three nations involved and beyond. It is premature to come to final conclusions about the implications of the agreement, but one thing is clear—the NAFTA debate has altered forever the way we think about trade policy, trilateral relations in North America, and the nation-state in a global economy. And the way in which the debate unfolds will reverberate in U.S. policy, impacting on neoisolationism and protectionism and U.S. relations east and west.

Several initial conclusions about the implications of NAFTA emerge from the period of negotiation and ratification. First, the prominence of what were once thought of mostly as nontrade questions (such as the environment, human rights, and labor standards) has led to new, unconventional approaches to trade policy. As a result, the substantive agenda of future trade negotiations has been redefined and made vastly more complex and politicized. Second, the attention given to these issues has spilled over into a general reordering of U.S.-Mexican relations, introducing innovative mechanisms for cooperation as well as new tensions. Third, NAFTA has prompted a rethinking of the meaning and scope of national sovereignty, both in trilateral relations and in the global arena more broadly. Fourth, even if free trade agreements among nations of different development levels promise macroeconomic benefits for all involved, they also serve as lightning rods for intense conflict and political debate. Finally, free trade debates have demonstrated an explosive ability to polarize domestic political forces in all three nations of North America, potentially leading to fundamental realignments and restructurings of political party systems. In light of these five points, it is fair to assume that the nature and substance of conflict and cooperation is likely to change over the next decade.

Unconventional Approaches to Trade Policy

Three years ago, an edited volume about a trade agreement would not have included chapters on the environment, labor standards, or human rights.

Rather, the scholarly debate would have focused on the sectoral economic impact of trade liberalization. Indeed, such studies continue to play an important role in projecting the expected economic impact of NAFTA. The brunt of the political debate, however, has centered on the environmental and social impacts of NAFTA. There are few empirical studies on the relationship between trade and the environment, but there has been no dearth of policy prescriptions and claims. Efforts to sort out the question of linkage between trade and other complex social issues are likely to generate conceptual battles for years to come. The debate in the North American context has been so intense that the repercussions are already felt in the General Agreement on Tariffs and Trade as well as in the European Community.

The melding of environmental and labor concerns into trade practice and theory has not been easy. Advocates of an aggressive integration of trade and nontrade issues assume that encouraging the harmonization of environmental and social costs among trade partners will remove the temptation to indulge in what has been described as environmental and social dumping. The core policy problem revolves around the difficulty of defining dumping in nontrade contexts. It is not easy to achieve a political consensus among diverse trade partners regarding the level of cost all are willing to bear in order to achieve uniformity of standards. Defining social dumping is further complicated by the near impossibility of harmonizing social systems that have led to rich differences among nations based on what is unique to each.

Little consensus has been achieved in the area of labor issues, despite years of efforts, because labor pricing varies dramatically in national markets due to differences in productivity, demography, and the historical evolution of national social policies. It is neither possible nor desirable to pretend that productivity differences do not exist by attempting to impose a uniform cost of labor. Similarly, the utilization of lower-cost labor cannot, per se, be defined as dumping. By that logic, the United States would be compelled to place countervailing duties on the exports of most of the underdeveloped world as well as on the products of those U.S. states where labor costs are lower than the national average. In much the same way, any attempt to harmonize the different social safety net and benefit packages of the nations of North America must run into ideological and practical barriers.

The EC has been in existence since 1958, but only now is its social charter being worked out. Even so, efforts to develop comprehensive social charter standards in the EC have pitted the lower-cost and more free-market nations of the EC, such as England, Spain, and Portugal, against industrial giants like France and Germany. Such conflicts will only intensify as each nation in Europe adopts its own approach to wrenching adjustments in social policy in response to economic stagnation and budgetary pressures. The tensions would surely be even greater should the nations of

North America move in the direction of rigorous social harmonization. This is evident from the health care debate now taking place in the United States. Ultimately, it is likely that the United States, Mexico, and Canada will agree on setting a floor for certain basic standards regarding bedrock issues like child labor, the right to strike, and the right to organize. The parallel agreements and trinational commissions negotiated by the Clinton administration already have prompted debates similar to those experienced by the EC regarding the scope of responsibility assigned to the Brussels bureaucracy and the desirability of strengthening such supranational authorities in the reading of social policy and regulatory authority.

The conceptual challenges of defining environmental dumping are similarly daunting. Distinguishing between protecting the environment and protecting inefficient producers is not an easy task. More fundamentally, environmental policies are essentially political, not market, decisions. Political decisions reflect the values and economic conditions currently prevailing in society: One society's dumping is another society's trade-off.

The United States has made a major investment in its commitment to the environment and other social issues. Robert Samuelson has pointed out that that commitment is so great that Americans have sacrificed gains in real take-home income in order to pay for those values. He explains the disconnect between productivity growth and lagging income gains as the result of a societal decision to "take more of our pay in forms other than money," that is, in environmental policy, health care benefits, and expanded concepts of legal rights. U.S. spending on health care, the environment, and legal services has grown from a total of 9.4 percent of GDP in 1972 to 16 percent of GDP in 1990, an estimated increase of approximately $420 billion annually over what was spent in 1972.

Although the United States might decide that it prefers to spend its productivity gains for health care and cleaner air and water, is it fair to ask poorer nations to adopt developed-world standards because rich nations fear losing their competitive cost edge? Every dollar taken out of a developing country's wages could mean the difference between a dinner of beans and one of meat. Samuelson feels compelled to remind the wealthy United States that there is no free lunch, but developing countries are never likely to need such lectures for they face agonizing allocation decisions under conditions of scarcity. The challenge to policymakers is to determine, beyond obvious and egregious acts of irresponsibility, a norm or cost level that might serve as a universal standard to determine when environmental dumping has occurred.

As Howard Wiarda points out in Chapter 5, the intertwining of the trade agenda with environmental, labor, and human rights concerns is the product of a political convergence in the United States—a marriage of convenience between nongovernmental organizations that have learned to leverage the U.S. Congress and traditionally protectionist forces in the labor and business communities. The political punch of this alliance has been intensified by the downturn in the U.S. economy that began in 1990, the wave of layoffs and restructuring in U.S. giants like IBM and GM, the defeat of George Bush, and the fear of national decline vis-à-vis Japan and Europe. Still, the long-term implications of the nontrade agenda are far from clear. Does it represent the shape of conflict for years to come, or is it merely a passing political ripple? The relationship between trade and nontrade issues could be the great policy challenge of the 1990s, or the debate could fizzle once the world economy regains its momentum. The economic, political, and conceptual ramifications of conditioning trade to a complex social and political agenda are sufficiently thorny to provide grist for conflict, creativity, or stalemate.

The Trilateral Issue Agenda

The landscape of the trilateral issue agenda has changed radically since the NAFTA negotiations began. On the U.S.-Mexican front, issues that had dominated the agenda in the 1980s, such as drug cooperation, debt rescheduling, and Central American security, either had disappeared or were greatly diminished in importance by the 1990s. The immigration issue faded but is now resurfacing.

By contrast, issues that had been secondary during the 1980s, such as environment, labor standards, and human rights, have come to the fore in the 1990s. This is largely a testimony to the creativity of the NGO community in utilizing the NAFTA negotiations as an opportunity to raise the profile of these issues. In spite of the severe environmental problems along the U.S.-Mexican border, it is unlikely that the border would have become an issue of national prominence were it not for the NAFTA debate. Similarly, U.S. interest in Mexican labor and human rights problems is unlikely to have been as acute had they not been viewed through the focusing lens of NAFTA.

There are two implications of the shift in the bilateral substantive agenda. First, NAFTA shines the spotlight of U.S. attention on a wide range of Mexico-related issues in a way not seen before in the post–World War II era. Second, NAFTA has gradually led U.S. policy toward greater interest in issues that many would describe as Mexican domestic issues, a stance that implies a more active U.S. involvement in what were traditionally defined as Mexican sovereign prerogatives.

The intensified public awareness of Mexico that has been generated by NAFTA is a double-edged sword. The days of benign neglect are over, but they may have been replaced with malign attention. Ironically, NAFTA may have inflamed the potential for U.S.-Mexican conflict in some areas even though its intention was the reverse. Mexico is a developing nation whose shortcomings are easy to sensationalize. The bombardment of negative press reports about Mexico and NAFTA could have the quietly pernicious, long-term effect of reinforcing negative stereotypes and hostility in the U.S. body politic. It would be easy for the average American, who listens to Ross Perot but spends little time thinking about Mexico, to absorb an image of a Dickensian Mexico—a nightmare of desperate poverty and widespread child labor, a nation intent on stealing jobs from Americans. The combined rhetorical firepower of Jesse Jackson, Patrick Buchanan, Ralph Nader, Ross Perot, and Jerry Brown has already been targeted at thin-skinned Mexico, which does not auger well for the future of bilateral harmony.

This is occurring just as Mexico is undergoing its own modernization and seeking closer ties with the United States. Mexico has always been exceptionally sensitive to its treatment in the U.S. media, often reproducing U.S. articles verbatim in Mexican newspapers. But it will have to learn to become more tough-skinned in this intensified era of intimacy. Indeed, Mexico may need to revive some of its old-fashioned, prickly defense of its national sovereignty to contain a meddlesome United States inclined toward self-righteous hectoring. Similarly, it is easy to imagine a situation in which every downturn in the U.S. economy or every plant closure or investment decision leads to a highly public process of finger-pointing. Trade disputes are likely to become more visible, as they have in the aftermath of the U.S.-Canada Free Trade Agreement.

In the case of Canada, NAFTA also has led to a reordering of bilateral relations. The heart of U.S.-Canadian affairs was, for over forty years, the sense of common identity and common goals from the standpoint of Cold War foreign policy objectives. The United States and Canada have been bonded in the military commitments of NATO and of their North American offshoot, the North American Air Defense Command (NORAD). With the disintegration of the Soviet Union, NORAD no longer has a clear raison d'être. And as the pressure of external threat is lifted, the United States and Canada are free to indulge in differences that previously would have been dwarfed by greater priorities.

It is in this post–Cold War context that the NAFTA debate has restimulated economic and trade resentments in Canada toward the United States. Although a trade dispute with Canada might make page three of a U.S. newspaper, such an item is front-page material in Canada. This has been intensified given the economic recession in Canada in the 1990s. Ironically, and similar to U.S.-Mexican relations, a trade vision that was intended to result in greater harmony between the two nations has actually had the paradoxical effect of increasing some forms of conflict.

Finally, NAFTA has unlocked a process of mutual discovery between Canada and Mexico, two nations that had rare contact in the past. This new relationship has added an entirely new dimension to North American relations. Clearly, Canada and Mexico would have slumbered on in blissful ignorance of each other's existence had it not been for NAFTA. As it is, a new realm of trade, investment, and diplomatic relations has been opened. The prospect of Canadian-Mexican alliances on a variety of issue areas vis-à-vis the United States is not the least likely outcome of NAFTA.

Sovereignty at Stake?

New sources of NAFTA-related tensions among the nations of North America are enhanced by the fact that many of them imply challenges to traditional notions of national sovereignty. Indeed, much of what might be described as the "new agenda" in trilateral relations is undergirded by transnational forces. Of course, interdependence has long been a theme in the literature about U.S.-Mexican relations, with frequent references to "silent integration" and the "intermestic" nature of the two societies. Still, NAFTA has been the catalyst for a qualitative shift in the issues considered on the bilateral agenda and the way in which people think about interdependence.

By definition, NAFTA embodies a set of trinational rules governing economic behavior. Acceptance of these rules has required fundamental modifications of traditional notions of sovereignty. All three North American nations have had to alter laws regarding foreign investment to accommodate free trade. As pointed out by Loaeza in Chapter 6 and Rugman in Chapter 4, both Canada and Mexico have sought to fundamentally retool their economic growth models by strategically inserting their own nation in a global trade scheme. NAFTA highlights global economic interdependence in an era of massive flows of investment and portfolio capital and in a world of instantaneous electronic communications. The Mexican leadership has tried to come to grips with these realities by reconceptualizing sovereignty, abandoning economic nationalism and the illusion of autarky. The U.S. leadership is only just beginning to grapple with the realities of global labor markets and investment flows.

NAFTA's integrative tendencies have been reinforced by the Wilsonian strands of the Clinton administration with regard to promoting universal democracy, combined with its Aquarian-age emphasis on the global environment. All have blurred the edges of national boundaries and softened the traditional worship of the nation-state. The emphasis on environmental affairs in NAFTA is supported by the awareness that ecosystems are transnational and transcend the nation-state. The U.S. concern with Mexican democratization is fueled by an implicit belief in the need for a world consensus on universal values over particularistic national and cultural histories. Increasingly, we are seeing a U.S. attempt to influence the domestic policies of its neighbors, whereas in the past, diplomatic objectives were limited and driven by a more narrow concept of the U.S. national interest.

Much of the push toward integration has been driven by a host of societal actors, including pressure groups, intellectuals, the media, and NGOs. As pointed out by both Wiarda in Chapter 5 and Weintraub and Baer in Chapter 7, a de facto free market of political and policy ideas now exists, and it has significant implications for traditional notions of national sovereignty. Most of the cross-border influence has been directed from Canada and Mexico toward the U.S. Congress. We should expect to see odd, new cross-border alliances, as was the case when Mexico's leftist intellectuals cooperated with the protectionism of Senator Fritz Hollings in holding high-profile hearings that were scathingly critical of the Salinas government. The Mexican government made extensive use of highly paid lobbyists to ensure passage of NAFTA. The internationalization of the North American political debate, at both the governmental and nongovernmental levels, is a major consequence of NAFTA.

The United States is accustomed to, if at times uncomfortable with, the idea of foreign nations attempting to influence its domestic policy. Still, important precedents have been set that are likely to have long-term implications. The United States has shown less and less tolerance for foreign influence, as witnessed by the reaction of critics like Ross Perot to foreign lobbyists. Furthermore, U.S. NGOs are targeting aspects of Canadian and Mexican policy for lobbying in those countries at a future date. Neither Canada nor Mexico is accustomed to overt foreign efforts to influence their policy community. For both, such activities constitute a new political offshoot of NAFTA with uncomfortable sovereignty implications.

In effect, NAFTA has provoked an unanticipated and unprecedented reassessment of trilateral mutual impacts and responsibilities. Canadians complain that proximity to the United States has placed pressure on their domestic health care system in the newly competitive cost climate of free trade. They observe that lower taxes in the United States lead to cross-border shopping and make it difficult to enforce a domestic value-added tax. Given these and many other cross-border impacts, governments must decide which portions of national policy they have an obligation to preserve and which they should share with their neighbors in free trade. It has been pointed out that national governments cede sovereignty when they agree to harmonized regimes on intellectual property or investment standards—why not environmental standards? Where are the boundaries to mutuality in cross-border policy consultation? The question is a valid one.

The answer, however, may not be very satisfying. Governments pursue their national interests on a case-by-case basis in trade negotiations. Major divergences were acknowledged in NAFTA in areas such as energy policy, agriculture, and government procurement. Just as nations will preserve what they feel to be their national interests in free trade negotiations, so, too, will they in other areas. Free trade does not erase national interests, nor can it result in absolute harmonization of conditions. Thus, Mexico might decide that its national interest is better served by placing priority on strict air emissions controls in Mexico City rather than on achieving food standards similar to those found in the United States. Similarly, the United States might determine that its negotiating leverage is best deployed vis-à-vis Mexico in the border areas, where U.S. citizens are at risk due to transboundary pollution, rather than in demanding uniform standards in the Yucatan peninsula. Canada has already decided that its national interest is best preserved by partially opting out of trinational commission dispute resolution mechanisms on environmental matters. In sum, NAFTA has ushered in an era of heightened sensitivity and creative tension regarding the cross-border impacts of national policies, but it has far from eliminated deeply rooted impulses to defend national interests.

Trilateral Relations in a New Era

One of the lessons of NAFTA is that the shape of conflict and cooperation is likely to be driven by the struggle to redefine sovereignty as described earlier. However, new patterns of cooperation are also likely to emerge as all three nations strive to minimize differences that unnecessarily impede the flow of commerce. New forms of consultation may become the norm in the areas of macroeconomic and financial policy. More deeply, a new spirit of common interest is likely to be the product of the sizable expansions in trade that can be expected as a consequence of NAFTA. This new spirit of partnership is already observable in Mexico's more positive view of its relationship with the United States. The reversal of decades of mistrust and a greater willingness to engage in cooperative policy ventures is one product of NAFTA.

NAFTA may well be a harbinger of broader global conflict centered around the differences between developed and developing nations in the areas of trade, environment, and social policy. Interestingly, this conflict is likely to reverse the overall post–World War II pattern of developing-world hostility to the industrialized community. With the demise of the Cold War, the Third World has ceased to become an ideological battlefront in a war against the West. Instead, the developing world is seeking the friendship that comes from economic cooperation. Today, it is the developed world that has begun to view less-developed nations as a threat to their standard of living.

This is true even though economists like Timothy Kehoe demonstrate convincingly that trade partnerships between nations of different economic levels are fruitful for all concerned. The conventional wisdom regarding trade liberalization remains as true for NAFTA as it has for other agreements—overall net gains in employment and trade are expected for all three countries. In Chapter 1, Kehoe points out that the gains anticipated from integration with Mexico are likely to be similar to those achieved by the accession of Spain and Portugal into the European Community. Similarly, there will be specific sectoral losses as a result of the shakeout in comparative advantage between the nations involved. As pointed out by Howard Rosen in Chapter 2, the politics of adjustment will require policies that address the human cost of achieving large-scale economic efficiencies.

Nonetheless, the intensified competition of an economically integrated globe has exacerbated fears of job loss in industrialized countries. Developed world tendencies toward protection underline the resentments of developing nations, which see export-led growth and market access as their principal opportunity for development. These tensions are visible in the desire of Eastern European nations to knock down EC trade barriers; in the African and Caribbean nations' effort to achieve European market access for tropical products; in developing nations' anxiety about agricultural and textile issues in the GATT; in the desire of newly industrializing Asian nations, such as South Korea, for greater access to the Japanese market; and in Latin American eagerness to form a deeper trade association with the United States. Around the globe, developing nations are knocking on the gates of the industrialized world's marketplace and meeting with an ambivalent reception. In the United States, the clout of Ross Perot reflects a worrisome surge of neoisolationism and neoprotectionism.

Environmentally and socially driven trade disputes are also likely to establish the pattern of future conflict between developing and developed countries. This will be especially true if the countries of North America embrace the notion that the logic of trade-dumping disputes and countervailing duty remedies can be applied to environmental and social issues. The U.S. antidumping regime is already viewed by developing nations as the main refuge of U.S. protectionism, and efforts to extend the logic inherent in that regime are viewed with great trepidation. It is easy to imagine an explosion of environmentally driven trade litigation and dispute resolution among the nations of North America.

Conflict between the developing world and industrialized nations will also center on the exigencies of the global commons. Although the global commons knows no national boundaries, the developing world harbors a residual mistrust of the unilateral proclivities of the industrialized world. This is inevitable given the industrialized world's leadership in environmental matters and the developing world's preoccupation with poverty. The more sensitive environmental activists recognize the social urgencies of developing nations, but they fear the global environment cannot be sacrificed while waiting for the developing world to attain prosperity. Meanwhile, complaints of U.S. unilateralism increasingly are heard from neighbors to the south—from the Brazilian defiance of world concern over the Amazon rain forest to the sotto voce worries of Chilean, Mexican, and Venezuelan policymakers about efforts by the United States to impose

U.S. environmental standards. They fear the return of the ugly American, this time robed in moral self-righteousness and good intentions. The grist for future conflict can be seen today as U.S. environmentalists point fingers at the appalling condition of the U.S.-Mexican border and as the United States offers to "help" Mexico enforce its own national laws; meanwhile, some Mexicans wonder if U.S. environmentalists represent a new brand of imperialist.

All of this is avoidable. Perhaps, as Tonra and Gilbreath suggest at the opening of Chapter 3, multilateral problems call for multilateral solutions. Most Latin American policymakers privately acknowledge their willingness to cede sovereignty on environmental issues, and their willingness seems to increase to the degree that these new global determinations are made in a multilateral context in which they have significant input. It may be easier to negotiate sovereignty within multilateral entities than in confrontations between advanced industrial and less-developed nations. To some, the issue is not whether there should be environmental standards reflected in trade rules but who will determine these standards and how they will be enforced.

Conclusion

In sum, NAFTA has energized a host of issues that had been lying just below the surface of trilateral relations. These are issues that indisputably have broader relevance to the global trade arena. The nontrade agenda, first introduced in a highly visible way in NAFTA, will reverberate in future GATT and EC negotiations. The debate over sovereignty has only just begun. And the North American policy arena will increasingly resound to a new score of unfamiliar issues and dilemmas. In short, NAFTA promises to be a microcosm of the issues at large in the new world order and disorder. The multiple challenges of neoisolationism, protectionism, and questions regarding the proper linkage between trade and nontrade issues have converged in NAFTA, which has proven to be a watershed for the future of North America and the world at large.

Acronyms

AD	antidumping
AFL-CIO	American Federation of Labor–Congress of Industrial Organizations
BC	British Columbia
BSI	British Standards Institution
CE	Communauté Européene (European Community)
CEN	European Standards Committee
CETA	Comprehensive Employment and Training Act
CNC	National Confederation of Campesinos
CNN	Cable Network News
COHA	Council on Hemispheric Affairs
CTM	Confederation of Mexican Workers
CSIS	Center for Strategic and International Studies
CVD	countervailing duties
DDT	dichloro-diphenyl-trichloro-ethane
DIN	German Standards Institution
DNC	Democratic National Committee
EC	European Community
ECU	European Currency Units
EDWAA	Economic Dislocation and Worker Adjustment Assistance Act
EIA	environmental impact assessment
EIS	environmental impact statement
EPA	Environmental Protection Agency
FDI	foreign direct investment
FIRA	Foreign Investment Review Agency
FTA	free trade agreement
FY	fiscal year
GAO	General Accounting Office
GATT	General Agreement on Tariffs and Trade
GDP	gross domestic product
GST	goods and services tax

IIE	Institute for International Economics
IJC	International Joint Commission
IPS	Institute for Policy Studies
IRA	individual retirement account
ISI	import-substituting industrialization
ITA	industrial training account
ITC	International Trade Commission
JTPA	Job Training Partnership Act
KPMG	division of Peat Marwick
MNE	multinational enterprises
NAC	North American commission
NAEC	North American economic community
NAFTA	North American Free Trade Agreement
NAM	National Association of Manufacturers
NAP	North American parliament
NATC	North American trade commission
NGO	nongovernmental organization
NIE	newly industrialized economy
NORAD	Northern Air Defense Command
NTB	nontariff barriers
OMB	Office of Management and Budget
PAN	Partido Acción Nacional
PCB	polychlorinated biphenal
PRD	Partido de la Revolución Democrática
PRI	Partido Revolucionario Institucional (Party of the Institutional Revolution)
R&D	research and development
SEA	Single European Act
SEDUE	Secretaría de Desarrollo Urbano y Ecología
SEDESOL	Secretaría de Desarrollo Social
SITC	Standard International Trade Classification
TAA	Trade Adjustment Assistance
TRA	trade readjustment allowances
UI	unemployment insurance
UN	United Nations
WARN	Worker Adjustment and Retraining Notification Act

The Contributors

M. Delal Baer is director of the Mexico Project and deputy director and senior fellow of the Americas Program at the Center for Strategic and International Studies (CSIS) in Washington, DC. She also chairs the Mexican Studies Department at the Foreign Service Institute of the U.S. Department of State. Baer's writings appear in the *Wall Street Journal*, the *Christian Science Monitor*, the *Washington Post*, and the *Journal of Commerce*. Her publications include "North American Free Trade," in the 1991 fall issue of *Foreign Affairs*, and *Strategic Sectors in Mexican-U.S. Free Trade* (with Guy Erb).

Jan Gilbreath is a policy analyst for the Program for U.S.-Mexican Policy Studies at the LBJ School of Public Affairs at the University of Texas at Austin and a research consultant at the Center for Global Studies, Houston Advanced Research Center. She is also a member of Governor Ann Richards's task force on U.S.-Mexican infrastructure issues in the Texas Department of Commerce. Gilbreath is the author of numerous articles on the environmental implications of NAFTA, which have appeared in such publications as the *Economist*, *El Financiero Internacional*, the *Wall Street Journal*, and the *Houston Chronicle*.

Timothy J. Kehoe is professor of economics at the University of Minnesota. He also serves as a visitor with the Federal Reserve Bank of Minneapolis and as special economic adviser to the secretary at the Secretaría de Comercio y Fomento Industrial in Mexico. Since 1985, Kehoe has been codirector of the MEGA (Models d'Equilibri General Aplicat) project at the Universidad Autonoma de Barcelona. He has written numerous articles that have appeared in such periodicals as *Journal of Mathematical Economics*, *Empirical Economics*, *Journal of Economic Theory*, and *Journal of Public Economics*.

Soledad Loaeza is director of the Center of International Studies at El Colegio de México, where she is also a research professor. She was previously a visiting fellow at St. Anthony's College in Oxford, England. Loaeza has published articles in *Foro Internacional*, *Revista Mexicana de Sociologia*, and *Nexos*. She is also a member of the editorial boards of *Nexos*, *Foro Internacional*, and the *Journal of Latin American Studies*.

Howard Rosen is executive director of the Competitiveness Policy Council. He has written numerous papers on international economics and trade, which have appeared in such publications as *Policy Analyses in International Economics* (Institute for International Economics) and the *Harvard International Review.* In 1981, Rosen worked with the U.S. Department of Labor on the *Report to the President on U.S. Competitiveness.* In January 1991, he prepared a paper for the United Nations Conference on Trade and Development. Rosen's article "Can American Industry Compete: Focus Must Be on Longer Term" appeared in the *San Diego Union* in February 1992.

Alan M. Rugman is professor of international business at the University of Toronto and a research director of the Ontario Centre for International Business. As a leading authority in international business, Rugman served as vice-president of the Academy of International Business in 1989–1990 and was made a fellow of the academy in 1991. Rugman was a member of Canada's International Trade Advisory Committee from 1986 to 1988, when the U.S.-Canada Free Trade Agreement was being negotiated. Since then, he has served on the Sectoral Trade Advisory Committee for Forest Products.

John Benjamin Tonra is a resident with the Political Science Department at the University of Dublin–Trinity College, Ireland, where he is teaching and conducting doctoral research in the areas of European Community politics and international integration. He is also an adjunct fellow with the Center for Strategic and International Studies. His articles have appeared in the *Journal of Commerce*, the *San Diego Union*, and the *World and I.* Tonra has previously worked in the Irish Department of Foreign Affairs and was a research associate on the Mexico Project and Canadian Affairs with the CSIS Americas Program.

Sidney Weintraub holds the William E. Simon Chair at the Center for Strategic and International Studies in Washington, DC. In addition, he is Dean Rusk Professor at the Lyndon B. Johnson School of Public Affairs at the University of Texas at Austin. Weintraub was a member of the U.S. Foreign Service from 1949 to 1975 and deputy assistant secretary of state for international finance and development from 1969 to 1974. He is the author of numerous articles in newspapers and journals, including "Canadian Anxieties and U.S. Responses: Introductory Thoughts" in Peter Karl Kresl's *Seen from the South,* and "Canada Acts on Free Trade" and "U.S.-Canada Free Trade," *Journal of Inter-American Studies.* His books include *Free Trade Between Mexico and the United States* (1984) and *A Marriage of Convenience: Relations Between Mexico and the United States* (1990).

Howard J. Wiarda is a visiting scholar with the Center for Strategic and International Studies Americas Program and a visiting professor at the National Defense University in Washington, DC. He has had a distinguished teaching career at the University of Massachusetts at Amherst and as a researcher at Harvard University's Center for International Affairs, the American Enterprise Institute, and the Foreign Policy Research Institute. He is the author of many books, most recently *The Democratic Revolution in Latin America* and the third edition of his textbook *Latin American Politics and Development* (with Harvey F. Kline).

Index

Academics, NAFTA and, 122–123, 130–131, 139–140
Acid Rain Memorandum of Intent (1980), 61
AD. *See* Antidumping laws
AFL-CIO. *See* American Federation of Labor–Congress of Industrial Organizations
African-Americans, NAFTA and, 134
Aghion, P., 25
Aghion and Howitt model, 25
Agriculture, 12, 127, 191
  Mexican, 83, 149
Air pollution
  economic output and, 85
  legislation on, 68
  Mexican standards for, 83
  See also Border pollution; Pollution issues
American Chamber of Commerce of Mexico, 04
American Federation of Labor–Congress of Industrial Organizations (AFL-CIO)
  influence of, 126, 132, 136, 139
  NAFTA and, 118, 123, 124, 125, 132
  See also Labor unions
American Society for the Prevention of Cruelty to Animals, 130
Anderson, Andrew, 109
Anderson, Benedict, 147
Anti-Americanism, 115, 146–147, 162
Antidumping laws (AD), 59, 103, 109, 112, 191. *See also* Dumping
Applied general equilibrium models, 9–12, 11 (table), 13, 16
Archey, William: on NAFTA, 122
Arias, Cristóbal, 173
Arizona Toxins Information Project, 128
Arrow, K. J., 24
Auerbach, A. J., 21
Auerbach and Kotlikoff model, 21
Authoritarianism
  economic reform and, 169
  undermined, 167
Automobile industry
  NAFTA and, 122, 147
  production sharing, 12
Automotive Parts and Accessories Association, 122

Bachrach and Mizrahi model, 10, 11
Backus, D. K., 24
Backus, Kehoe, and Kehoe model, 24, 25, 32
Baer, M. Delal, 130
Baldwin, R., 22–23
Baldwin model, 22–23
Barlow, Maude, 114, 115
Barrio, Francisco, 173
Barrios, Jonguitud, 168
Bartlett, Christopher, 104
Basel Convention, 58
Bentsen, Lloyd, 134
Bilateralism, 80–81, 154, 155, 159
Black Caucus (Congressional), NAFTA and, 134
Boeker, Paul, 123
Bonior, David, 135
Border development bank, 82
Border pollution
  concerns about, 62, 75, 76–77, 80–81, 88, 117, 125, 137, 190
  environmentalists and, 192
  NAFTA and, 128
  See also Air pollution; Pollution issues
Boundaries, blurring, 55, 188
Boundary Waters Treaty (1909), 60, 62
Bourassa, Robert, 108
Bracero program, 74, 120
Brady Plan, 171
British Standards Institution (BSI), 72
Brookings Institution, 131
Brown, Deardorff, and Stern model, 10, 11, 12
Brown, Jerry, 123, 139, 187
BSI. *See* British Standards Institution
Buchanan, Patrick, 139, 187
  NAFTA and, 123, 129, 130
Bush, George, 145, 186
  NAFTA and, 3, 121, 127, 131, 133, 135, 136, 139, 140, 175
Business Roundtable, 121

Calvo Doctrine, 161, 179n4

Camarena, Enrique, murder of, 175
Campbell, Bruce, 115
Campbell, Don, on FTA, 114
Campbell, Kim, 54
Canada
  decentralization in, 107–108
  exports from, 9, 64
  labor market programs in, 45 (table)
  Mexico and, 187–188
  NAFTA and, 7, 97, 111, 113, 187–188
  relative size of, 4–7, 5 (figure), 9
  separatism in, 107–108
  training programs in, 46 (table)
  UI in, 43, 44 (table)
  U.S. trade with, 98–99
Canadian Royal Commission on Economic Prospects, 63
Cananea copper mine, 167
Capital flows, 4, 19–22
  border controls and, 55, 72
Capital-labor ratios, 19, 21, 22
  differences in, 20, 30–31
Cárdenas, Cuauhtémoc, 138, 177
  decline in popularity of, 171, 179
  economic reform and, 169
  hard-line attitude toward, 170
  opposition by, 145, 146, 168, 176
Cárdenas, Lázaro, 145, 163, 168
Carter Center, Mexican elections and, 178
"Cassis de Dijon" decision, 70
Castro, Fidel, 160
Catholicism, Mexican identity and, 150
CBC, economic nationalists and, 115
Cecchini Report, 69
CE (Communauté Européene). *See* European Community
CEN. *See* European Standards Committee
Cenelec, 71
Center for Science in the Public Interest, 127
Center for Strategic and International Studies (CSIS), 130, 131
CETA. *See* Comprehensive Employment and Training Act
Chamber of Commerce, U.S., 121, 122
Chamber of Deputies (Mexico), influence of, 170
Chapter 19 panels (FTA), 112
Charter of Rights and Freedoms, language issues and, 108
Child labor, concerns about, 119, 120, 125, 135, 137, 185, 187
Child Labor Coalition, 128
Citizens' Trade Campaign, 129
Civil disobedience, PRI and, 172
Clean Air Act (1970), 75
Clean Air Act (1990), 39 (table), 45, 61
  JTPA and, 43
Clinton, Bill, NAFTA and, 121, 126, 131, 136, 139, 140, 175
Club of Rome, 67
CNC. *See* National Confederation of Campesinos
COHA. *See* Council on Hemispheric Affairs
Collantes, Cesar, 123
Colosio, Luis Donaldo, on environmental enforcement, 86
Command-and-control model, 57
Commerce Department, U.S., 110, 112
Commission for Environmental Cooperation, 53, 87
Common Agricultural Policy, 18
Communauté Européene (CE). *See* European Community
Community, strengthening, 156
Community Nutrition Institute, 127, 128
Comparative regional analysis, x–xi, 12, 13, 16
Competition, increasing, 12, 66, 106, 191
Comprehensive Employment and Training Act (CETA), 37
Confederation of Mexican Workers (CTM), 163
Conflict resolution, 56, 59, 65, 147, 190, 191
  environmental, 80, 86–88
Congress, Mexican
  hearings by, 157n3
  influence of, 170
Congress, U.S.
  Japanese FDI and, 110
  NAFTA and, 131–135
  special interests and, 109
Consolidated Omnibus Budget Reconciliation Act (1985), 41
Consumer Federation of America, 127
Consumer standards, 101, 127–128, 133
  concerns about, 135, 137
  differences in, 55
Cooperation, 156
  mechanisms for, 183
  patterns of, 190
  Third World and, 190
Coronado, Elaine, 123
Corporatism, erosion of, 167, 174
Council of Ministers (of EC), 74
  environmental policy and, 67
  New Approach and, 70
  qualified majority voting by, 70–71, 90n17
Council of the Americas, 121–122
Council on Environmental Quality, 75
Council on Hemispheric Affairs (COHA), 131
Countervailing duty (CVD) laws, 59, 103, 109, 112
  disputes over, 191

Court of International Trade, 127
Cox and Harris model, 10, 12
CSIS. *See* Center for Strategic and International Studies
CTM. *See* Confederation of Mexican Workers
Cuba, Mexican relations with, 160
Cultural identity, ix–x, 104, 149, 152, 156
Cultural nationalism, Canadian, 97, 113–114, 115
Customs Service, U.S., suit against, 127
CVD. *See* Countervailing duty laws

Decentralization, 107–108, 175
  economic, 108–111
Defense Conversion Act (1990), 39 (table), 43, 45
Defense Department Reauthorization Bill (1990), 43
De la Madrid Hurtado, Miguel, 165
  criticism of, 169
  economic nationalism and, 153
  foreign policy of, 154
  unions and, 167
Democratic Party
  AFL-CIO and, 136, 139
  free trade and, 131
  Hispanic vote and, 132–133
  NAFTA and, 123, 125, 133
  pressures on, 131–132, 140
Democratization, 119, 127
  economic reform and, 169–174
  NAFTA and, 176–177
  promotion of, 179, 188
Department of Labor, U.S., certification process by, 50n10
Deregulation, 159, 166
Dervis, de Melo, and Robinson model, 13
Devarajan and Sierra model, 13
Díaz, Porfirio, foreign investment and, 161
DIN. *See* German Standards Institution
Dinosaurios, 168, 169, 173
Dirty industries, 92n50
  exports from, 84
  migration of, 80
  See also Pollution havens
Dislocation
  assistance for, 37, 40
  short-term, 118, 139
  trade-related, 35, 45, 47, 118
Dodd, Christopher, 177
Dollar, appreciation of, 5
Dolphin protection program, 59
Dornbusch, Rudiger, 123
Drug issue
  concerns about, 119, 120, 127, 131, 134, 135, 138, 155, 186
  as foreign policy issue, 133
Dumping, 137
  disputes over, 77, 191
  environmental, 184, 185
  social, 184
  see also Antidumping laws
Dunkel draft, 57
Dutch disease, 165

EC. *See* European Community
Echeverría, Luis
  foreign policy of, 154
  waste by, 152
Economic Commission for Latin America, 161
Economic crisis, Mexican, 152, 154–155, 162, 163, 164–166, 168, 186
Economic development, 4, 63, 151, 160
Economic Dislocation and Worker Adjustment Assistance Act (EDWAA), 37, 38 (table), 42, 43
  effectiveness of, 40
  enrollment in, 47
Economic nationalism, 115, 145, 153
  abandoning, 188
  growth of, 110–111
  See also Nationalism
Economic openness, 18, 145, 175, 178
  support for, 165–166, 179
  See also Openness policy; Political openness
Economic Policy Institute, 131
Economic reform, 177, 179
  aggressiveness of, 167–168
  democratization and, 169–174
  ISI and, 169
  reversibility of, 178
Eden, Lorraine, 106
EDWAA. *See* Economic Dislocation and Worker Adjustment Assistance Act
EIAs. *See* Environmental impact assessments
EISs. *See* Environmental impact statements
Ejido system, 10, 174
Electoral process
  reform of, 166–167, 170, 172
  undermining, 172–173, 177
El Paso–Ciudad Juárez, pollution in, 76
Emerson, Ralph Waldo, quotation from, 117
Employment. *See* Jobs issue
Endangered species, 58, 86
Endangered Species Act, 86
Energy policy, EC, 63–64, 74
Environmental Action, 127
Environmental Defense Fund, 92n48
Environmental impact assessments (EIAs), 69, 76
Environmental impact statements (EISs), 53, 78, 86
Environmental issues, x, 119, 122, 131, 134, 135, 186

Canadian-U.S., 59–65
concern for, 57, 65, 67, 72, 75–76, 84, 85, 88, 128, 185
free trade agreements and, 54, 55, 63, 64, 87
GATT and, 53, 55, 57, 88, 130
growth and, 56–57, 85
labor issues and, 184
Mexico and, 74–75, 79, 137
NAFTA and, 53, 54–55, 77–80, 80–88, 89, 125, 128, 129, 133, 183, 188
resolving, 87, 89, 132, 137, 140
trade and, 55–57, 63, 69–72, 78, 184, 185, 192
Environmentalists
concerns of, 55, 59, 87, 192
influence of, 109, 136, 139
NAFTA and, 83–84, 118, 125, 127–128
Third World and, 191–192
Environmental laws, 58, 73, 79, 84, 85
as trade barriers, 128
Environmental Protection Agency (EPA), U.S., 75, 128
on Mexican environmental statutes, 79
pollution regulation and, 85
Environmental standards, 60, 63, 81, 185
challenging, 56
divergent, 64–65
funding for, 74
harmonization of, 65, 80, 82–84, 178, 184, 189
imposing, 85
industrial location and, 72–73
Mexican, 79, 89
nationalization of, 75
public disclosure of, 79
U.S., 137, 192
violations of, 65
EPA. *See* Environmental Protection Agency, U.S.
European Committee for Electrotechnical Standardization, 70
European Committee for Standardization, 70
European Community (EC), ix, x, 9
enforcement mechanisms of, 66–67
environmental policy and, 55, 56, 63–64, 66–74, 88
integration in, 70, 111
NAFTA and, 125, 184
regional development funds from, 18
social charter of, 184–185
Spain and, 3, 13–19, 191
trade barriers in, 191
European Court of Justice, environmental issues and, 67, 68, 70, 71
European Free Trade Association, 71
European Inventory of Existing Commercial Chemical Substances, 69
European Parliament, environmental policy and, 67
European Standards Committee (CEN), 71
European Telecommunications Standards Institute, 70
Exchange rates, 5, 31, 167
swings in, 16
Exogenous changes, 13, 14, 105–106
Export-led growth model, 145, 151, 191
Exports, 112
growth and, 27
index for, 25

Farm Bureau, 126
FDI. *See* Foreign direct investment
Federal Law for the Prevention and Control of Environmental Contamination (1971), 75
Feinberg, Richard, 123
Fifth Action Programme for the Environment, 67, 73
FIRA. *See* Foreign Investment Review Agency
Fischer, S., 23
Florida Fruit and Vegetable Association, 126–127
Foley, Thomas, 134
Foreign direct investment (FDI), 178
Canadian, 98, 102 (table), 110
EC, 98, 99–100
global stocks of, 98–100, 99 (table), 101 (figure)
Japanese, 110
restricting, 110, 161, 162
triad, 98, 99–100, 99 (table)
U.S. and, 109
See also Foreign investment
Foreign investment
GDP and, 16, 22 (figure)
imports and, 16
laws restricting, 10
liberalizing, 21
in Mexico, 92n54, 161
per capita, 23 (figure)
See also Foreign direct investment
Foreign Investment Review Agency (FIRA), 110
Foreign Policy, Cárdenas article in, 177
France
labor market programs in, 45 (table)
training programs in, 46 (table)
UI in, 43, 44 (table)
Free trade. *See* Trade
Friends of the Earth, 53, 127
FTA. *See* United States–Canada Free Trade Agreement
Fundidora Monterrey steel mill, 167

GAO. *See* General Accounting Office
GATT. *See* General Agreement on Tariffs and Trade
GDP. *See* Gross domestic product
General Accounting Office (GAO), 83
JTPA review by, 37
General Agreement on Tariffs and Trade (GATT), 48, 63, 89, 111, 119, 184, 191, 192
dispute resolution and, 59, 86, 87
environmental issues and, 53, 55, 57, 58, 88, 130
Kennedy Round of, 40
Mexico and, 59, 75, 159, 165
Tokyo Round of, 40
trade issues and, 57–58, 84
Uruguay Round of, 35, 78
General Law for Ecological Equilibrium and Environmental Protection (1988), 76
Gephardt, Richard
Mexican environment and, 79
NAFTA and, 78, 134, 135
German Standards Institution (DIN), 71–72
Germany
labor market programs in, 45 (table)
training programs in, 46 (table)
UI in, 43, 44 (table)
Gingrich, Newt, 135
Globalization, 111, 188
information technology and, 103–104
MNEs and, 97, 103
NAFTA and, 101
national responsiveness and, 104
pressures of, 114, 115
sovereignty and, 101, 103–104, 104–107, 105 (figure)
Goods and services tax (GST), 107, 115
Gore, Al, and debate with Ross Perot, 129
Great Lakes, pollution of, 61–62
Great Lakes Water Quality Agreement (1972), 61
Greenpeace, 127
Gross domestic product (GDP)
foreign investment and, 16, 22 (figure)
growth of, 17, 17 (table), 18, 32
Grossman, Gene M., study by, 25, 85
Grossman and Helpman model, 25
Growers
jobs issue and, 136–137
NAFTA and, 126–127, 135
Growth, 118, 163, 164, 171, 173, 188
acceleration of, 152, 185
environmental issues and, 56–57, 85
NAFTA and, 22–27
openness and, 24, 31–33
political reform and, 152
Grubel-Lloyd index, 26, 27, 32, 33
GST. *See* Goods and services tax

Harmonization, 64–65, 69, 70, 71, 88, 111
pressures of, 114
social, 184–85
trade and, 189
See also Standardization
Hazardous wastes, 79
handling, 58, 77, 81, 83, 84
legislation on, 68–69
Health standards, ix, 114, 137, 189
concerns about, 135
harmonization of, 80, 82–84
spending on, 185
Helms, Jesse, PAN militants and, 176
Helpman, E., 25
Heritage Foundation, 131
Hernández Galicia, Joaquín, 168
Hills, Carla, on health and environmental standards, 83
Hinojosa and Robinson model, 10
Hispanic community
influencing, 176, 178
NAFTA and, 123, 125, 132–133, 134
racism and, 138
Hollings, Fritz, 189
Honda Canada ruling, 112
Howitt, P., 25
Huerta, Victoriano, 151
Hufbauer, Gary, 130
Humane Society, 130
Human rights
concerns about, ix, 119, 127, 136, 137, 177, 178, 183, 186
trade and, 185
Human Rights Commission of OAS, 176
Hunter, Markusen, and Rutherford model, 10
Hurtig, Mel, 114, 115
Hydro-Quebec, 64

IIE. *See* Institute for International Economics
IJC. *See* International Joint Commission
Immigration issue, 18, 127, 157n8, 186
Imports
foreign investment and, 16
GDP and, 17
liberalization of policy on, 159, 165–166, 174
Import-substituting industrialization (ISI), 161–162
changes in, 164, 166, 169
nationalism and, 163
Import-substitution model, 145, 151, 164
Income
distribution of, 180n8
gains in, 122, 140, 185
per capita, 6–7, 6 (figure), 33, 85
real, 5, 166

Individual retirement accounts (IRAs), 47, 48
Individual training accounts (ITAs), 47
Industrial migration, 84–86, 89
  environment policy and, 72–73
"Infant-industry" thesis, 163
Information technology, 103–104
Infrastructure, development of, 80–81, 82
Inland Joint Response Team, 77
Institute for International Economics (IIE), 130
Institute for Policy Studies (IPS), 131
Integration, ix, 70, 104, 111
  industrial, 74
  media and NGOs and, 189
  MNEs and, 97
  NAFTA and, 111, 188
  nationalism and, x
  sovereignty and, 106
Interdependence, x, 155, 162, 188
Interest rates
  capital flows and, 21
  differences in, 30–31
  real, 20
International Boundary and Water Commission (1944), 74
International Boundary Commission (1889), 74
International Brotherhood of Teamsters, suit by, 127
International Joint Commission (IJC)
  nonbinding judgments by, 60
  water quality and, 62
International Trade Commission, U.S. (ITC), 110, 112, 113
  Mexican agricultural exports and, 83
Investment, x, 4, 100, 119
Investment Canada, 110
Investment flows, 72, 188
  border controls and, 55
IPS. *See* Institute for Policy Studies
IRAs. *See* Individual retirement accounts
ISI. *See* Import-substituting industrialization
Isolationism. *See* Protectionism
ITAs. *See* Individual training accounts
ITC. *See* International Trade Commission, U.S.

Jackson, Jesse, 139, 187
  NAFTA and, 130, 134
James Bay–Great Whale project, 64
Japan
  labor market programs in, 45 (table)
  prejudice against, 110, 126, 133
  UI in, 43, 44 (table)
Job Corps, 37
Job-search assistance, 36, 37, 40, 41, 43
  TAA and, 47
  See also Unemployment insurance
Jobs issue, 118, 122
  concern about, 37, 114–115, 124, 126, 129, 132, 133, 134, 135, 136–137, 140, 190, 191
  NAFTA and, 130–131
Job Training Partnership Act (JTPA), 36–37, 38 (table), 41, 42, 45
  Clean Air Act and, 43
  effectiveness of, 40, 50nn7, 13
Johansen, L., 3
Johnson, Eddie Bernice, 134
Jordan, Barbara, 134
JTPA. *See* Job Training Partnership Act

Kantor, Mickey, 82
Kehoe, P. J., 24
Kehoe, Polo, and Sancho model, 13–14
Kehoe, T. J., 24
KPMG Peat Marwick, model constructed for, 10
Krueger, Alan B.: study by, 85

Labor, 35, 49, 186
  environmental issues and, 184
  NAFTA and, 19, 35, 124–126
  restrictions on, 42, 63, 120
  trade and, 185
  See also Workers
Labor Department, U.S., pollution regulation and, 85
Labor market programs, 35, 38–39 (table)
  international comparison of, 45 (table)
  proposed changes for, 45, 47–48
  survey of, 36–37, 40–43
Labor mobility, 9, 19
  increase in, 124
  lack of, 18, 125
Labor standards, ix, 119, 183
  violation of, 65
Labor unions, 119
  control of, 163
  decline of, 125–126, 132
  independence for, 174
  influence of, 136, 139
  NAFTA and, 124–126
  See also American Federation of Labor–Congress of Industrial Organizations
Land ownership, laws regulating, 10
La Paz agreement (1983), 75, 81
  criticism of, 76, 77
"Larry King Live" show, Perot-Gore debate on, 129
League of Nations, Mexico and, 151
Levin, Carl, 133
Levine, R., 25
Levy and van Wijnbergen model, 10

Liberal-Democratic Party, rule of, 180n7
Liberalization, 10–11, 36, 147, 190
criticism of, 145
currency swings and, 16
environmental issues and, 56
impact of, 3–4, 14, 26, 35, 184
of import policy, 159, 165–166, 174
pressures for, 171
Limits of Friendship (Pastor and Castañeda), 162
Living standards, 6, 167
Lobbying, 127
Mexico and, 161, 176
López Portillo, José, 165
economic nationalism and, 153
foreign policy of, 154
waste by, 152
Lowi, Theodore, on interest group liberalism, 121
Lucas, R. E., 22
Lustig, Nora, 131

Maastricht Treaty. *See* Treaty on European Union
Maquiladoras, 74–75, 92n50, 124
problems with, 56, 79
Marine Mammal Protection Act, 59
Market economy, 109, 167, 191
McCloskey, Michael, on environmental funding issues, 88
McQuaig, Linda, 115
Media
development of, 147, 152–153, 187
integration and, 189
Medicare system, protecting, 114
Meech Lake accord (1990), failure of, 108
Mexican-U.S. Integrated Border Environmental Plan (1992), 80
Mexican War (1846–1847), 117, 160
Mexico
Canada and, 187–188
democratization of, 188
economic crisis in, 152, 154–155, 162, 163, 164–166, 167, 168, 186
foreign intervention in, 147, 153, 160–164, 175, 177, 178
foreign investment in, 17 (table), 21
foreign relations of, 152–155, 156
GATT and, 59, 75, 159, 165
GDP of, 30
growth rates in, 4, 17 (table)
NAFTA and, 7, 103, 180n22, 187–188
population of, 18–19, 19 (figure), 20 (table), 23 (table), 82
prejudices against, 120, 126, 135, 138, 139, 186–187
reforms in, 137–138
relative size of, 4–7, 5 (figure), 9
Middle class in Mexico
consumption by, 153
growth of, 174
ISI model and, 163
public affairs and, 152
MNEs. *See* Multinational enterprises
Modernization, 187
criticism of, 145
economic, 149, 174
identity and, 149, 156
social, 152
Montreal Protocol, 58
Morici, Peter, on U.S.-Canada talks, 63
Mulroney, Brian, 62
Multinational enterprises (MNEs), 55, 97, 108
environment and, 103
globalization of, 101, 103–104, 106
Japanese, 103
largest, 98, 99 (table)
national responsiveness and, 104
Multisectoral general equilibrium models, 10
Muñoz Ledo, Porfirio, 177

NAC. *See* North American commission
Nader, Ralph, 139, 187
NAFTA and, 123, 130
NAEC. *See* North American Economic Community
NAFTA. *See* North American Free Trade Agreement
NAM. *See* National Association of Manufacturers
NAP. *See* North American parliament
NATC. *See* North American trade commission
National Association of Manufacturers (NAM), 121, 122
National Confederation of Campesinos (CNC), 163
National Consumer League, 127
Nationalism, x, 135, 138
cultural, 97, 113–114, 115
historical dimensions of, 147, 148–152, 162
ISI model and, 163
potential for, 146
See also Economic nationalism
National Press Club, 176
National treatment provisions, 111, 113–114
National Wildlife Federation, 92n48, 129
NATO, Canada and, 187
Natural Resources Defense Council, 92n48, 127
Neoisolationism, 183, 191, 192
Networking, 123–124, 128
New Approach, 70, 71

New development paradigm, 165, 166
New Left, NAFTA and, 128
Newly industrialized economies (NIEs), 103
New York Times, 177
NGOs. *See* Nongovernmental organizations
NIEs. *See* Newly industrialized economies
1992 Program of EC, 22, 35, 63, 106
Nitrogen oxide, 64
  increase in, 56
  reducing, 61
Nongovernmental organizations (NGOs), ix
  alliances with, 178
  integration and, 189
  leverage by, 185–186
Nonintervention, principle of, 160, 161, 162, 176
Nontariff barriers (NTBs), 10, 87
  reducing, 9, 12, 111
  trade and, 185, 186, 192
NORAD. *See* North American Air Defense Command
North American Air Defense Command (NORAD), Canada and, 187
North American commission (NAC), 113
North American Economic Community (NAEC), 111–113
North American Free Trade Agreement (NAFTA)
  analyzing, ix, 3, 14–15, 98, 192
  applied general equilibrium estimates of, 9–12, 11 (table)
  environmental issues and, 53, 54–55, 77–80, 80–88, 89, 125, 128, 129, 133, 183, 188
  impact of, 3–4, 10–11, 16, 101, 174–179, 183, 184, 189–190
  modifications to, 127
  opposition to, 117–118, 119, 120, 123–130, 135–136, 137, 140, 146–147
  problems with, 111–112, 118–121, 134–135, 139, 140
  support for, 118, 121–123, 139–140
North American parliament (NAP), 113
North American trade commission (NATC), 112
NTBs. *See* Nontariff barriers

OAS. *See* Organization of American States
Office of Management and Budget (OMB), U.S., trust funds and, 48
Ohmae, Kenichi, on globalization, 106
Oil resources, 9, 160, 161
  foreign exchange from, 164, 165
  importance of, 152, 155
OMB. *See* Office of Management and Budget
Omnibus Budget Reconciliation Act (1981), 41
Omnibus Trade and Competitiveness Act (1988), 40, 41, 42, 48
Ontario, FTA and, 107
Openness policy, 17, 27
  growth and, 24, 25, 31–33
  See also Economic openness; Political openness
Opposition parties (Mexico)
  criticism by, 146
  electoral problems and, 147
  NAFTA and, 177, 178
  support for, 168
Organization of American States (OAS), 176
  Cuba and, 160
  See also Human Rights Commission of OAS
Organized labor. *See* Labor unions
Output, 7
  increase in, 21, 24, 26–27, 30–31, 33
Overlapping-generations framework, 21

PAN. *See* Partido Acción Nacional
Paper organizations, NAFTA and, 128
Parastatals, changes for, 167–168, 174
Parmenter, Meagher, McDonald, and Adams model, 13
Partido Acción Nacional (PAN), 176
  mobilization of, 170–171
  resurgence of, 172
  stances of, 168
Partido de la Revolución Democrática (PRD), 171
Party of the Institutional Revolution (PRI), 159, 168, 176
  authoritarianism and, 162, 172–173
  discontent with, 146, 165, 166–167
  dominance of, 163, 164, 172
  economic reform and, 169, 170, 171
  resurgence of, 170, 171–172, 173, 179
Pastor, Robert, 123
Pemex, 165
Per capita income, 6–7, 33
  alternative measures of, 6 (figure)
  environment and, 85
Performance bonds, 78–79
Perot, Ross, 139, 187, 189
  debate with Al Gore, 129
  NAFTA and, 123, 129, 130
  neoisolationism and, 191
Peseta, appreciation of, 16
Peso, appreciation of, 5, 16
Pesticide issue, 58, 65, 83, 126
Phytosanitary standards, 10, 84
Pillsbury Company, 127
Political community
  foreign influence on, 189
  imagined, 147

Political culture
changes in, 152
prosperity and, 153
Political openness, 166, 174, 176
economic reform and, 171
pressures for, 170, 171
PRI and, 179
slowing, 159–160
See also Economic openness; Openness policy
Political policies, 149
shaping, 160
Political reform, 167
economic expansion and, 152
"Polluter pays" principle, 57, 67, 73, 90n4
Pollution abatement, cost of, 72, 84, 92n54
Pollution havens, creation of, 55. *See also* Dirty industries
Pollution issues, 57, 84, 85, 119, 120, 127, 133, 135
resolving, 137, 140
See also Air pollution; Border pollution
Pollution taxes, 82
Porter, Michael, 101, 106
PRD. *See* Partido de la Revolución Democrática
Prebisch, Raúl, 161
Prejudice, 110, 120, 126, 133, 135, 136, 138, 139, 186–187
PRI. *See* Party of the Institutional Revolution
Pricing, 159
realistic, 167
Privatization, 159, 166, 167, 169, 171, 174, 175
Procompetitive effects, 12
Products
development of, 24, 25
standardization of, 101
Protectionism, 110, 126, 127, 131, 134, 136, 138, 153, 183
challenges of, 159, 192
Mexican, 151
Third World and, 191
U.S., 103, 112, 166
Public Citizen, 53, 127
Public Voice, 127
Purchasing-power parity, 5, 6, 31

Quebec, separatism of, 107, 108
Quotas, ix, 10

Racism, 136, 138
Radical fringe, NAFTA and, 129–130
Rainbow Coalition, NAFTA and, 130, 134
R&D. *See* Research and development
Rangel, Charles, 133
Reagan, Ronald, TAA and, 41
Real exchange rate
indices for, 15 (table), 16 (figure)
movements in, 15
Recession, 120, 136
Reich, Robert, on MNEs, 103
Reid-Southam, Angus, poll by, 113
Relocation assistance, 37, 47, 137, 140
Remittances, net, 18 (table)
Renelt, D., 25
Research and development (R&D), 24, 104
Review of U.S.-Mexican Environmental Issues, 83
Revolution of 1910, 150, 151, 161
Reyes Lujan, Sergio, on environmental enforcement, 85
Richey, Charles, ruling on EIS, 86
Rio Accords. *See* Rio Declaration on Environment and Development
Rio Declaration on Environment and Development (Rio Accords), 57, 74
Rivera-Batiz, L., 25
Rivera-Batiz and Romer model, 25
Robinson, Burfisher, Hinojosa-Ojeda, and Thierfelder model, 10
Roland-Holst, Reinert, and Shiells model, 10, 12
Romer, P. M., 22, 25
Rostenkowski, Daniel, 134
Rugman, Alan, 109

Safety standards, 137
concerns about, 135
harmonization of, 80, 82–84
Salinas de Gortari, Carlos, 3, 93n58, 171, 176
criticism of, 145, 146–147
economic reform and, 168, 170, 174
electoral reform and, 173, 177
environmental policy and, 54, 78–79, 86
foreign policy of, 154
liberalization by, 156, 165
and political reform, 170, 173
popularity of, 169, 170
on poverty, 163
unions and, 167
Salutin, Rick, 114, 115
Samuelson, Robert, 185
Sanitary regulations, differences in, 55, 84
Schott, Jeffrey, 130
Schwartz, Alan M., 62
SEA. *See* Single European Act
Secretaría de Desarrollo Social (SEDESOL), 86
environmental enforcement by, 78, 79
goals of, 76
Secretaría de Desarrollo Urbano y Ecología (SEDUE), 76, 78
SEDESOL. *See* Secretaría de Desarrollo Social

SEDUE. *See* Secretaría de Desarrollo Urbano y Ecología
Segunda vuelta (second round), 172, 177–178
Self-determination, 153
 concern for, 156
 economic, 150
 limits to, 154
Serra Puche, Jaime, 82
Services, ix
 exemption from national treatment, 111
 standardization of, 101
Shelton-Colby, Sally, 123
Shoven, J. S., 3
Side agreements, 88, 137, 140
Sierra Club, 92n48
 NAFTA and, 53, 127
 suit by, 86
Single European Act (SEA) (1985), 66, 67, 70, 71
SITC. *See* Standard International Trade Classification level
Smith, Wesley, 131
Sobarzo model, 10, 12
Social issues, x, 109, 148, 164
 trade and, 184
Social reform, 109
Social safety nets, 125, 184
Solidarity program, 171
Southern Arizona Environmental Management Society, 128
Sovereignty
 awareness of, 105, 106
 concerns about, ix–x, 114, 154, 156, 161, 183, 188–190, 192
 globalization and, 101, 103–104, 104–107, 105 (figure)
 integration and, 106
Spain
 EC and, 3, 13–19, 191
 foreign investment in, 17 (table)
 growth rates in, 17 (table)
 population of, 18, 19 (figure), 20 (table), 23 (table)
 and real exchange rate, 15
 regional development funds for, from EC, 18
Spanish model, 13–19, 14 (table)
Specialization, 24, 26–27, 32
 impact of, 25, 33
Standard International Trade Classification (SITC) level, 9, 32
Standardization, 72–73, 138
 acceptance of, 101
 floor for, 185
 increase in, 69, 72, 106
 See also Harmonization
State ownership, overcoming, 159, 167
St. Lawrence River, pollution of, 61
Stockholm Conference on the Human Environment (1972), 67
Stokey and Young model, 24, 25
Strange, Susan, 106
Structural development funds, 73
Sulphur dioxide, 64
 increase in, 56
 reducing, 61
Super 301 trade law, 103, 110
Supreme Court, U.S., environmental controls and, 85–86
Sustainable development, 56, 57, 58, 78

TAA. *See* Trade Adjustment Assistance program
Tariffs, 166–167
 elimination of, ix, 9–10, 111
 environmental, 73
 extraordinary, 58
 lowering, 12
Tax reform, 14, 174
Teléfonos de México, privatization of, 167
Textile industry, 147, 191
 growth of, 12
 job loss in, 136
Think tanks, NAFTA, 130–131
Third World
 economic cooperation and, 190
 environmental issues and, 58–59, 191–192
 protectionism and, 191
Tijuana–San Diego area, pollution in, 76, 77
Tipping fees, increase in, 62
Toronto Star, economic nationalists and, 115
Torricelli, Robert, 177
Trade, ix, 18, 179
 Canadian, 100, 102 (table)
 changes in, 119
 by commodity, 8–9 (figure)
 direction of, 7 (figure)
 environment and, 55–57, 63, 69–72, 78, 184, 185, 192
 increase in, 78, 122, 190
 international discussion of, 57, 183
 nontrade issues and, 184, 185, 186, 192
 by sector, 7, 9
 unconventional approaches to, 183–186
Trade Act (1974), 40, 51n17
Trade Adjustment Assistance (TAA) program, 39 (table), 40–43
 aims of, 42, 50nn8, 11, 12
 proposed changes for, 45, 47–48, 49
 training component of, 42
 workers certified for, 41–42
Trade Adjustment Assistance Trust Fund, 48
Trade agreements, ix, 191
 negotiating, 89n1, 183
Trade disputes

environmentally and socially driven, 88, 191
settling, 87
Trade Expansion Act (1962), 40
Trade laws, abuse of, 112
Trade readjustment allowances (TRAs), 40–41, 42
Trail Smelter Arbitration, 60
Training, 37, 41, 43, 49, 137
international comparison of, 46 (table)
JTPA and, 50n7
spending on, 47, 140
Transboundary pollution. *See* Border pollution
TRAs. *See* Trade readjustment allowances
Treaty of Rome, harmonization and, 69, 70
Treaty on European Union (1992), x, 66, 71
environment and, 68, 69, 73–74
legislative power and, 67
Trela and Whalley model, 10
Triad, 115
changes in, 103, 186–188
FDI in, 98, 101 (figure)
global flows in, 100 (table)
integration and, 97–100
NAFTA and, 190–191
Tuna-dolphin conflict, 59

UI. *See* Unemployment insurance
Undocumented workers, arrest of, 157n8
Unemployment
long-term, 36, 37
reducing, 36
Unemployment insurance (UI), 42, 137
aims of, 36, 38 (table), 48
international comparison of, 44 (table)
review of, 43, 49
spending on, 40–41, 48, 140
training and, 47
See also Job-search assistance
Unions. *See* Labor unions
Union Treaty. *See* Treaty on European Union
Unitarian Church, 130
United Kingdom
labor market programs in, 45 (table)
training programs in, 46 (table)
UI in, 43, 44 (table)
United Methodist Church, 130
United Nations Codex Alimentarius Commission, 58
United Nations Conference on Environment and Development (1992), 57
United Nations International Comparison Program, purchasing-power parity and, 6
United States
Canadian trade with, 98–99
economic decentralization in, 108–111
foreign investment in, 21
GDP of, 30
intervention by, in Mexico, 160, 161
labor market programs in, 45 (table)
Mexican cultural differences with, 148, 155, 156
Mexican trade with, 166
population of, 19 (figure), 20 (table), 23 (table), 82
relations with, 147–148, 151, 154, 155–156, 159–160, 162, 179, 183, 189
relative size of, 4–7, 5 (figure), 9
training programs in, 46 (table)
UI in, 43, 44 (table)
United States–Canada Free Trade Agreement (FTA) (1989), 10, 12, 13, 62–63, 105–106, 156, 187
Canadians and, 97, 111, 113
environmental issues and, 54, 55, 63, 64, 87
jobs issue and, 114–115
NAFTA and, 130–131
negotiations for, 154
problems with, 107, 109, 111–112, 114
United States–Canada Free Trade Association, 11
United States Council of the Mexico-U.S. Business Committee, 122

Veracruz, occupation of, 151, 160
Verbeke, Alain, 109
Villa, Pancho, 160
Villaseñor, Eduardo, resignation of, 173

Wages
controlling, 159
minimum, 119
substandard, 124
Wall Street Journal, 122, 177
WARN. *See* Worker Adjustment and Retraining Notification Act
War of Independence (Mexico), nationalism and, 150
Washington Convention, 58
Water projects, 81, 82
Water quality, 61, 68
Whalley, J., 3, 10
Wilson, Woodrow, 151
Worker Adjustment and Retraining Notification Act (WARN), 37, 40
Workers
exploitation of, 125
government assistance for, 35–36
undocumented, 157n8
See also Labor
World Bank, loans from, 86
Wright, T. P., 24

Young, Andrew, 134
Young and McCleery model, 10

About the Book

The North American Free Trade Agreement (NAFTA) is the first example of a free trade agreement involving partners of vastly different levels of development. As a result of the unconventional issues raised in the debate over NAFTA, trade matters will never again be viewed purely in economic terms.

This book explores the unconventional dimensions of the NAFTA debate. How, for example, might different environmental regulatory frameworks and compliance levels affect investment flows among three NAFTA countries? Does the European Community experience with harmonized environmental regulation and with integrating lower-wage economies with more advanced industrialized economies have relevance in North America? In what ways has intensified regional economic integration modified the course of domestic political evolution in Mexico and even altered the meaning of national sovereignty for all three nations? Addressing these and other questions, the authors grapple with some of the thorniest dilemmas of a relationship that encompasses free trade, the environment, social policy, and political development.